RELATIONAL DATABASE PRACTICES:
BRIDGING THE GAP BETWEEN THE THEORY OF DATABASE DESIGN AND REAL-WORLD PRACTICES

Malcolm Hamer

Dedicated to the memory of

James Clifford, 1950 – 1995

and

John Simopoulos, 1923 – 2015

Malcolm Hamer is an IT Consultant and Director at Acumen Solutions, a business and technology consulting firm with offices in the US and UK, serving clients of all sizes from many sectors, including consumer products, professional services, pharmaceuticals, communications, media, financial services, and government. Before becoming an IT consultant he worked for over 20 years in technology in global organizations in the telecommunications, banking, and securities industries – architecting, building, and operating large global infrastructures and services, including one of the first global corporate data networks, one of the first global corporate email services, and one the first online banking services. He also worked as Lecturer in Telecommunications at the Open University in the UK and, before becoming an IT consultant, worked for two years in a New York based start-up. He holds degrees in Physics from Oxford University and an MBA from New York University. He is co-author of *Telecommunications: a Systems Approach* (with Gaby Smol and Mike Hills), *Telecommunications Systems* (with Gaby Smol), and *Telecommunications Users' Handbook* (with Michael Corby and Steve Donohue). He has written articles and presented papers on a wide range of IT topics throughout his career.

CONTENTS

i

PREFACE

The two principal aims of this book are (a) to provide an easy-to-read introduction to relational databases (Chapters 1 to 5), and (b) to bridge the considerable gap that exists between what is generally taught in university database courses (or in vendor-provided database courses) and what actually goes on in database design in the real world of business and professional databases (Chapters 6 to 18).

This book should be of interest to the following readers:

- People who are taking, or have taken, a database course, either in a university or in a vendor-provided training program, and who want to build on the knowledge acquired in that course so as to be better prepared to deal with databases in the real world.

- Senior technology managers who want to understand the subject of relational databases more deeply, in order to be able to make better decisions about the architecture of complex systems of which relational databases are a part.

- People who want to know about relational databases purely out of interest in the topic and who seek a broad overview of the subject and its importance as one of the cornerstones of present-day Information Technology.

Chapters 1 to 5 provide an introduction to the most important concepts in relational databases and database design. This part of the book will allow someone with a basic understanding of computer programming to learn the fundamental concepts that underlie the design of relational databases, *without* going into the details of the Structured Query Language (SQL). If you have recently completed an introductory course on relational databases, the contents of the first five chapters should already be familiar to you. However, I encourage you to read them as reminder of the key concepts and to make sure that you are familiar with the terminology used in the rest of the book.

For the hands-on database designer or application programmer, this book is intended to complement the reference manuals of whichever database management system (DBMS) you are going to be working with (for example, Oracle, Microsoft SQL Server, or IBM DB2). This book deals with the concepts, principles, techniques, and practices of database design, so that you can put to more effective use the "tools of the trade" – which include a DBMS (such as Oracle), the SQL language, and stored procedures.

Today, databases underlie almost all significant business and professional computer applications. Apart from a few non-relational databases, developed for high-volume transaction processing, most of the new databases created since the mid-1980s have been relational databases; and although you may have read about database systems based on "new" models for "big data", these complement, rather than replace, relational DBMSs. Relational databases are, and are likely to remain, the foundation of the majority of business and professional computer applications.

My interest in databases was sparked in 1984. Prior to that, I had paid very little attention to databases. I had, from time to time, tried to read books about databases; but I had quickly lost interest. I had no pressing need to develop a database and it seemed to me that the way data was being organized in databases simply didn't make sense. (These books described the ideas underlying the pre-relational "hierarchical model" and "network model" databases, in which data is organized into a hierarchy of records, with records one level up the hierarchy acting as "parent" records to the "child" records under them.) The only time that I had been forced to build a database, prior to 1984, was in 1982. I had volunteered to write a computer program to support a fund-raising "telethon" for the Parent Teachers' Association of a Manhattan public school. I soon realized that I would need to create a database of some sort in which my program could place its information. My home computer in those days was a Radio Shack TRS80 (or "Trash 80", as it was affectionately known by most of its users). Apart from a BASIC interpreter, I did not have much in the way of software for my TRS80 – certainly nothing as "state-of-the-art" at that time as dBase II. So I wrote a BASIC program that created and updated some TRSDOS files. The structure I used for these files was simply the first data structure that came into my head.

Looking back at the contents of these files, and stretching the truth only a little, I could describe them as consisting of four tables: "parents", "students", "addresses", and "telethon_calls". The database design, if I could call it such, was free of any kind of "hierarchical" structure (although I certainly would not claim that it was truly relational). This simple exercise taught me that it is possible to design a database without invoking the structural concepts that I had read about in the various books that I had half-heartedly tried to read in prior years – such as "parent" records and "child" records (even though, in this particular exercise, I was literally dealing with parent and child records!). I spent the evenings of the following week keying in the details of 595 students and 510 sets of parents, and then printing out the call sheets for the first telethon. After the telethon was over, and I had entered the pledges and address corrections, I didn't think any more about databases for the next two years.

In 1984 I took a course at New York University Business School (now the New York University Stern School of Business) on Database Management Systems, taught by James Clifford (to the memory of whom this book is dedicated). Fifteen minutes into the first class on relational databases I was excited and enthralled by the concept of relational databases that Jim was explaining to the class. The idea was so simple, so powerful, and (in retrospect) so obvious. Having heard the idea, I immediately found it hard to imagine how anyone could have struggled with those awful pre-relational databases without yelling, "This can't be right!" (That's certainly what I had felt when I had previously tried to read about databases.) Never had an idea felt so right to me on first hearing it.

My enthusiasm for relational databases, although in part due to the fact that I found the concept so elegant, was further strengthened by Jim's teaching style and wonderful sense of humor. I would describe very few teachers that I have been taught by at school or university as having been inspirational, but Jim certainly deserved this description.

Over the next fifteen years I took every opportunity that I could find to look at different relational database designs, underlying different applications in different organizations and industries. Whenever possible, I talked to the designers of these databases about the ideas on which they had based their designs.

I was working overseas in 1995 when Jim died, and I did not hear about his death until sometime later. I felt sad that I had not kept in touch with him. I went to buy a copy of his last book. While thumbing through other books in the "Databases" section in the book shop, I was surprised to see how little the contents of most books had changed since I took Jim's course in 1984. Based on the research I had done on real-world database designs in the intervening years, it occurred to me how difficult computer science graduates must find it when they start their first database-related job. I also noticed that the majority of books that I looked at contained the same example of a University Administration database that had appeared in the book that I studied in 1984 when taking Jim's course. (Jim, by the way, felt this example was boring and, breaking with tradition, used a Museum, which he called the "These Are A Few Of My Favorite Things Museum", as the basis of the examples in class and the term project.)

I was finally motivated to write down my observations and thoughts about database design when my friend, John Simopoulos (to the memory of whom this book is also dedicated), called me from London and asked me several questions about relational databases. My first emailed answer, which I had initially intended to be only a few pages long, quickly evolved into the first three chapters of this book. I later expanded my answer until, eventually, it had become so lengthy that I decided to turn it into this book. John, by the way, was a Philosophy don at St. Catherine's College, Oxford and is the only person that I have known who has, in real life, designed and built an actual University Administration database. When I asked him at the time why he, a Philosophy don, was spending his time building a database, he replied, "We philosophers are practical men." Without John's considerable patience and encouragement while reading and correcting the gradually-expanding answer to his questions I would not have completed this book.

I would also like to thank John Edkins of the Department of Computer Science at the University of Wales, Aberystwyth for his encouragement and his many helpful suggestions. His insights into which aspects of relational database design his students find the most difficult to grasp, and how to address those difficulties, were particularly helpful in making the first five chapters easier to read.

And finally, I would like to thank my wife, Cecilia, for her many comments and suggestions on the various drafts of this book; and Eric Guckelberger, who reviewed and made many improvements to the final draft.

Malcolm Hamer

CHAPTER 1

DOING IT WITH TABLES

Introduction

In the first five chapters of this book I will give a general introduction to relational databases. The purpose of this general introduction is twofold. First, if you have never taken a course on relational databases, it will allow you to use this book as a self-contained text – taking you from the basics of relational databases (Chapters 1-5) to the practices of database design in the real world of business and professional databases (Chapters 6-18). Second, if you have attended a course on relational databases in the past, but have not studied or worked with relational databases for some time, the first five chapters will provide a reminder of some of the concepts and terminology that will be used in the rest of the book.

Throughout this book I have assumed a basic understanding of computer programming, sufficient to grasp what is going on in the example SQL queries that I present in the text. This does *not* mean that you need to be proficient in SQL to understand the examples. In all the examples, the main focus is on what is happening in the tables in the database (where data is stored), rather than on the queries that would be used to extract data from these tables, or insert data into the tables. I use the SQL examples simply to show that particular database designs allow the desired information to be successfully retrieved from the database, rather than to explain the details of how to construct SQL queries. I explain, in the text, what these example SQL queries are aimed at achieving and I show the results of the queries; so you do not need to study the SQL examples in detail if you don't want to.

In case you *do* want to study the SQL queries, I have kept them as simple as possible. You should be able to get a fair grasp of what is going on in the queries if you are familiar with one or more computer programming languages. If you are familiar with a programming language you will, I hope, be able to distinguish between the three basic components of a programming language and understand the roles of those three components:

(a) The "reserved words" of the language – words like IF, THEN, or PRINT in standard programming languages (although in SQL a number of different reserved words are used);

(b) The named "variables" (like "x", "y", "AB7", or "sales"); and

(c) The "arithmetic operators" (like +, -, /, and *) and "logical operators" (like OR and AND).

If you are reading this book purely out of interest in the topic, rather than as preparation for working on a database, I believe you will find the level of detail in this book just about right. I believe that it also contains the right level of detail for a senior technology manager who wants to understand the subject more deeply, in order to be able to make better decisions about the architecture of complex systems of which relational databases are a part.

1

When it comes to hands-on use of a Database Management System (DBMS) such as Oracle, Microsoft SQL Server, or IBM DB2, this book is intended to complement the reference manuals of the DBMS that you are going to be working with. I have therefore avoided duplication of the contents of those manuals, which in any case vary somewhat from system to system.

I will not take up your time here telling you in detail why databases are important. If you have read this far then I assume that you already believe that they are. Almost all computer applications need to retrieve data, and store the results of their operation for later retrieval. This cannot be done effectively for multi-user applications, or complex single-user applications, unless that data is stored in an organized way, rather than simply written serially into a file (like a Microsoft Word document file). To store data in an organized way you need to use a DBMS – unless you intend to write, from scratch, all the software needed to perform the functions of a DBMS for a specific application (which of course would be a huge waste of effort). DBMSs are thus essential tools in building most applications that store and retrieve data. DBMSs manage all the details of where to put the bits and bytes and how to get them out again.

Although a DBMS is an essential part of any system that stores any significant amount of data, a DBMS becomes useful only after you have instructed it to build an empty database of a specific design, ready for users to start inserting data into that database. The "database design", according to which the database is created by the DBMS, is therefore an essential first step in bringing the database into existence. The primary focus of this book is on the creation of practical database designs for real-world applications, and on understanding database designs that others have created.

The Early Days of DBMSs

DBMSs have existed since the 1960s. The earliest DBMSs were based on the "hierarchical model", in which data is organized in a hierarchy, much like the way that books were traditionally classified in libraries. The drawback of this type of database was that, to get to a piece of data, you had to "navigate" the database through a defined hierarchy – one which might make sense to some users but not others. So, in the same way that librarians, using traditional book-classification systems (such as the Dewey Decimal System), had to choose to categorize a library book called "The Philosophy of Cooking" under either Philosophy or Food, a hierarchical database required that a decision be made about whether telephone numbers were to be arrived at by the path:

company→division→department→employee→phonenumber, or

company→site→building→floor→office→phonenumber

The next generation of DBMSs were based on the so-called "network model", which allowed "horizontal" and "diagonal" links to be added, supplementing the vertical hierarchy. For example, if the vertical structure contained the two paths

company→division→department→employee, and

company→site→building→floor→office→phonenumber

you could add a diagonal link crossing over from "employee" to "phonenumber". But databases using these network DBMSs were still difficult to build and difficult to use. A lot of thought had to go into what queries users *might* make of the database; and, if the designer got it wrong, the user would have great difficulty in getting to the required data.

The Relational Model

Relational DBMSs represent the third type of DBMS – the type almost universally used today. The concept of a relational database was introduced by E.F. Codd in 1970, in a seminal paper, A Relational Model of Data for Large Shared Data Banks, *Communications of the ACM, Volume 13, Number 6, June 1970*, pp. 377-387. ("ACM" is the Association for Computing Machinery, founded in 1947.)

Codd had a revolutionary idea, which now seems so obvious that it is hard to put oneself in his place, working in database systems in 1969-70, and imagine how difficult it must have been to break away from the ideas used in DBMSs up until then.

Edgar Frank Codd (known as "Ted" to his friends) was born in Portland, Dorset in the UK in 1923. He studied Mathematics at Exeter College, Oxford, and also (separately) Chemistry. He moved to the US in 1949 and there he joined IBM. He developed his ideas on the Relational Model while working at the IBM Research Laboratory in San Jose. (He is also well known for the subject of his 1963 University of Michigan Ph.D. thesis – "Cellular Automata" – familiar to early computer programmers worldwide as "The Game of Life".) Codd died in 2003 at age 79 at his home in Florida.

What Codd's 1970 paper said was, basically, "let's do it with tables". More specifically, he proposed a completely new approach to representing data in a database as follows:

- Databases can be built using sets of **tables**, each having a name and one or several columns.

- Each of the columns of each table will have a name.

- At least one of the columns of each table will be designated as a **key column**, ready to hold "key" data elements. The value of the key uniquely identifies a particular row in the table. A key can consist of one column, or several columns taken together. (The concept of a key was already incorporated into the earlier database models.) When rows of data are added to a table, each value of the key may occur only once, so that each row is unique and the key uniquely identifies a particular row in the table.

- Once the "empty" tables are created, data can be inserted in the form of **rows** added to the tables.

3

Theoretically, there would be no limit to the number of rows that could be added, although in practice the amount of storage available on the computer that holds the DBMS would set a limit to the maximum size of the database.

Let's start with a simple example – the one that writers of books about databases have been using for over four decades: a University Administration database. (I will introduce other examples later.) This example consists of three tables that might look like this (after a small amount of data has been added to the database):

Table name: **students**

student_id	first_name	last_name	sex	date_of_birth
200800101	Edgar	Glick	M	1993-01-25
200800102	Alice	Baker	F	1993-04-20
200800103	Robert	Cunningham	M	1992-09-22
200800104	Charles	Dillard	M	1993-03-13
200600001	Sally	Sparrow	F	1990-05-28
200600002	John	Liu	M	1989-12-26

Table name: **courses**

course_number	course_title	credits
M101	Mathematics	4.5
P101	Philosophy	4.5
M207	Introduction to Programming	3.0
P321	Life, the Universe, and Everything	3.0
M342	Database Design	3.0

Table name: **enrollments**

student_id	course_number	term	year
200800101	P101	1	2008
200800101	M101	1	2008
200600001	M342	1	2008
200600002	P321	1	2008

Each table has a name (for example, "students") and each column of each table has a name (for example, "student_id", "first_name", "last_name", and so on).

Obviously a real database that has been fully "populated" with data would contain many more rows of data than this; and there would be many other tables in addition to these three. Also, although a print-out of the database contents might look something like the above example, the bit-by-bit details of exactly how the data is stored within the computer would be up to the programmer who wrote the software of the DBMS. However, the way that the data would be stored in a relational DBMS would represent the tabular structure shown here in some fairly direct way.

The above example does not show which columns represent the key data elements. This information would be represented in the database somehow, and in this example would indicate that the following are the key columns:

4

- In the table "students", the key is "student_id".

- In the table "courses", the key is "course_number".

- In the table "enrollments", the key consists of the two columns "student_id" and "course_number", taken together.

In Codd's original theoretical model (but not in the actual relational DBMSs that were eventually built), he said that associations between the tables would be established by use of exactly the same names for columns in two or more different tables. Thus, calling a column "student_id" in both the "students" table and the "enrollments" table would establish that "student_id" represented exactly the same data element in both tables. This turned out to be an unnecessary condition. I will say more about this later.

Of course, if you want to get your papers published by the ACM, it is better to avoid using mundane words like "table" and "row". So, in order to make his theory sound more technical, Codd used the terms **relation** and **tuple** (pronounced "too-pull") to mean "table" and "row". Also, rather than just saying "this table has three columns", Codd introduced the terminology "this relation is of degree three".

Relational DBMS Products Emerge

There was great excitement in academic circles about Codd's ideas. However, although early relational DBMSs were used in universities within the next few years, it took about twelve years for reliable DBMS software (suitable for the business world) to be written, debugged, and brought to market. Two of the first DBMS products to be adopted by the business world in the early 1980s were Ingres and Oracle.

For over a decade after that (well into the 1990s) the old "network" DBMSs continued to be widely used for existing business applications, because relational DBMSs turned out to consume a lot of computing power. Even today, some high-performance systems still use non-relational DBMSs for this reason. However, it would be unthinkable today to use anything other than a relational DBMS as the foundation of a completely new application (although other types of database may be used to complement a relational database, for example, for storing high-volume transactional data).

As relational DBMSs were created and marketed, much of Codd's terminology was dropped in favor of down-to-earth terms like "table" and "row". By 1985, nobody was using Codd's original jargon, with one exception: databases based on tables continued, and still continue, to be known as "relational databases". The term **relational** means "based on *relations*", that is, "based on tables". It has nothing to do with the concept of a "relationship" – although one often talks about relationships when talking about databases. This has caused some confusion, some of which was intentionally generated by the vendors of early-1980s products. Vendors whose DBMSs were not truly relational made heavy use of the word "relationship" in their marketing materials to try to trick potential customers into thinking that they were going to get a relational DBMS.

Some of the early theoretical concepts had to be modified when practical relational DBMSs came to be developed. In particular, the requirement that columns in different tables that contain the same data element be given the same name was dropped. It had been found that establishing a permanent association between tables in this way was both too complicated and unnecessary. Instead, the equivalence of the two columns is established at the time the user does a query. For example, consider the tables "students" and "enrollments". It would be possible to give the name "student_id" to a column in the "students" table and the name "student_number" to a column in the "enrollments" table, even though these columns represent exactly the same thing. (Of course this very confusing for the database users and it is therefore a very bad idea; but the point of this example is that there is nothing to prevent you from doing this.) When performing a query that involves taking data from both tables, and combining the data, the user would simply tell the DBMS *at the time of the query* that the two things are the same, using a statement within the query like:

students.student_id = enrollments.student_number

The two sides of this statement define a particular column in a particular table using the "tablename.columnname" notation, in which the name before the period is the name of the table and the name after the period is the name of the column in that table. Note that I am not recommending the use of two different names (like "student_id" and "student_number") for the same thing. This is not a good practice. The point of this "bad" example is this: the designer of the database, and the users of the database, need to know that these columns will hold the same data element; *but the DBMS does not need to "know" this fact.* Each query tells the database to make such an association at the time the query is executed. As soon as the query has been executed, the DBMS immediately "forgets" about the association, and approaches the next query with an "open mind". A relational database can be pictured as consisting of a number of "free-floating" tables that are completely unconnected with one another in the database. The connections exist in the mind of the database designer and in the minds of the database users; but, for the DBMS, these connections do not exist outside the context of the queries.

Interestingly, an attempt was made in 1992 to partially revive the concept of association through identical column names, which was then referred to as a "natural join". However, most DBMS vendors have not implemented this optional feature. Experience has shown that the standard method of associating tables with one another (via explicit statements within the query) is a completely satisfactory approach. Trying to establish association via identical column names has the side-effect of creating unwanted column-associations where the database designer has used the same name, such as "date", for different things – such as date of birth and date of enrollment.

Query Languages

Having defined what a relational database was, Codd's next step was to define a **query language** that users would use to interact with relational databases. Query languages had existed since the earliest databases. However, because the data in a relational database was to be stored in a radically different way, the relational model required a completely new query language.

Before we look at how relational query languages evolved, I will first explain two ways in which queries can operate, using simple examples based on a single table. Consider the example "students" table that I showed earlier. Here it is again:

Table name: **students**				
student_id	first_name	last_name	sex	date_of_birth
200800101	Edgar	Glick	M	1993-01-25
200800102	Alice	Baker	F	1993-04-20
200800103	Robert	Cunningham	M	1992-09-22
200800104	Charles	Dillard	M	1993-03-13
200600001	Sally	Sparrow	F	1990-05-28
200600002	John	Liu	M	1989-12-26

In this table the key column is "student_id". If we want to retrieve information about a *particular* student, for instance, the student with student ID '200600001', we would issue a command to the DBMS to tell it to find the row in the "students" table for which "student_id = 200600001". The DBMS would then return the values of the other data elements in this row: "Sally", "Sparrow", "F", "1990-05-28". Such a query is a **key-based query**.

Although queries using the values of keys are the most common way that data is located in tables, sometimes users will want to do queries that involve the values in non-key columns. The relational model allows for the selection of rows from a table based on the values in *any* column, or any combination of columns. For example, a user may try to retrieve a list of all students whose first names are "John". Because non-key data elements are rarely unique, the result of such a **non-key-based query** is usually the retrieval of several rows (whereas single-table key-based queries return single rows).

Relational DBMSs internally generate sorting indices for key columns. These indices allow the DBMS to more quickly and efficiently locate rows in tables when data is retrieved by means of key values, but not when data is retrieved by non-key values. (These sorting indices are internal to the operation of the database, so users of the database are not aware of their existence.) Because retrieval of data according to values in non-key columns cannot take advantage of sorting indices, it places a heavier processing load on the DBMS than retrieval of rows based on the key. Consequently, it takes longer to execute non-key-based queries. However, provided that users are not doing it all the time, use of non-key-based queries is generally not a problem. If users are found to be performing a lot of queries that retrieve data based on non-key columns, the Database Administrator (the person responsible for making sure that the database is operating efficiently) can decide to instruct the DBMS to generate a secondary set of sorting indices for those non-key columns. This will speed up queries based on the contents of those columns.

Codd's first attempt to design a query language for relational databases used an approach which was later referred to as **relational algebra**. (Don't try to understand the use of the word "algebra" in this situation. In this context the word has no strict mathematical meaning. Someone adopted the term because they couldn't think of anything better.) A relational-algebra query language is a "procedural" language that tells the DBMS, more or less step by step, how to retrieve the data. The reserved words (the verbs, prepositions, and conjunctions of the query language) in the early relational-algebra query languages included words like SELECT, PROJECT, and JOIN.

However, after playing with this kind of query structure for a while, Codd decided that there was a better approach, which was referred to as **relational calculus**. (This is another arbitrary and meaningless term, chosen, I assume, because calculus is a more advanced part of mathematics than algebra.) A relational-calculus query language is a "declarative" language that allows you to tell the DBMS *what* you want, instead of *how* to get it. The reserved words used in early examples of this type of query language were words like RETRIEVE, FROM, and WHERE. An example of a query in a relational-calculus language would look something like this:

```
RETRIEVE
    students.student_id,
    students.first_name,
    students.last_name
FROM
    students,
    enrollments
WHERE
    students.student_id = enrollments.student_id AND
    enrollments.course_number = 'P101'
```

In this example I have combined the features of several early relational-calculus languages in order to make the example easier to follow; so this example does not exactly match a specific language. (Some early languages used RANGE OF instead of FROM.) In this example the word RETRIEVE is followed by the names of the columns from which the data in the result is to be taken. These are defined using the "tablename.columnname" notation. The word FROM is followed by the names of *all* the tables involved in the query (in this example, "students" and "enrollments"), not just those tables whose columns appear in the RETRIEVE clause.

The WHERE clause has two parts. The first part tells the DBMS that "student_id" in the table "students" is the same thing as "student_id" in the table "enrollments" (something that the DBMS does not "know" until you tell it). The second part of the WHERE clause is the condition that is to be used in retrieving the data, namely, that we want only students who are enrolled in course number 'P101'.

In this example, the output would be a list of students, showing their student IDs, first names, and last names. In the example tables shown earlier there was only one student who was enrolled in course 'P101', so the result of this query would look something like this:

```
student_id          first_name          last_name
----------          ----------          ----------
200800101           Edgar               Glick
```

Ingres, a successful early relational DBMS product, used a version of relational calculus, called QUEL. QUEL was also used in the Britton-Lee IDM 500 "Intelligent Database Machine". However, other early DBMSs, such as Oracle and IBM's earliest relational DBMSs, used query languages based on relational algebra. These relational-algebra query languages included the original SQL (not to be confused with the present-day SQL) and SEQUEL (not to be confused with the way that "SQL" is sometimes pronounced).

Relational calculus turned out to be a much better approach for a query language than relational algebra. Relational-calculus languages were easier to use and they left it to the DBMS software to select the best way of retrieving the data. By contrast, relational-algebra languages allowed users to write queries that caused the DBMS to do far more work than was necessary. For instance, a user who was a novice, or just cantankerous, could write queries containing a series of table JOINs, one after another, with some SELECT and PROJECT instructions acting on the results of these JOINs. (The action of SELECT was to choose some of the rows in a table; the action of PROJECT was to choose some of the columns.) A JOIN is an operation that combines tables, generating large temporary tables in the computer's memory. Three or more JOINs in a row would generate a gigantic temporary table, which is bad news as regards the performance of the DBMS. A more knowledgeable user would intersperse the JOINs with SELECTs and PROJECTs, so that the size of each intermediate result would be minimized. To put the way that the query is executed entirely in the hands of the user thus turned out to be a poor choice.

Because of the superiority of relational calculus, universities soon started to favor DBMS products that used relational calculus (like Ingres). The vendors of the DBMSs based on relational algebra soon realized that they had backed the wrong horse. They therefore "upgraded" their query languages to relational calculus. The definitive version of the resulting relational-calculus language was the one developed by IBM for their DBMS product "SQL/DS" (which stands for "Structured Query Language/Data Store"). To distinguish it from the earlier relational-algebra SQL, the language itself was initially referred to by the DBMS product name "SQL/DS". When defining SQL/DS, presumably in an attempt to hide the fact that they had originally bet on the wrong approach, IBM and Oracle retained the verb SELECT (which was the hallmark of the original relational-algebra query languages like SEQUEL), but adopted the remaining words from QUEL, so that SQL/DS ended up using SELECT, FROM, and WHERE. (A useful mnemonic for the changes that were made to SQL at this point is to imagine that "DS" stood for "Dump everything except Select".) Nowadays everyone uses a modern version of the SQL/DS query language, which is now shortened to "SQL" and sometimes pronounced "sequel" – thus helping to erase all memories of the relationally algebraic past.

The most important reserved words you find in modern SQL are SELECT, FROM, WHERE, INSERT, SET, UPDATE, and DELETE, together with the reserved words used to form complex conditional statements, such as AND and OR, and word-pairs, such as GROUP BY and ORDER BY, which are used in sorting the data that is returned by a query. In total there are over 300 reserved words. However, many of these are for special purposes. You will not use them very often, if ever. Two other important word-pairs are CREATE TABLE, which brings a new table into existence, and DROP TABLE, which gets rid of it. For the tables that form the database, use of these two commands is normally restricted to the Database Administrator. However, users of the database can also use these commands to create temporary tables. Temporary tables exist only for the duration of the execution of a multi-step SQL query and are used to hold intermediate results while doing the query.

Although the original query languages that were based on relational algebra (like SEQUEL) have been almost forgotten, the relational-algebra term **join** has been re-purposed to mean "the association of one table with another table, within an SQL query, by means of the part of a WHERE clause that defines the two tables' common attribute, that is, the column that appears in both tables". For instance, in the earlier example, the condition:

WHERE students.student_id = enrollments.student_id

establishes a join between "students" and "enrollments", by way of the column "student_id" that they have in common. The condition that establishes a join (like the condition above) is sometimes referred to as a **join condition**. In the less-usual case of two tables needing to be tied together by matching the values of *two or more* attributes that appear in both tables, the join condition for these tables would consist of two or more *separate* equality conditions within the WHERE clause – one for each of the common attributes.

While on the subject of terminology, I should also mention that the terms **SQL query** and **SQL command** tend to be used interchangeably. Although the "Q" in SQL stands for "query", the term "SQL command" is a more accurate generic term when you are talking about data insertions, updates, and deletions (which, strictly speaking, are not queries). In this book I use the term "query" when I am focusing on the retrieval of existing data from a database and "command" when talking about SQL commands more generally.

DBMSs Today

A brief note on the DBMS market today: two of the early players in the field of relational databases – IBM and Oracle – are still very much in the DBMS business today, with their IBM DB2 and Oracle DBMSs. Ingres still exists as an open-source product (now owned by Actian Corporation), but this is a niche product. The head of the Ingres project at the University of California, Berkeley, Robert Epstein, later founded Sybase, whose successful Sybase DBMS was taken over by Microsoft (via a rather complex series of transactions) in 1993 and became Microsoft SQL Server. Oracle is the leader of the "big three" today, with Microsoft SQL Server in second place, and IBM DB2 in third place (although DB2 is often the DBMS of choice for banks and other organizations that handle large quantities of data and require highly-reliable platforms for their data processing).

Schemas, Subschemas, and Views

Before going on to the next topic, I want to briefly mention three pieces of jargon that you might come across in the context of relational databases: schema, subschema, and view.

Throughout this book I use the term **database design** to mean the complete set of tables used to build a particular database for a particular purpose. Although "database design" is the sensible term to use, a database design is sometimes also called a **schema**. This piece of jargon was not Codd's. It originated elsewhere, within the pre-relational DBMS world. However, you will still hear it used today. (For instance, it is often used by database experts when they want to scare off non-technical managers who might want to interfere with their work.) Unfortunately the word "schema" has been pressed into service in many other contexts and has become a technology buzzword that has lost its original precise meaning. I therefore recommend the use of the more down-to-earth term "database design".

The term **subschema** is another a pre-relational term that is sometimes used in the context of relational databases. Subschema means "a view of a database, presented to a particular group of users, in which they can see only a subset of the data contained in the database". A subschema might be created, for example, to hide sensitive information (such as Social Security Numbers) from certain users. When these less-privileged users sign on to the database they are assigned to the subschema, rather than the full database.

In the context of a relational database, a subschema has the specific meaning of "a view of the database in which only certain tables, and/or certain columns of certain tables, can be seen or updated by a group of users". A more down-to-earth term for a subschema is simply a "view". However, the term "view" has now acquired a more restricted meaning, which will be explained in a moment. So, to avoid confusion, it is better to use the term **database view** as a translation of "subschema".

The term "view" is nowadays understood to mean "a virtual table defined in SQL by means of an CREATE VIEW query". Such a virtual table does not actually exist in the database; but queries can be directed at it as though it existed. For example, the results of a query to list all students and the courses that they are taking could be defined as a view, using the following SQL command. Note that I have written this command in an easy-to-read format, by splitting it over several lines, and by progressively indenting the various lines to indicate which lines are inside which clause. You can spread SQL commands across several lines like this, without affecting their operation. I strongly recommend that you make a practice of doing this, even if those around you are too lazy to do it.

```
CREATE VIEW course_signups AS
  (SELECT
      students.student_id,
      students.first_name,
      students.last_name,
      courses.course_number,
      courses.course_title
  FROM
      students,
      enrollments,
      courses
  WHERE
      students.student_id = enrollments.student_id AND
      enrollments.course_number = courses.course_number
  )
```

The above SQL command is in two parts, one nested inside the other:

- The outer part of the SQL command is the CREATE VIEW statement that tells the DBMS, "create a virtual table called 'course_signups' according to the instructions contained within the parentheses that follow".

- The inner part, contained within the parentheses, is a SELECT statement.

If this inner SELECT statement were executed on its own, without the outer CREATE VIEW statement, it would yield the following results:

```
student_id   first_name  last_name   course_number  course_title
----------   ----------  ---------   -------------  ------------
200800101    Edgar       Glick       P101           Philosophy
200800101    Edgar       Glick       M101           Mathematics
200600001    Sally       Sparrow     M342           Database Design
200600002    John        Liu         P321           Life, the Universe, and Everything
```

Note that, in these results, information about students who are enrolled in more than one course (in this example, just Edgar Glick) is repeated for each course that they are enrolled in.

What the outer statement (the CREATE VIEW statement) does is to create a virtual table called "course_signups", with the column names and contents shown above. I repeat: this table does not actually exist in the database.

Once the CREATE VIEW command has been executed, users can direct queries at "course_signups" as though it were a real table. When a user composes and executes an SQL command directed at this virtual table, the DBMS translates that command into operations on the real tables in the database, such that the final results are those that would have been obtained if the virtual table were a real table.

For example, a user can get the full details of all students who are enrolled in course 'P101' using a very simple SQL command directed at the "course_signups" view as follows:

```
SELECT *
FROM
   course_signups
WHERE
   course_signups.course_number = 'P101'
```

In this command the asterisk symbol is a wild-card symbol, used in many programming languages to mean "any value" or "all values". (Note that, as in most programming languages, an asterisk in SQL can be a wild-card symbol or a multiplication sign, depending on the context within which it appears.) When used on its own in the SELECT clause, the asterisk acts as a wild-card symbol meaning "all of the columns" (in the "course_signups" view). The results of such a query, using the data in the above example, would be:

```
student_id first_name  last_name    course_number  course_title
---------- ----------  ---------    -------------  ------------
200800101  Edgar       Glick        P101           Philosophy
```

In summary, because the term "view" may still, in certain contexts, be used in its original sense of "subschema", there is potential for confusion between this meaning and the newer meaning. It may help to avoid confusion if you use the term **table view** to mean "view" in the sense of the above example, and the term "database view" to mean subschema, that is, a restricted view of the database as a whole.

Normalization

After 1970, Codd did more work on the relational model and came up with another very important concept – the need to "normalize" the database design. **Normalization** of a database means "choosing a set of tables, and columns for those tables, that is such that no modification anomalies can ever occur".

The term **modification anomaly** is used here to mean "deletion anomaly, insertion anomaly, or update anomaly". For the time being we will consider only deletion anomalies and insertion anomalies. Update anomalies are a special class of modification anomaly which we will look at in later chapters. I will use the generic term "modification anomaly" when talking about all types of anomaly, but I will refer specifically to "deletion anomaly", "insertion anomaly", and "update anomaly" when giving individual examples.

An **insertion anomaly** occurs in a database when it is impossible to place a new piece of information into the database because another piece of data would have to be inserted first. A **deletion anomaly** occurs when the deletion of a no-longer-needed or no-longer-valid piece of data causes a still-needed piece of data to be lost from the database.

For example, suppose that, in designing a University Administration database, we decided to represent courses *only* in a table called "enrollments_notnorm", with columns "student_id", "term", "year", "course_number", "course_title", "credits", and "teacher_id". A row is to be added to this table for every student currently enrolled in a course; and a row is to be deleted for every student who completes a course (or withdraws from a course). Such a table, with a few example rows, might look like this:

Table name: enrollments_notnorm						
student_id	term	year	course_number	course_title	credits	teacher_id
200800101	1	2008	P101	Philosophy	4.5	T0042
200800101	1	2008	M101	Mathematics	4.5	T0105
200600001	1	2008	M342	Database Design	3.0	T0088
200600002	1	2008	P321	Life, the Universe, and Everything	3.0	T0042

The values of "student_id" associate the rows in this table with rows in the "students" table (not shown here); and the values of "teacher_id" associate the rows in this table with rows in a "teachers" table (also not shown here). This "enrollments_notnorm" table exhibits both insertion anomalies and deletion anomalies, as follows:

- *Insertion:* If the university decides to add to a new course to the curriculum, it cannot do so without at least one student enrolling in the course. This is because a row cannot be added to the enrollments table without a value of "student_id" to go in the first column, which is the key column. (Obviously one could imagine various ways of "kludging" the design, for example, defining an imaginary student with ID '000000000' who is used as a placeholder. However, this would be an example of bad database design.)

- *Deletion:* At the end of the term/semester/year, when all rows are deleted from the "enrollments" table to reflect the fact that all students have completed their courses, the courses vanish from the database. The courses cannot be found when the first student wants to enroll in one or more courses at the start of the next term/semester/year.

These anomalies arise from the fact that we have tried to place information about courses in the table that records enrollments. (Further anomalies of a similar nature arise from the fact that we have also placed "teacher_id" in this table.) To prevent such anomalies arising, we need to split this "enrollments_notnorm" table into a number of separate tables. Specifically, we need to modify the database design to include the following tables:

- A table called "courses", with columns "course_number", "course_title", and "credits". This will record the basic information about the courses that are on offer. (This table was shown in the first example of the database design near the start of this chapter.)

- A table called "enrollments", with columns "student_id", "course_number", "term", and "year". This will record which students are enrolled in which courses, without holding any other information about either the students or the courses. (This was also shown in the first example of the database design near the start of this chapter.)

- A table called "course_teachers", with columns "course_number" and "teacher_id". This will record which teachers are assigned to teach which courses, without holding any other information about either the teachers or the courses. (Note that, in this example, I have assumed that a separate "teachers" table already exists. I could have created a more extreme example of a problematic table by cramming information about teachers into the "enrollments_notnorm" table as well.)

So, along with the tables "students" and "teachers", we now have a total of five tables, in place of the three tables that we started with in the anomaly-ridden design (which consisted of only the tables "students", "teachers", and "enrollments_notnorm"). This five-table part of the complete database design (a design which would, in practice, have many more tables than these five) is illustrated below. Note that, in order to save space, I have shown the empty tables, before any data is inserted into them. I will do this whenever I want to give an overview of a database design, without going into detailed examples of table contents.

Table name: **students**				
student_id	first_name	last_name	sex	date_of_birth

Table name: **courses**		
course_number	course_title	credits

Table name: **enrollments**			
student_id	course_number	term	year

Table name: **teachers**					
teacher_id	first_name	last_name	sex	date_of_birth	date_of_hire

Table name: **course_teachers**	
teacher_id	course_number

Having examined the three tables that we started with ("students", "teachers", and "enrollments_notnorm") – to see if there are any modification anomalies – and having corrected the design so as to eliminate these anomalies (as illustrated above), we would next take a close look at all the other tables in the database design. For each table, and the tables associated with it via shared keys, we would consider (a) what happens when we try to add new information into the database, and (b) what information might be unintentionally lost when we delete things from the database. If any potential anomalies were encountered, then we would address these as we did in the above example – by splitting certain tables into two or more tables.

Normalization thus consists of breaking up tables into two or more tables with fewer columns, until all possible insertion and deletion anomalies are prevented. There are complicated sets of rules for determining when a database design is fully normalized. However, once you have done a few designs following these rules, you will soon get a "feel" for normalization and be able to do it instinctively.

15

Normalization is thus rather like learning to drive a car: you start by thinking of each separate step, but eventually it ceases to be a step-by-step, rules-based process and becomes intuitive.

I will return to the subject of normalization in Chapter 4.

The Story So Far

To summarize what we have covered in this chapter:

- Almost all modern DBMSs are relational, that is, they are based on tables. They use a standardized query language called SQL. SQL is a relational-calculus or "declarative" style of query language, which uses reserved words like SELECT, FROM, and WHERE.

- Databases are created in a relational DBMS according to a "database design" (or "database schema", if you're trying to impress someone), consisting of a set of tables. You bring the empty database into existence using a series of CREATE TABLE commands.

- To comply with the relational model, one or several columns (in some cases, all columns) of each table must be designated as key columns. The value (or set of values) that appears in a key column (or in the two or more key columns) must be unique within the table. This means that the value of "the key" uniquely identifies a row in the table. It also means that every row as a whole is sure to be unique, regardless of what values appear in the non-key columns.

- Once the tables have been created, users can start inserting data, in the form of rows added to one or several tables. Later they, or others, can retrieve, modify, add to, or delete some or all of the data. (Some users will be given read-only rights in the database, while others will have full add/delete/modify rights.)

- In the relational model, no table is in any way "senior" to any other: all tables are created equal. There is no such thing as a "record", as there was in the older types of database. Instead, data is placed in the tables, which represent an expression of the data in its most basic form, with no in-built assumptions about how it is going to be used.

- When users perform queries involving two or more tables, the user tells the DBMS at the time of the query which columns in each table correspond to which columns in the other tables involved in the query. (This is done by means of equality conditions in the WHERE clause of the query.) There is no permanent association between the tables, outside the context of queries.

- A database design is said to be normalized if it is such that no modification anomalies can ever occur. Normalization of a database design (if the design is not already normalized) involves breaking up tables into two or more tables with fewer columns, until all possible modification anomalies are prevented.

Summary of Jargon

Jargon	How common	Sensible term/explanation
Relational model	Universal	Doing it with tables
Relation	Now rare	Table
Tuple	Now very rare	Row
Relation of degree 'n'	Now very rare	Table with 'n' columns
Key	Universal	A designated column of a table (or a designated set of columns – in some cases *all* the columns), each value (or set of values) of which may only occur once in the table, so that each row of the table is sure to be unique and so that the key uniquely identifies a particular row.
Relational algebra	Now rare	A style of query language in which the user tells the DBMS exactly *how* to execute the query, using reserved words such as SELECT, PROJECT, and JOIN.
Relational calculus	Now rare, apart from in some research papers	A style of query language in which the user tells the DBMS *what* he or she wants, using the reserved words SELECT (originally RETRIEVE), FROM, and WHERE.
Join (or join condition)	Very common	*Originally*: in a relational-algebra-based DBMS, the creation of a temporary table, while executing a query, by combining two tables via matching attribute values. *Today*: a condition in a WHERE clause that associates two tables (named in the FROM clause) with one another.
Normalization	Universal	Tinkering with a relational database design to eliminate the possibility of modification anomalies.
Schema	Fairly common	Database design (that is, the table names, their column names, and the designation of key columns).
Subschema	Widely understood but not often used	Database view, that is, a view of a database, presented to a group of users, in which they can see and update only a subset of the data contained in the database.
View	Very common	*Originally:* subschema (see above). Better referred to as a "database view". *Today*: a virtual table, defined by an SQL command that operates on one or several real tables. Better referred to as a "table view".

CHAPTER 2

THINKING ABOUT DATA MORE CLEARLY

The Entity-Relationship Model

Following Codd's revolutionary idea, researchers started thinking more clearly about data in an abstract sense. They saw how misguided all the pre-1970 attempts to structure data within databases had been, and how the world of data really isn't hierarchical at all. Throwing out all the dreadful hierarchical diagrams from the early 1960s, they sought ways of modeling the "true" structure of data. In 1976, an ideal approach was found by Peter Chen.

Peter Chen, a Harvard Ph.D. who served on the faculty of MIT and UCLA (and later, in 1983, became Distinguished Chair Professor at Louisiana State University), published a now-famous paper, The Entity Relationship Model – Toward a Unified View of Data, *ACM Transactions on Database Systems, Volume 1, Number 1, March 1976*, pp 9-36. Chen's Entity-Relationship Model, or "E-R Model" for short, included both the model in concept and a practical way of drawing an "E-R Diagram" to represent the model.

Chen used six fairly straightforward terms in his model: data entity (or more simply, "entity"), entity set, relationship, cardinality, attribute, and key attribute. I will now explain these terms, in most cases paraphrasing Chen's definitions.

The first term, **data entity**, means "something, in which we are interested, that exists and which is distinguishable from other similar things". Thus, a car might be called a data entity, even though there may be thousands of cars of the same model and color, because we can distinguish a particular car from the others by its chassis number. By contrast, a grain of sand is not a data entity because, no matter how interested we might be in grains of sand, there is no practical way of telling one from another. The point of the phrase "in which we are interested" is to make it clear that, in building a data model, we can ignore things that are irrelevant to the database that we are planning to design. For example, a parking ticket may be distinguishable from other parking tickets by way of a serial number on the ticket, and it certainly has a lot to do with cars; but we are not interested in parking tickets if we are building a database for a car manufacturer such as Ford in order to record details of all the cars that Ford has built.

An **entity set** is "a collection of all similar entities". How you define your entity set depends on your view of the world. For example, Ford might define an entity set as "all cars made by Ford", whereas the police might be interested in "all cars registered in this country". (When you eventually start to draw your E-R diagram and then design your database, you will soon get tired of saying "entity set". In fact, most people just talk about "entity" when they mean "entity set", except when they need to make clear the distinction between a particular entity and the entity set.)

The third term, **relationship**, means "an association between two or more entity sets". For example, suppose that I define as entities: *student*, *teacher*, and *course*. One relationship might be *student is enrolled in course*. The relationship *is enrolled in* associates students with courses. Similarly, another relationship might be *teacher is teaching course*.

Conceptually, it is possible to have three-way relationships. However, these can generally be expressed as two or three two-way relationships. This makes it very much easier to represent the relationships in a database design. Chen's model therefore assumes that all relationships are expressed as two-way relationships.

It is also possible, and quite common, to have a relationship between an entity set and itself. (Note that I used "entity set" here because it sounds odd otherwise.) Thus, you might have: *student is sibling of student*. Acknowledging the existence of this relationship shows that you are interested in the fact that some students are siblings of other students and you want to record this in the database that you are going to build.

As with entities, it is important to limit the identification of relationships to those that are relevant to the purpose of the database that you are about to build. Thus, a possible relationship is: *student has dated student*. This might be interesting to some of the student population, but certainly doesn't belong in the design of a University Administration database.

Another common example of a type of relationship is a set-membership (or "generalization") relationship. This type of relationship is often referred to as an *is a* relationship or, in order to confuse database-design novices, an *isa* relationship. An *is a* relationship records the fact that members of one entity set are also members of a broader entity set. For example, you might have relationships such as the following: *student is a universitymember*, and *teacher is a universitymember*. In this example *universitymember* is the more general entity set.

Chen's fourth term, **cardinality** (of relationships), means "for the entities at one end of a relationship, how many entities at the other end of the relationship can have that relationship to them". (The concept of cardinality was already recognized before Chen defined it very specifically in the context of the E-R model.) There are three possibilities for cardinality: one-to-one, one-to-many, and many-to-many. For example, *student is a universitymember* is one-to-one: although the entity sets *student* and *universitymember* both contain many entities, one particular student can only be himself or herself as a university member. He or she can't be two members. But the relationship *student is enrolled in course* is a many-to-many relationship, because each individual student can be enrolled in several courses, and each course may have many students enrolled in it.

An example of a one-to-many relationship is *student has on loan librarybook*, because a student may borrow several books at once, but a specific book (assuming that we are recording each individual copy) can be on loan to only one student at a time.

The fifth term that Chen used (which was a term widely used before he gave it a specific meaning) was **attribute**. In the context of the E-R model this means "a property, in which we are interested, of the entities in an entity set; or a property of a relationship". So, for example, the attributes of the entity *student* that we might include in our data model might are first name, last name, sex, date of birth, and student ID number. Note that these are attributes of the student himself or herself. Things like room number, home address, and so on, are *not* attributes of the student. They are attributes of other entities (such as room or dwelling). The student's room still exists, and his parent's house still exists, even if he quits college and goes to work in another country.

An important point about the E-R model is that relationships, like entities, can have attributes (although they do not have to, whereas entities do). Before looking at attributes for relationships, we will first go on to Chen's sixth term – "key attribute".

Key attributes are attributes that uniquely identify an individual entity. For an entity set to be represented in a database, it is essential that one of its attributes, or a combination of two or more of its attributes, be designated as the key that will uniquely identify any individual entity in that entity set, and distinguish it from all the other entities in the entity set. Examples of key attributes are (a) the chassis number on a car, and (b) the serial number on a DVD player taken together with the name of the manufacturer. In this second example, the manufacturer needs to be considered a part of the two-attribute key because two different manufacturers may use a similar serial-number scheme, so that two DVD players, of different make and model, may end up having the same serial number.

Key Selection

The selection of good key attributes out of various candidates is sometimes difficult. If the members of the entity set are clearly unique, but the entities do not possess an absolutely reliable key attribute or attributes, then it may be recognized (during the building of the data model) that a key attribute needs to be "created". For example, to identify individual students it is not adequate to use their names. Two students may have the same name. In some countries it may be possible to use students' National Identity Numbers or Social Security Numbers as Student ID numbers. Such numbers are guaranteed to be unique. But where there is no such number, or where privacy laws prohibit the use of such a pre-existing number by a university, it may be necessary to make it a condition of setting up the database that unique Student ID numbers be issued to all students. We may refer to such a key attribute as an **artificial key** because it is not a key attribute that the entity natural possesses. Note that, in this example, the artificial key is imposed on the real world: students have to be told what their Student ID numbers are. These numbers are also likely to be used on student-identity cards.

Another example of a situation where an artificial key is required is for an entity like an address. The lines of an address itself do not form good key attributes, because of the various different formats that an address may have. (There may or may not be an apartment number; the building may have a name instead of a number; abbreviations, like "St." for "Street", may be used or not; and so on.) For this reason we need to create an artificial key, such as an "address ID number", that will be assigned programmatically as each address is entered into the database, and will then be used as the key. In this example the artificial key is used only in the database: it is not forced on the real world. Artificial keys that are used only within a database are much more common than artificial keys that are forced on the real world (like a student ID number, which is necessitated by the need to build one or more university databases and, for practical reasons, has to be adopted for use in the real world).

When you are drawing your E-R diagram, and you add an entity that requires an artificial key, you should make a note on the diagram that the attribute's key is an artificial key. You should also record whether or not the artificial key is to be forced on the real world or used only for the purposes of recording information in the database.

Another solution to the problem of finding key attributes for entities that do not have good already-existing keys is to operate a **forced key** system. This means that you decide to use, as key attributes, some already-existing but not-necessarily-unique attributes (such as people's first name, last name, and middle names or initials). To make this scheme work you have to write a program that controls the interaction between the user and the database during data entry. This program will check each new name that the user enters and reject the attempted use of a name if the combination of first name, last name, and middle name or initials already exists in the database. The user will then need to provide additional initials, or make up a middle name, in order to provide a unique key for the database. This may sound messy; and typically it is. However, there are some situations where it may be better than the other options. One example of a forced key, which is now very well known, is the creation of email addresses. In order to come up with unique email addresses in large organizations, email system administrators sometimes have to ask users who have very common names to invent middle initials or names, resulting in strange email addresses like "john.x.y.z.smith@bigbank.com" or "david.treasury.wong@bigcompany.com".

Attributes of Relationships

Having looked at the attributes of entities, we now turn to the topic of attributes of relationships. As mentioned earlier, relationships sometimes, but not always, have their own attributes. The attributes of relationships typically define:

- When the relationship applies (for example, the term and year that a student is taking a course). In this case the attributes of the relationship may be a pair of dates – a start date and an end date – or attributes that represent a period of time, such as a term and a year.

- When the relationship was established (for example, the date of becoming a member of a club). In this case the attribute of the relationship is a single date.

- When the relationship will end (for example, the expiry date of a subscription). In this case the attribute of the relationship is also a single date.

- Who established the relationship (for example, who donated the work of art to the museum). In this case the attribute of the relationship may be a name.

These additional attributes are generally not key attributes of the relationship itself; but there is no reason why they cannot be. For example, if the relationship represents an event that can occur more than once, but the individual events are not important enough to be represented in the E-R model as an entity set in their own right, you can maintain a record of the separate events by making the "date" attribute of the relationship a key attribute. For example, in the relationship *student has dated student,* an attribute "date_of_occurrence" of the relationship could record the date of each date. This attribute thus becomes a key attribute of the *has dated* relationship.

Another point to note about relationships, which will become clearer in a moment when we look at how to use an E-R diagram to derive a database design, is that each relationship exists in the context of the particular entity sets at each "end" of the relationship. Each relationship therefore needs to be distinguished from other instances of an identical relationship in a different part of the model.

For example, there may be many *is a* relationships in various parts of the model. We need to be able to talk about each one in its own right. The information about which entity sets are at the two ends of the relationship is therefore a defining attribute of the relationship. When the relationship is shown on an E-R diagram, there is no doubt about where the relationship fits into the model; so there is no need to label the relationship as connecting the entities that it does. But if we need to write about the relationship in a separate document, it is necessary to include information about the entity sets between which it operates.

The individual entities in an entity set are identified by the values of their key attributes. It follows that the key attributes of the two entities at each end of a relationship represent the necessary (and, in most cases, sufficient) information to distinguish the relationship from all other relationships in the E-R model. The attributes of a relationship are thus:

- The key attributes of the entity sets between which the relationship operates.

- Any attributes that the relationship possesses in its own right (which are typically non-key attributes, but may sometimes be key attributes).

For example, if the entity *course* has, as its key attribute, "course number", and the entity *student* has, as its key attribute, "student ID number", then the relationship *is enrolled in* that connects *student* to *course* acquires the key attributes from both entities: "student ID number" and "course number". The relationship *is enrolled in* might have, as its own attributes, "term" and "year".

22

Summary of Jargon (Part 2)

Jargon	Definition
E-R Data Model (or E-R Diagram)	A data-oriented description of the piece of the real world for which you want to build a database.
Entity (or Data Entity)	Something, in which we are interested, that exists and which is distinguishable from other similar things.
Entity Set	A collection of all similar entities.
Relationship	An association between two entity sets.
Cardinality (of a relationship)	How many entities can be on each end of the relationship: one-to-one, one-to-many, many-to-many.
Attribute	A property, in which we are interested, of the entities in an entity set, or of a relationship.
Key Attribute	An attribute that uniquely identifies an individual entity within an entity set; or, less commonly, an attribute of a relationship that uniquely identifies one of several instances of the relationship that occur between the same two entities.

Drawing an E-R Diagram

There are no hard-and-fast rules about how to represent a data model on paper. The original scheme for drawing an "E-R Diagram" was as follows:

- Represent entity sets by rectangles. Inside each rectangle write either the entity name (for example, "student"). Alternatively, you can use the entity set name (for example, "students"). Although this is technically more correct, it has the disadvantage of clashing with the grammar of the relationship names (which should be based on singular subjects and objects, for example, "is enrolled in"). In the following example I will use the singular form, for example, "student".

- Represent relationships by diamond-shaped boxes. These are connected by lines to the rectangles that represent the entities to which they refer. Write the description of each relationship (for example, "is enrolled in") inside its diamond-shaped box. Relationships are typically written as though they had singular subjects and objects. (If you have chosen to label the entity-set rectangles with plural names, do not worry too much about grammatical agreement between the entity sets and the relationships.)

- Put arrows on the relationship lines to show which way the "verb" in the relationship operates (for example, the verb "is enrolled in" operates in the direction from "students" to "courses"; so the arrow points towards "courses").

- Represent the cardinality of the relationship on the two lines that attach the relationship diamond to its entities (for example, '1' on each line for one-to-one, '1' and 'n' for one-to-many, and 'm' and 'n' for many-to-many).

- Show the attributes of each entity and each relationship by writing the name of each attribute inside an oval, placed close to the rectangle or diamond. Attach each oval, by a line, to its entity rectangle, or to its relationship diamond.

- Underline the <u>attribute names</u> that are key attributes.

- For relationships, you can take it as a "given" that the key attributes of the two entities connected by the relationship are attributes of the relationship; so you do not need to create ovals for these attributes. Draw attribute ovals only for the attributes that belong to the relationship itself.

There is no need to follow this original scheme exactly. Many variants have been used. (The number of different shapes used in the diagram is generally reduced in computer programs that are used to draw E-R diagrams.) The ovals (containing the attributes) were not a great idea in the first place. Some people prefer to use rectangles for the attributes, and circles for the entities. But even so, the attributes still tend to clutter up the diagram.

One fairly good approach to drawing an E-R diagram is to leave the non-key attributes off the diagram and record them on a separate sheet; then move the key attributes inside the entity rectangles, under the entity names. (They should still be underlined, to make it clear that they are key attributes.) Similarly, if any of the relationships have key attributes then these should be placed inside the relationship diamonds and underlined. The following is an example of such a simplified diagram. (The separate lists of non-key attributes for the entities and relationships are not shown here.)

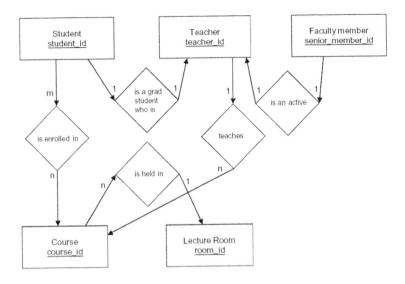

Here are some useful guidelines to follow when creating an E-R diagram:

- Identify all the entities first, before thinking about the relationships.

- If you think that you have identified a three-way relationship, think again. There is always a better way of describing what is going on – a way that can be represented in terms of relationships between two entities.

- When choosing the name of the relationship, if your first attempt sounds muddled, consider reversing the direction of the "verb". For example, instead of *is being taken by* for *course→student*, try *is enrolled in* for *student→course*.

- Make sure attributes are all single valued (for instance, length or width, but never "dimensions").

- Think carefully about what attributes the relationships may have (in their own right), for example, attributes associated with time.

- Do not be afraid to include a number of *is a* relationships, for example, *capitalized-software is a depreciable-asset*. These relationships can be very useful.

- When two entity sets are connected by an *is a* relationship, the less-general entity set can have additional attributes that do not apply to the more-general entity set. For example, in an accounting database, the entity *capitalized-software* may have an attribute "programming language used", which would be nonsense for the more-general entity set *depreciable-asset* (because that entity set would typically include things like equipment). However, the less-general entity set *must* have all the attributes of the more-general entity set. So, if the attributes of

25

the general entity set *depreciable-asset* are "asset ID", "initial book value", "date of purchase", "depreciation term", "supplier name", and "product name", then the attributes of the more-specific entity set (*capitalized-software*), would consist of all of the above, plus "programming language used". In other words, when going from the more general to the less general entity set, you can add attributes (in this example, "programming language used"), but you cannot drop attributes.

- Relationships are allowed to have both their ends going to the same entity set, for example, the relationship *is a sibling of*, which connects at both its ends to the entity set *student*.

- Some entity sets will need two or more key attributes (for example, "manufacturer" and "serial number") to uniquely identify an individual entity in the set. In this case the key is formed by these key attributes taken together. However, these two or more key attributes are kept as distinct, separate, single-valued attributes. They are not in any way combined on the diagram.

To make the point that there are no hard-and-fast rules about the symbols that are used in an E-R diagram, below is an E-R diagram showing the generalization relationships between classes of quadrilaterals. In this diagram each entity set (except for the most-general, *quadrilateral*) is represented by the quadrilateral shape itself!

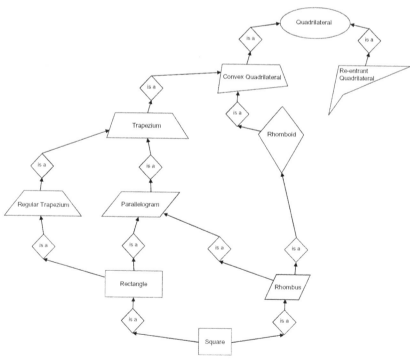

Using an E-R Diagram to Design a Database

Some database designers like to leap straight into designing a database, without taking the time to draw an E-R diagram first. While this may be acceptable for a very simple database (for example, one with only three tables), or one very similar to one that the designer has built before, it is generally a bad idea to skip the E-R diagram step. Drawing the E-R diagram forces you to think very clearly about the data that you are dealing with, before you start to do the database design. It greatly simplifies the task of designing the database. It also provides a valuable reference document that can be used in the future by someone else who needs to extend the scope of the database by adding more tables, or adding columns to existing tables.

Before looking at how an E-R diagram is used to create a relational database design, there is one very important thing to note: Chen's Entity-Relationship Model stands on its own, completely separate from Codd's Relational Model for DBMSs. Because the creation of the first databases pre-dated Chen's Entity-Relationship model by about fifteen years, there was nothing like an E-R diagram in use during the time of the earlier hierarchical DBMSs and network DBMSs. However, there is nothing in the E-R model to prevent it from being used, and useful, in the context of non-relational DBMSs.

Nevertheless, if you were to draw an E-R diagram and then try to translate it into a hierarchical database design or a network database design, it would become painfully obvious how unsuited to its intended use a hierarchical DBMS or network DBMS really is. By contrast, when you use an E-R diagram as the starting point for doing a relational database design, everything falls into place so easily that the strength of the relational model is made even more apparent.

Starting with an E-R diagram, the following steps are all that it takes to design the database for a relational DBMS:

- First, create a table for every entity set, giving it a column for each attribute. Make sure that your key attribute or attributes really work as a key.

- Second, create a table for each relationship, giving it a column for each of its own attributes (if there are any) plus – this is essential – columns for the key attributes of the two entity sets between which the relationship operates. The relationship's own attribute or attributes will generally not be additional key attributes of the relationship, but one of them might be (such as a date or an order reference number).

- Third, take a good look at the design to see if it is already normalized. (As explained earlier, there are rules for determining this; but they are really tedious. Normalization as an "art", rather than a "science", is a much easier task.) If you spot a problem, it is generally solved by splitting "entity" tables (vertically) into two or more tables, with fewer columns, and adding "relationship" tables as necessary. I will return to the topic of normalization again in a moment.

- Don't be afraid to have tables with only one column, containing a single key attribute, for example, a table called "faculties" with a single key column called "faculty_codes". This table records the existence of all the faculties in a university, using abbreviations such as "SCI" for Science. (A second column, giving the full names of the faculties would normally be included if there were a need to create reports in which the name appeared in full. However, this may not be the case with some entities. In such cases a single column is enough.) Such an entity-representing table allows the database user to enter all the faculty codes into the database before any teachers (or other entities that have relationships with faculties) are added to the database.

- Last, in order to create the actual database, you will need to decide on the **format** of each attribute (sometimes referred to as the **type** or **datatype** of the attribute), for example, "floating point decimal number", "integer", "character string of variable length", "binary value", and so on. You will need to take account of the specific formats supported by the DBMS that you are going to use. I will give specific examples of formats later.

Naming Tables

The process of turning an E-R diagram into a database design requires that you use a certain amount of common sense, particularly when it comes to naming tables. Tables that represent entity sets are fairly easy to name. The names should be reasonably short, but not cryptic, and preferably plural. The names should also reflect the basic nature of the entity, not its immediate use in the database. So, "students", "courses", "addresses", "customers", and "emailaddresses" are all fine. By contrast, the following are *not* good choices for table names:

- "studentsofuniversityofhongkong" (too long).
- "stu" (too short and cryptic).
- "table142" (makes life impossible for the user, since it conveys no useful information).
- "studentaddresses" (limits the applicability of the table, preventing broader use).

In the last example it would have been be better to create a table called "addresses" that can hold anyone's address, rather than creating a table specifically for the addresses of students.

Although, as mentioned earlier, relational DBMSs do not force you to use the same column names for the same attribute in two different tables, it is a very good practice to keep them the same, otherwise you will make life needlessly difficult for everyone.

When it comes to naming relationships, things are not as easy. Using the entire text of the description of the relationship from the E-R diagram generally makes the name too long. If you can find a single word that captures the essence of the relationship, that is ideal. It does not have to be a verb: use of a noun is fine, and in many cases is better. So, for the name of the table that represents the relationship *is enrolled in*, "enrollments" is a good choice.

Unfortunately, if you look at the table names used in many real-world databases, you may find relationship-representing tables with names built from the names of the tables that represent the entities that the relationship connects, for example, "students_courses". While a name like this has the advantage of clearly indicating that the table is a relationship between students and courses, it has the big disadvantage of not telling you what the table is all about: although we can probably guess that it is about enrollment, it could possibly be about a waiting list for a fully-booked course. On the whole, "enrollments" is a much better choice for the name of such a table.

By the way, you may come across another, even-more-confusing naming convention for the naming of relationship-representing tables, based on using names like "students_courses_intersect". I don't know where this naming convention comes from. Personally, I find it really annoying; and I certainly don't recommend it.

In some circumstances it is acceptable to give relationship-representing tables names that are derived from the names of the two entities between which the relationship operates, provided that (a) there is no sensible alternative, and (b) the meaning is clear – for example, "course_teachers", which is unambiguous.

Before I leave the topic of table naming, I want to prepare you for the real world by warning you that you will encounter truly dreadful table-naming practices in many database designs. This is a great shame because carefully chosen table names make the job of the person who later has to modify or extend your database design much easier. They also make it much easier for expert users who type their own SQL queries to create reports. You will hear many excuses for sloppy table-name selection, such as: "Even application programmers don't see the table names because they interact with a software layer that hides the actual names"; "The DBMS doesn't allow table names longer than 30 characters and it's hard to come give every table a meaningful name within 30 characters"; or "I'm too busy to worry about the person who will be maintaining the design". None of these excuses is acceptable.

Normalization

Once the initial database design has been finished, the next thing that you have to do, before creating the database, is to normalize the design. (This was described very briefly earlier. I will go into the subject in more detail in Chapter 4.) If you are very lucky, the design may already be normalized, particularly if you were thinking very clearly when drawing the E-R diagram. If you have given the entities an excessive number of attributes, the first-attempt design, derived immediately from the E-R diagram, will probably be non-normalized. (There really isn't a better word for this condition. "Abnormal" might be misunderstood, and "abnormalized" sounds silly.)

For a database to be normalized, at a minimum the non-key attributes should be what is called "**fully functionally dependent** on the key attributes". The term "fully functionally dependent", sometimes abbreviated to "FFD", is not a great piece of terminology, but we are stuck with it.

If an attribute is "functionally dependent" on another attribute it means that if we know the latter we can find out the former. For example, we might say that the attribute "sex" is functionally dependent on the attribute "first_name" – because if we are told the first name we can determine the value of "sex". Obviously this is not always true in practice; but for the sake of this example we will pretend that it is true.

Fully functionally dependent means that the relationship is such that the value of the dependent attribute is directly and completely determined by the value of the other attribute. For example, if we are given the room number of a particular classroom, we can go and measure the height of that room's ceiling. The value of "ceiling_height" is thus FFD on "room_number" within the building. This situation is subtly different from the dependency "first_name" → "sex", where the value of "first_name" is not sufficient information to allow me to find the entity (that is, the particular student) and make enquiries about his or her sex. The functional dependency arises from constraints operating in the real world on the values of "first_name" and "sex", such that we can rule out certain combinations, like "John" and "F". For an attribute of a student, like "sex", we find *full* functional dependency only on "student_id". For example, if we are given the value of "student_id", we can go and find that particular student and ask him or her about his or her first name and sex. So, in the same way that the ceiling height is directly and completely determined by knowing the value of "room_number", the values of "first_name" and "sex" are directly and completely determined by knowledge of the value of "student_id".

Following the rule that all the non-key attributes must be fully functionally dependent on the key attribute (or key attributes), the entity set "students", with key attribute "student_id", can have attributes like "first_name", "last_name", "sex", and "date_of_birth". However, it should not have attributes like "home_address", "room_number", "phone_number", or "major_subject", because these are not essential attributes of the student himself or herself.

It is sometimes tempting to include in a data model, and in the resulting database design, non-key attributes that are not essential attributes of the entity in question – to save all the effort of thinking about what the other entity sets are that these attributes belong to, and what the relationships are between those entity sets and the main entity set that you are dealing with. However, this temptation should be resisted. You may think you are saving yourself work by having a smaller number of entity sets, each festooned with attributes; but in fact you are sowing the seeds of problems for the database users – problems which will take you a lot more time to fix once the database is live.

Creating the Database

Once you have arrived at a set of tables that you believe to be normalized, you are just about finished. Now you can write the CREATE TABLE statements to bring your database into existence on your DBMS.

These statements will look something like the following. The details may vary from one DBMS to another. (By the way, I am *not* going to use this example in its entirety in the chapters that follow. Instead, I will simplify it by using just the first five tables and modifying the "teachers" table to include all the information about teachers, such as first name, last name, and so on.)

CREATE TABLE students (student_id varchar(9), first_name varchar(40),
                last_name varchar(40), sex char(1), date_of_birth datetime)

CREATE TABLE courses (course_number varchar(8), course_title varchar(40),
                credits decimal(3,1))

CREATE TABLE enrollments (student_id varchar(9), course_number varchar(8), term char(1),
                year int)

CREATE TABLE teachers (teacher_id varchar(9))

CREATE TABLE course_teachers (teacher_id varchar(9), course_number varchar(8))

CREATE TABLE faculty_teachers (teacher_id varchar(9), faculty_member_id varchar(9))

CREATE TABLE student_teachers (teacher_id varchar(9), student_id varchar(9))

CREATE TABLE faculty_members (faculty_member_id varchar(9), first_name varchar(40),
                last_name varchar(40), sex char(1), date_of_birth datetime,
                date_of_hire datetime)

CREATE TABLE lecture_rooms (room_id varchar(8), room_name varchar(20))

CREATE TABLE room_use (room_id varchar(8), course_number varchar(8), day char(3),
                start_hour int, start_minute int, end_hour int, end_minute int)

The descriptors like "varchar(40)", "char(1)", "int", and "datetime" after each column name are the definitions of the format of the column: "varchar(40)" means "variable length character string of up to forty characters", "char(1)" means "a character string of exactly one character", "int" means "integer", and "datetime" means a date or a date plus a time. These descriptors are important. It is particularly important to give the columns that represent the same attribute the same format in different tables. For instance, it would be a bad idea to make "student_id" an integer in one table and a character string in another, because logical and mathematical operations on the data might then go wrong – particularly when you are testing for equality of values of two data elements. This would be disastrous if the columns were key columns, because join conditions would then fail to operate correctly.

Incidentally, I used the term **data element** in the previous paragraph to mean a *particular value* of an attribute, that is, the contents of a particular cell in a table. I recommend that you maintain this distinction between "attributes" and "data elements". It is then clear, when you say "attribute", that you are talking about the attribute *in general* (for instance, when talking about a particular column of a table or talking about the attributes of entities in the data model). When you say "data element" it is clear that you are talking about a particular value of an attribute. However, you will find that some people use the two terms interchangeably.

While on the subject of terminology, I should also point out that the term **cell**, which is understood by anyone who has used a spreadsheet program like Microsoft Excel, is not used very often in the context of databases. This is a shame, because it is a very clear and useful term. In this book, I will use the term "cell" wherever it is appropriate.

In the above example of a set of CREATE TABLE statements, I have not mentioned anything about key columns. As explained in Chapter 1, key columns are an essential part of the relational model. I will describe how the definition of key columns is addressed in Chapter 3.

After the CREATE TABLE commands have been executed (and the empty tables thus brought into existence), and the key columns have been designated, the database is more or less ready to use. There may be some additional things that the Database Administrator (DBA) will want to do to ensure that the database performs well when a lot of users are using it; but these will not be described here.

When you look at the relational database design that derives from an E-R diagram, it becomes clear why it is useful to have the E-R diagram for future reference. Because entity sets *and* relationships both become tables, it is quite hard to "reverse-engineer" an E-R diagram from the database design. Obviously it is possible; but it takes time and some familiarity with how the database is used. It is far better to draw the E-R diagram first. If a copy of the E-R diagram is available for other designers to refer to in the future, it is then a lot easier for them to extend the database by adding columns to tables, or by adding new tables. Trying to do this, without a copy of the E-R diagram to refer to, is difficult and tedious.

There are various software products that claim to draw E-R diagrams for you, given a finished database design. Some products do this, in addition to allowing you to use the product to draw E-R diagrams from scratch. Others do nothing other than draw an E-R diagram after the fact (from the finished database design). Using the after-the-fact diagram-drawing function is of limited value. In this case, all the software does is draw rectangles containing table names and column names, and then draw connecting lines between the column names in different rectangles where the column names match. It does not allow for the possibility that the designer might have chosen, just to be difficult, to make the column names of the same attribute slightly different in two tables. Also, such a diagram does not distinguish between entities and relationships: everything is just a rectangle and you have to work it out for yourself. It seems to me that the main purpose of software that draws after-the-fact E-R diagrams is to allow undisciplined database designers to create such a diagram so that they can check off "E-R Diagram" on the list of documents that they are required to produce.

The above comments about E-R diagram software apply only to software used to draw E-R diagrams after the fact, not to software used to create E-R diagrams when starting the process of designing a database. Software that helps you draw E-R diagrams is useful: it creates neat diagrams and allows you to store the diagrams electronically, or send drafts via email to colleagues.

A Brief Note on the Writing Conventions Used in this Book

You have probably noticed by now that I have adopted the following conventions for the way that I write various things. (I will try to be consistent throughout the rest of the book.) There are no universally-accepted standards; these are just the standards that I have chosen to use. They are as follows:

- In example SQL commands, I write the reserved words, like SELECT, FROM, and WHERE, in uppercase. I have written all other parts of SQL commands (table names, column names, and so on) in lowercase. I have done this so that the reserved words stand out. (For clarity, I have also put reserved words in uppercase where I refer to them in the text.) If you find yourself having to write SQL commands in your work, you need not write the reserved words in uppercase (unless this is the convention followed in the organization in which you work). My personal preference is to write everything in lowercase. I feel that this looks neater. It is easier on the eye and more in keeping with the style of modern programming languages. (Note, however, what I say below about the case-sensitivity of DBMSs.)

- Where I refer to tables names and column names in the text, I enclose the names in quotation marks, for example, "students" and "student_id". Note that, when you write SQL commands, you should never enclose tables names or column names in quotation marks. However, single quotation marks are used in SQL commands to enclose literal values like text strings and dates, as in:

  WHERE student_id = '20080001'

  Note, however, that the reserved words used to define special non-literal values, like NULL, are never enclosed in single quotation marks.

- Where I refer to entities and relationships in the text, I put entities in italic text and relationships in underlined italic text, for example, *student is enrolled in course*.

- When I introduce new terms I write them in **bold** typeface.

Case-Sensitivity in DBMSs

Although I mentioned above that my personal preference is to write SQL entirely in lowercase, you should follow the conventions of the organization in which you are working. You should pay particular attention to the extent to which the DBMS that you are working with is case-sensitive. Different DBMSs adopt different conventions for case-sensitivity. A particular DBMS may, by default or by the way it is configured, adopt different case-sensitivity rules as regards (a) reserved words, (b) "object names", and (c) "user data":

- Most DBMSs are *not* case-sensitive as regards reserved words; so you can use uppercase, lowercase, or mixed case for the reserved words.

- Some DBMSs are case-sensitive by default, or can be configured to be case-sensitive, as regards **object names**, that is, the names of tables, columns, and temporary variables. For instance, where object naming is case-sensitive, you cannot, within an SQL command, refer to the table "students" as "STUDENTS" or "Students". You must type its name exactly as it was defined when the table was created.

- Most systems are case-sensitive by default as regards the "user data", that is, the data that is placed in the database. This means that users, and developers of application software that interacts with the database, must make sure that they follow whatever rules have been established for the database. So, for example, if the values for male and female are agreed as 'M' and 'F', everyone must use uppercase 'M' and 'F'. Nevertheless, a wise SQL writer might decide to write queries in such a way as to allow for some users not following the rules, writing WHERE clauses containing conditions like

    WHERE sex ='F' OR sex = 'f'

- Some systems can be configured to be case-*in*sensitive as regards user data. Whether or not such an option is used depends on the situation. For example, it may be used if the database is going to be populated with data taken from two older databases – one containing all-uppercase data and one containing mixed-case data – where the easiest way to avoid problems is to opt for case-insensitivity. By contrast, in situations where distinguishing case is important, for example, where case-sensitive usernames for a website are to be stored in the database, it may be better to leave the DBMS configured as case-sensitive.

- Some DBMSs tie together the case-sensitivity settings for object names and for user data. In these systems, if you want to maintain case-sensitivity for user data you will be forced to accept object-name case-sensitivity, whether you like it or not.

The Database Design Process Summarized

To summarize what we covered in this chapter – a good database design process is one where you proceed roughly as follows:

1. Study the part of the real world that is of interest. Think very hard about the entities that exist in it, and the relationships between those entities.

2. Draw an Entity-Relationship diagram. Write down the attributes of each entity and the attributes of each relationship (if they have attributes). Note the key attributes of each entity and, at a minimum, put these key attributes on the E-R diagram. (You can write the non-key attributes on a separate sheet of paper, or in a spreadsheet, if there is not enough room for them on the diagram.)

3. Translate the E-R diagram into a first-attempt database design, by turning each entity into a table and each relationship into a table. (You do not need to worry about the formats of the attributes at this stage.) A very compact and useful way of writing down a database design, which can usefully be employed at this third step, is to write each table name followed, in parentheses, by its attribute names, with the names of the key attributes underlined. (Note: this format has nothing to do with SQL. It is just a useful convention for documenting the database design.) For example:

    students (student_id, first_name, last_name, sex, date_of_birth)

    courses (course_number, course_title, credits)

    enrollments (course_number, student_id, term, year)

4. Take a long, hard look at this first-attempt design and try to normalize it. Identify any modification anomalies that might arise during the insertion of data and the deletion of data. Adjust the design to eliminate these anomalies. (I'll explain this in more detail in the next chapter.) Once you are satisfied, you then have your database design.

5. Now identify the formats of each attribute. At this point it is often useful to create a catalog (for instance, in a spreadsheet) of all the column names that you have used, what tables they are used in, what their formats are, and any standard values that you are planning to use (such as 'M' or 'F' for "sex"). For example:

Column name	Appears in these tables	Format	Restrictions on values
student_id	students, enrollments	varchar(9)	
first_name	students	varchar(40)	
last_name	students	varchar(40)	
sex	students	char(1)	Must be 'M' or 'F'
date_of_birth	students	datetime	
course_number	courses, enrollments	varchar(8)	
course_title	courses	varchar(40)	
credits	courses	decimal(3,1)	
term	enrollments	char(1)	Must be '1', '2', or '3'
year	enrollments	int	

This catalog will help you check that you have used the same format for a column name in every table in which it appears. It also acts as a useful reference sheet for anyone who needs to extend the database later on.

6. Create the database using CREATE TABLE commands (or whatever mechanism the DBMS that you are using provides for database creation).

CHAPTER 3

NULLS, KEYS, AND CARDINALITY

The Final Steps in Creating Tables

At the end of the last chapter I gave an example of how a database can be created using a series of CREATE TABLE commands. The following three commands were part of that series:

CREATE TABLE students (student_id varchar(9), first_name varchar(40),
                        last_name varchar(40), sex char(1), date_of_birth datetime)
CREATE TABLE courses (course_number varchar(8), course_title varchar(40),
                        credits decimal(3,1))
CREATE TABLE enrollments (course_number varchar(8), student_id varchar(9),
                        term char(1), year int)

Although the database that would be created by commands like these could, in theory, be used right away, in practice there are a few other things that we need to do before telling users that the database is ready for them to start entering data into it.

To start with, the database designer would almost always do the following when creating the various tables that constitute the database:

- Tell the DBMS which column or columns in each table are the "key" columns (that is, which columns will hold the data element or elements that represent the key for each row of data).

- Apply constraints on the values that can appear in some of the columns, for example, designating non-key columns that are allowed to contain **NULL** values (generally referred to simply as NULL columns) and designating columns that are *not* allowed to contain NULL values (referred to as NOT NULL columns).

NULL and NOT NULL Constraints

The concept of a NULL needs a little explanation and I will deal with it first. A NULL value means that no data at all has been inserted in a particular cell. It is referred to, in an SQL command, by the reserved word NULL. However, in the database itself, it is *not* represented by the word NULL, even though this is how it is displayed or printed when the contents of an empty cell are selected in a query. NULL is a distinct state. It is different from the text-string 'NULL' and it is different from a space. Another point to note about NULL is that, in a WHERE clause, the reserved word NULL cannot be used with an equals sign in a condition. For example, if there were a "middle_name" column in the "students" table and you wanted to test for the condition that this is empty, you would write:

WHERE students.middle_name IS NULL

or, to check that a middle name is present:

WHERE students.middle_name IS NOT NULL

If you wanted to include a column like "middle_name" in the "students" table, and allow the column to be empty in some rows (as in the above example), you would need to designate the column as a NULL column (meaning "NULL allowed") when you create the "students" table.

Conversely, for other columns like the "sex" column in the "students" table, you would probably want to tell the DBMS that the column is a NOT NULL column. This means that the DBMS must not accept a new row of data, to be added to the table, if the "sex" element is missing. You would do this if you want the DBMS to enforce the collection of this piece of data about all students when their information is entered into the database.

Although the NOT NULL condition is a way of enforcing the collection of certain pieces of information, it may not be the only mechanism that is used to enforce this. In most systems, the majority of database users do not interact directly with the DBMS. Instead, most users interact with application software, which in turn interacts with the DBMS behind the scenes. This application software can also enforce the collection of required data elements, giving error messages like "Sex is a required field. Please select Sex and click Submit again." Such application software is thus the first line of defense against the omission of important information. The NOT NULL condition in the database is the last line of defense. Because data may be inserted into the database in ways other than through application software, for example, by expert users who interact directly with the database using SQL commands, it is generally a good idea to designate NOT NULL columns, even when application software is enforcing the collection of the information.

The designation of columns as NULL or NOT NULL applies only to non-key columns. The DBMS will not allow a NULL to be inserted into a column that has been designated as a key column. There are thus three classes of column:

(1) Non-key, NULL (that is, NULL allowed).

(2) Non-key, NOT NULL.

(3) Key (which can never be NULL).

For a non-key column, if you do not provide the DBMS with a NULL/NOT NULL constraint, then the DBMS will apply a default condition. This is typically NULL, but the default condition may vary, depending on which DBMS is being used and how it is configured.

It is therefore a good practice to explicitly define each column as NULL or NOT NULL, rather than assume anything about the default condition. It is also a good idea to choose NOT NULL unless there is a good reason for allowing NULLs.

Columns can be designated as NOT NULL or NULL within the CREATE TABLE commands, for example:

```
CREATE TABLE students
  (student_id varchar(9) NOT NULL,
   first_name varchar(40) NOT NULL,
   last_name varchar(40) NOT NULL,
   sex char(1) NOT NULL,
   date_of_birth datetime NOT NULL
  )
```

Designation of Key Columns

In the first section of this chapter I said that the database designer will "almost always" supply the information about the key columns (as well as the NULL/NOT NULL conditions for the non-key columns). You may be wondering what "almost always" could mean when it comes to key columns. I will now explain this.

You may be puzzled by my next statement; but it is important to know this: *most relational DBMSs do not, by default, enforce the fundamental rules of the relational model.* In particular:

- Unless you specifically instruct the DBMS to apply row-uniqueness rules to each table, most DBMSs will allow rows to be inserted into a table that are exact duplicates of existing rows.

- Most DBMSs will allow you to create tables without any key columns.

Thus, if you want a relational DBMS to truly operate according to the relational model, you must define key columns for every table. This will automatically guarantee the uniqueness of every row, because the designation of a key column (or key columns) will cause the DBMS to check that each value (or set of values), entered in the key column (or columns) is unique. If this condition is met, then each row as a whole will be unique, even if the values in the non-key columns are all the same.

Because most DBMSs will allow you to operate with keyless tables, you could, if you wanted to, create a database in which you do not designate any key columns at all (although this would be a dreadfully bad idea). Provided that you, and all your users, know which columns are meant to be the key columns, and provided that no user enters a row of data into a table that duplicates the "key-column" values of already-inserted rows, then the database would be usable. However, in this keyless scenario, if users start to insert rows into the tables with duplicate key values, then everyone will start to get nonsensical results when trying to perform queries involving those tables.

Although a keyless database would give valid results up until the point where users start inserting rows with duplicate "key-column" values, its performance would not be very good, in terms of how much load it places on the computer on which the DBMS is running and how long it takes to do things. This is because, as mentioned earlier, a DBMS generates sorting indices for columns that are designated as key columns. (These indices are internal to the operation of the DBMS: the user does not need to worry about how they work.) The DBMS uses these indices to quickly locate rows in the table. Without any designated key columns, the DBMS has to work a lot harder when it retrieves and updates data.

I mention the possibility of using keyless tables (a) so that you understand the importance of the step of designating the key columns of each table, and (b) so that you won't panic if you come across databases containing keyless tables.

Assuming that you are going to create a database that operates in the normal way (with designated key columns in all tables), you will need to designate the key columns, either as you create the tables or shortly after you create the tables. In tables with a single key column, the key column can be designated simply by inserting the reserved words PRIMARY KEY in the CREATE TABLE statements, for example:

```
CREATE TABLE students
  (student_id varchar(9) PRIMARY KEY,
   first_name varchar(40) NOT NULL,
   last_name varchar(40) NOT NULL,
   sex char(1) NOT NULL
   date_of_birth datetime NOT NULL
  )
```

Note that there is no need to include the words NOT NULL in the description of "student_id" because a key column is, by definition, never NULL.

If there are two or more key columns in a table, then the method of designating these as jointly forming the key is a bit more complicated and can vary between DBMSs; so I will not give examples here. You should consult the manual for whichever DBMS you will be working with.

Note that the term **primary key** is often used in DBMSs, rather than simply "key", although they amount to the same thing. Use of the term "primary key" in database design arose from the desire to distinguish between a column that *is* used as a key column, and other columns that *might* have been used as a key column, but were not. For some entity sets there may be two or more **candidate keys** – two or more attributes between which a choice of key is made, whose values uniquely identify a particular entity. The rejected candidate will often become a column in the entity-representing table. It may turn out to be useful to use the rejected candidate key in certain queries as a means of selecting a particular row in the table, rather than the attribute that you selected as the key. Even though this may be the case, it is not necessary to tell the DBMS that you have this in mind. You need only designate the key that you decided to use – the primary key – when you create the table in question; and so the reserved word PRIMARY in PRIMARY KEY is essentially redundant (although the DBSM may require that it always be used).

Cardinality of Relationships

In Chapter 2, when describing how to draw an E-R diagram, I went to the trouble of labeling each relationship with its cardinality (one-to-one, one-to-many, or many-to-many). But when I showed how the database is brought into existence, using a series of CREATE TABLE statements, there was no mention of cardinality or how it might be incorporated into the database design. I am now going to look at how we might handle cardinality.

Consider the following examples of relationships and their cardinalities:

A. *student is enrolled in course* – which is many-to-many (which we abbreviate to "m-n", where "m" is used to stress that "n" is not necessarily equal to "m"). Each student may be enrolled in several courses, and each course may have many students enrolled in it.

B. *student has on loan librarybook* – which is one-to-many ("1-n"). Each student may borrow several library books at once, but each individual book (identified by some kind of tracking number) can be on loan to only one student at any one time.

C. *student has selected major* – which is also one-to-many, although the many is now on the student side of the relationship ("n-1"). We will assume, at least for now, that each student is allowed to select only one major subject. Thus, many students may select a particular major, but each student may select only one major.

D. *student lives in dormroom* – which is one-to-one ("1-1"). We will assume that this is a university with plenty of dorm rooms and that all students get their own rooms.

The relationship-representing tables for these four relationships might look like this (before any rows of data are inserted):

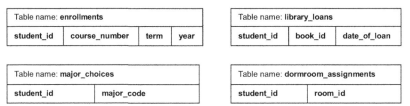

The key columns in each of these four tables are the first and second columns, taken together.

If we leave these four tables exactly as they are, then, by default, they will allow many-to-many relationships to be represented. For example, in the "dormroom_assignments" table there is nothing to prevent a user assigning fifty students to the same room. The condition that the key be unique is satisfied in all fifty rows because, although the room number is the same, the student ID is different; so the key as a whole ("student_id" and "room_id", taken together) is different in every row. Similarly, there is nothing to prevent a user assigning fifty rooms to one student. In this case the value of "student_id" is the same in all fifty rows; but the fact that "room_id" is different in each row guarantees the uniqueness of the value of the key.

This many-to-many situation is just what we want for the "enrollments" table. However, for the other three tables, we might want to enforce cardinality rules B, C, and D. In order to apply a cardinality rule, we can use a column-constraint function called **UNIQUE**. When a column is defined as UNIQUE, it means that the DBMS will allow each value to appear only once in that column. In a table with a single key column, that key column is, by definition, already unique. However, when two columns are taken together as the key (which is what we find in most relationship-representing tables), the values in each column, considered separately, may not be unique. So, we can add the UNIQUE constraint to either of the two key columns, or to both the key columns, as a way of enforcing the cardinality rules. Specifically:

> *To enforce cardinality rules, you designate, as UNIQUE, the column that corresponds to the "many" side of the relationship in a one-to-many relationship, or to both columns in a one-to-one relationship.*

Applying this to the above tables, we would leave the "enrollments" table as it stands, but make "book_id" UNIQUE in "library_loans", "student_id" UNIQUE in "major_choices", and both "student_id" and "room_id" UNIQUE in "dormroom_assignments". The effect of these UNIQUE rules is that the DBMS would not allow the rows that appear below in "strikethrough" text to be added to the tables:

- In this many-to-many table, all the entries are acceptable because no UNQIUE constraint applies:

Table name: **enrollments**			
student_id	**course_number**	**term**	**year**
200800101	P101	1	2008
200800101	M101	1	2008
200600001	M101	1	2008
200600002	M101	1	2008

- In this one-to-many table, the last row is not allowed because it violates the constraint that "book_id" must be unique. Book 'BN927999' has already appeared in the third row:

Table name: **library_loans**		
student_id	**book_id**	**date_of_loan**
200800101	BN178279	2008-02-17
200800101	BN106483	2008-02-17
200800101	BN927999	2008-02-14
~~200600001~~	~~BN927999~~	~~2008-02-18~~

- In this many-to-one table, the last row is not allowed because it violates the constraint that "student_id" must be unique. Student '200600002' has already appeared in the third row, with a major of 'PPE'.

Table name: **major_choices**	
student_id	**major_code**
200800101	PPE
200600001	PPE
200600002	PPE
~~200600002~~	~~BIO~~

- In this one-to-one table, the last two rows are not allowed. The third row is not allowed because student '200600002' has already been assigned a room in the second row; and the fourth row is not allowed because room 'SR00999' has already been assigned to a student in the first row.

Table name: **dormroom_assignments**	
student_id	**room_id**
200600001	SR00999
200600002	SR12643
~~200600002~~	~~SR12688~~
~~200800101~~	~~SR00999~~

This approach prevents the violation of cardinality rules, which reflect an aspect of the real world that has been recorded in the E-R model.

Is it a good idea to enforce cardinality like this? In many cases, no. If the users do not interact directly with the database, but enter the data through application software (which in turn interacts with the database), then it might be a better approach to enforce the cardinality rules in the application software. There are two reasons for this:

- First, if the application software does *not* check whether an entry is allowed, then it faces the possibility of receiving an error message back from the DBMS when it tries to add a rule-violating row to a table. The logic required to handle this situation, and tell the user that the entry is not possible, therefore has to be programmed into the application software. It is often easier to write the application software to proactively validate the attempted entry, and immediately tell the user that there is a problem, rather than to write the software so that it can deal with the error messages being returned by the DBMS (and then do something about the duplicate that the user has tried to enter).

- Second, the rules in the real world that give rise to cardinality rules in the E-R model are quite often changed during the life of the database. It is generally easier to deal with these changes by changing only the application software, rather than by changing the database design. (In most cases, if you change the database design, you have to make changes to the application software anyway.)

Examples of real-world changes that might affect cardinality rules are:

- Because of complaints about students hoarding library books, the library imposes a one-book-at-a-time rule.

- The university changes the one-major rule and starts to allow students to choose dual majors.

- Because of increased student intake, the University has to start asking students to share rooms.

If the cardinality rules are built into the application software, ideally in a parameter-driven way, they can be changed without changing the database design (that is, without applying or removing UNIQUE constraints). Parameter-driven application software, ready to deal with all possible variants of each cardinality rule, can be quickly changed by changing the value of a parameter. This parameter could be held in a file on a server, or even in a "settings" table in the database, so that the change can be put into effect quickly and easily.

So, in summary:

Cardinality-enforcement is often better left to the application software, and not done via UNIQUE constraints on the individual columns that represent part of the multi-column key of a relationship-representing table (although UNIQUE constraints could be used in this way if there is no other choice).

CHAPTER 4

NORMALIZATION OF RELATIONAL DATABASE DESIGNS

Normalization: an Art, not a Science

I mentioned in Chapter 1 that normalization is better practiced as an art, rather than a science. This may seem a strange statement to make about a subject as down-to-earth as designing a database. The trouble with normalization is that it is not a "mechanical" exercise. That is, nobody has managed to write a program into which you can feed the specification for a non-normalized database (the table names, column names for key attributes, and column names for non-key attributes) and out of which will come a fully normalized database. Normalization is an intellectual exercise. It can be performed only by a human being (or at least it can be performed only by a human being at present). It requires an understanding of the meaning of the data entities and relationships.

Probably the best way to illustrate this point is by an example. Imagine that you have just received an interstellar message (in English) from the University of Betelgeuse at Lambda Alnitak (UBLA), asking you to take a look at a first-draft design for their new database and to try to normalize it for them. Let us also imagine that you do not speak Betelgeusean. In an attachment to the message the table names and column names have been summarized for you (see below), with the column names for the key attributes underlined (in accordance with standard intergalactic practices):

slodushok (<u>slodush-hoog</u>, frooblenawk, frooblegink, koolpukak, lalacab, snorkwij, froodink)

cjarpsnashtoikli (<u>cjarpsnashtoikli-hoog</u>, cjarpsnashtoikli-ginkax, cjarpsnashtoiklinacklehoop)

falajajok (<u>falajaj-hoog</u>, frooblenawk, frooblegink, koolpukak)

tquirkstubbixok (<u>tquirkstubbix-hoog</u>)

proikwistquot (<u>tquirkstubbix-hoog</u>, <u>falajaj-hoog</u>)

bibiproikwistquot (<u>tquirkstubbix-hoog</u>, <u>slodush-hoog</u>)

tquirkstubbixcjari (<u>cjarpsnashtoikli-hoog</u>, <u>tquirkstubbix-hoog</u>, splandelwiz, yoidelwiz)

cjarpsnashtoiklisprankon (<u>cjarpsnashtoikli-hoog</u>, <u>slodush-hoog</u>, splandelwiz, yoidelwiz)

cabbiproik (<u>cab-hoog</u>, cabnawk, snizzumpo, squarjard, sjargarra)

cabbiproiksloosh (<u>cab-hoog</u>, <u>cjarpsnashtoikli-hoog</u>, betelrog, <u>druxni</u>, draxni)

Without speaking Betelgeusean, and without knowing anything about Betelgeusean society (let alone how things operate in their universities), how could you even begin to determine whether this database design is normalized? For example, are "koolpukak", "lalacab", "snorkwij", and "froodink" fully functionally dependent on "slodush-hoog"; or are they only indirectly associated with "slodushok"? Any answer to this question would be a wild guess. The tables "tquirkstubbixok", "proikwistquot", and "bibiproikwistquot" look pretty safe because they contain only key attributes. But wherever you see tables with non-key attributes, you are left wondering how their non-key attributes depend on their key attributes.

In this imaginary situation you are in exactly the same situation as a computer program that might be written to attempt normalization: *you have no clue what is going on!*

This is why I describe normalization as an "intellectual" activity and not a "mechanical" one. You have to think hard about whether each non-key attribute is fundamentally an attribute of the entities in the entity set from which the table was derived (or of the instances of a relationship from which the table was derived). You also have to think hard about a number of subtle rules that govern the values that attributes may take. This is why it is impossible to write down a set of rules for normalization that could be translated into a computer program, operating without any regard for the real-world meaning of the attribute names.

A Brief History of Normalization

The problem of anomalies arising from insertions and deletions (and, in some special cases, from updates to data values) was identified by Codd while he was doing research for his 1970 paper. He and others continued to work on the problem for the next eleven years. The problem, as originally stated ("How do you normalize a database design?"), remains unsolved, inasmuch as it was originally hoped that an algorithmic solution could be found. However, a milestone was reached with the publication of a paper by Ronald Fagin, A Normal Form for Relational Databases that is Based on Domains and Keys, *ACM Transactions on Database Systems, Volume 6, Number 3, September 1981*, pp. 387-415. In this paper Fagin defined a condition, which he called **Domain/Key Normal Form** (or DK/NF), and showed that a database design consisting of tables that meet this condition will have no insertion or deletion anomalies. He also showed that a design that is free from insertion and deletion anomalies must be in DK/NF. More will be said about this later. (By the way, it is not clear why the abbreviation is usually written as "DK/NF" rather than "D/KNF", or just "DKNF"; but "DK/NF" is how it is written in most papers and textbooks.)

As I mentioned in Chapter 1, I will use the generic term "modification anomaly" in order to avoid having to keep writing "insertion or deletion anomaly".

As with any new science, the terminology of normalization was initially very confused. As different types of modification anomaly were identified, and a remedy for each one was found, new levels of normalization were defined. When writing about normalization, Codd referred only to the *state of individual tables*, rather than the state of the database design as a whole. He defined **first normal form** (or 1NF) as the least-normalized state that a table can be in. A table in 1NF is just any old table (as long as it has an appropriate key column, or key columns, so that you can be sure that its rows will be unique).

Codd defined **second normal form** (or 2NF) as the state of any table in which all non-key attributes are functionally dependent on the whole key (that is, on the key column if there is only one, or on all the key columns taken together if there are two or more). He then went on to define **third normal form** (3NF) as the state of any table in which, in addition, there are no "transitive dependencies" (situations in which the value of a non-key attribute depends on another non-key attribute, which in turn depends on the value of the key).

Note that the definitions of the normal forms are cumulative; that is, at each level the conditions of all the lower levels must be met in addition to the conditions that must be met to get to the new level in question. (It is traditional, in database textbooks, to follow this statement with a diagram of concentric circles, to explain what "cumulative" means. I am assuming that you share my view that this is a waste of time.)

Codd's naming scheme (1NF, 2NF, 3NF) was disrupted by the publication of work by Ray Boyce, who defined the next level of normalization as **Boyce-Codd Normal Form** (or BCNF). For a table to be in BCNF "every determinant must be a candidate key". A candidate key is an attribute that could be used as a key. A determinant is an attribute whose value determines what value another attribute will have.

Boyce died in 1974 and his work in the field of relational databases was cut short; so he did not lend his name to any other normal forms. The next level of normalization, **fourth normal form** or 4NF (which would have been 5NF if Codd's original naming scheme had not been uninterrupted), addressed problems caused by "multivalued dependencies". This is a very confusing term. What it was meant to describe was a situation where a non-key attribute may take more than one value for a given value of the key. For example, if students are allowed to have two or more major subjects, and if the database designer made the mistake of making "major" a column in the "students" table, the value of the key ("student_id") would no longer uniquely determine the value of "major". Like the problems addressed by the changes needed to place a table in 2NF, 3NF, or BCNF, this is just another example of the fundamental mistake of associating, with an entity, attributes that are not fundamental properties of the entity (that is, they are not fundamental attributes like "first name" or "sex").

If you take the time to first draw an E-R diagram, and think very clearly about the entities and the relationships, before you start to design the database, these problems are much less likely to arise. This is evident when you look at the examples used in many textbooks on databases. The examples used to illustrate the various levels of non-normalization look very contrived. They would be unlikely to be arrived at starting the database design from a good E-R model.

As work continued on normalization, it became clear that modification anomalies could occur as a result of operations involving two or more tables, even though the tables themselves seem free from the problems identified in earlier research. This led to the definition of **fifth normal form** (5NF) which is the *state of a database as a whole* when "all join constraints are logically implied by keys and, for every table, the size of the domain of the key attribute (or key attributes) is greater than or equal to the value of ^nC_r where 'n' is the number of columns in the table and 'r' is n/2 rounded down to the nearest integer". This is a very complicated condition that involves the concept of a "join" that I explained in Chapter 1. (The "combination function", ^nC_r, means the value of n!/r!(n-r)! where n! is the product of the integers from 'n' down to 1.)

The definition of 5NF also involves the concept of the **domain of an attribute**, that is, the set of all possible values that it can take. For example, the domain of the attribute "sex" is just "male or female", if we look at it in a logical (or "abstract") sense. If we look at it in a "concrete" sense, as it would be represented in the database, we might say that its domain is "M or F" (or possibly "m or f"). Similarly, an attribute such as the "height" of a person might be said to have an abstract domain of "a number of feet expressed as any positive real number", or to have a concrete domain of "any decimal value, represented to two decimal places, from 0.01 to 10.00".

It is far from clear what was meant by "size of the domain" in the definition of 5NF. Clearly the size of the "sex" domain is 2; but what is the size of the "height" domain? The size of the concrete domain of "height" in the above example seems to be 1000, because the values go in steps of a hundredth of a foot from 0.01 to 10.00. But the size of the abstract domain is effectively infinite (since there are infinitely many real numbers, even within a range of values like 1 to 10). Clearly, research on normalization during the mid to late 1970s was producing results that were becoming increasingly difficult for a normal person to use in practical database design work.

As mentioned earlier, the final stage in the definition of normalization was Fagin's 1981 paper, which again broke away from Codd's naming scheme and defined DK/NF as the next (and final) stage after 5NF. Fagin's paper seemed, at least at first sight, to eliminate a lot of the confusion surrounding normalization. Not only did his definition of DK/NF represent the holy grail of normalization (that is, complete elimination of modification anomalies), but it also seemed to provide a rule that was somewhat easier to understand than the 5NF rule. Fagin said that all the tables in a database are in DK/NF if, for every table, "every constraint on the table is a logical consequence of the definition of the keys and the domains [of all the attributes]". He defined a "constraint" as any rule that applies to the allowable values of an attribute that is precise enough that we can determine whether or not it is followed for any particular value of the attribute.

The complexity of Fagin's rule is hidden in the very broad scope of the term "constraint". It includes, for example, edit rules, intra-table constraints, inter-table constraints, functional dependencies, multivalued dependencies, and join dependences – in other words, everything that was covered in the definitions of the lower normal forms, plus anything else you care to define as a constraint. I find rules like this one very difficult to deal with; and I am sure that many other people do too. First, it is easy to learn it by heart, but hard to see what it means until you have had a lot of practice. And second, it is generally explained by means of counterexamples, where tables are concocted that break the rule.

Fagin's rule is rather like an instruction for how to drive a car that says, "Drive at a steady and moderate speed, staying on the correct side of the road, and not colliding with other vehicles or pedestrians." This is a valid statement; but does not tell you how to actually drive a car. Also, the counterexamples that appear in most textbooks are rather like a driving instructor who gets into the car with you and, by way of instruction, just shows you photographs of the accidents his former students have been involved in while under his tutelage.

In a similar way, when you study normalization counterexamples, you are unlikely to arrive at a point where you say "OK, I get it". You may understand the implications of each example in isolation; but it is difficult to build a clear mental picture of what Fagin's rule requires you to do. As a result, a few days after studying the subject your understanding of the rule quickly fades and you are left with only a vague idea of what it meant.

Learning to Perform Normalization

If you go to the "Database" section of a library or bookstore, and look up "normalization" in a sample of twenty books, you will find that:

- Few books devote more than 2% of their pages to the topic.

- They almost all use the same example of a University Administration database – the same example that has been copied from textbook to textbook since the early 1980s.

- They almost all give you the feeling that the author does not really understand the subject of normalization.

- Some of the more modern books cut short the lesson on normalization, and make a statement something like: "If you follow my unique methodology for database design then everything will turn out normalized".

This is a sign that normalization is a subject that lacks a clear theoretical foundation and which is therefore very hard to teach. This brings me back to my point about normalization being more an art than a science. Like flying an airplane or performing surgery, it is best learned by closely supervised practice and is impossible to learn just by reading a manual. Once you have mastered it, you can do it without much conscious thought. You will sometimes make mistakes; but you will make fewer mistakes the more you practice.

Of course, there are practical problems in learning normalization through supervised practice. First, it takes too much time. Database courses in universities, as well as courses provided by DBMS vendors such as Oracle, rarely have enough total class time to accommodate more than about an hour on the topic, perhaps followed by an assignment. Coaching in normalization requires much more time than this, with smaller groups of students. Second, once you have learned the basics, and start to practice database design, the feedback you get on your design (from users) typically comes a long time after you have done the design. An anomaly may not be identified until six months later, when a user tries to enter data relating to a new procedure or situation. By contrast, errors by student pilots and student surgeons are obvious to the student within seconds. The long feedback loop for errors in database design makes for little or no on-the-job improvement in design skills.

The difficulties facing someone who wants to learn how to design normalized databases are thus considerable. It is no wonder therefore that many real-world relational databases in use today are based on designs that are not fully normalized (that is, they are not in DK/NF). Does this matter? In many cases the answer is "no", or at least, "not at first". Typically only a small number of well-trained users are given "raw" SQL access to a database. Most users will interact with the database via application software that constrains the things that they can do. This software will execute the necessary database updates behind the scenes, by sending SQL commands to the DBMS. The software will generally be written to do this in a way that does not cause any problems. So, for example, if an anomaly prevents a row being added to Table A until a row has been added to Table B, the application software, when asked to add data to the database, will issue an SQL command to add the required row of data to Table B before it adds a row to Table A.

Problems with the lack of full normalization are more likely to be felt later, by a database designer who is called upon to extend the original database design (adding new tables, and adding new columns to existing tables). If the original database design was not normalized then he or she may find that the design starts to look ugly when the additions are made to the non-normalized design. Also, he or she will typically find that more and more logic needs to be added to the application software to hide anomalies from users.

Good-Enough Normalization

Given that some of the rules for the higher normal forms are very complicated, two reasonable questions are:

- Is there a level of normalization that is good enough for most practical purposes?
- Is there a set of simple rules that will generally achieve this level of normalization?

The answer to the first question is clearly yes: minor modification anomalies can be masked from non-expert users, and expert users can work around them; so complete (DK/NF) normalization is not essential. The answer to the second question is also yes: it is possible to express the most important aspects of the most important rules in a more down-to-earth form.

The following is an attempt to present the rules for good-enough normalization as a set of do's and don't's that can be applied to data modeling and database design, in order to arrive at more-or-less-normalized designs:

(1) Make sure your keys are good keys:
  - Make sure that they are directly associated with the entity.
  - Taking into account the real-world rules that govern the part of the real world that you are modeling, make sure that each value of the key attribute (or, for a multi-attribute key, each combination of values) can occur only once, and that each value uniquely identifies a particular entity.
  - Make sure that there is nothing that happens in the real world that detaches any of the key attributes from the entity. For example,

"chassis number" is a good key for a car, but "license plate number" is not so good.

(2) Do not include attributes in the key that are not necessary to make it unique. For example, if unique student IDs have already been assigned to students, do *not* make the key "student_id" *plus* "date_of_birth".

(3) Make sure that non-key attributes depend on "*the key, the whole key, and nothing but the key*". For example:

- "Color" is an acceptable non-key attribute for a car. The value of the "color" attribute for any particular car can be determined by inspecting the car, once you know (from the car's chassis number) that you are looking at the right car. In other words, "color" is fully functionally dependent on "chassis number". (Note that the value of a non-key attribute like color may change – for example, if the car is re-sprayed. That is all right. Non-key attributes are allowed to change. It is the key attributes that must be constant.)
- By contrast, "owner" is a bad choice of non-key attribute for a car because it is not an intrinsic property of the car itself. You cannot determine the value of "owner" by inspecting the car. (To represent owner you should have a separate "ownership" table in the database. This table derives from the relationship *owner owns car*, which ties the car to its owner.)

(4) Do not use, as non-key attributes, things that the entity may have more than one of. For example, "major" is not a good non-key attribute for *student* if the university allows students to have two major subjects. (Actually, "major" is not a good non-key attribute for *student* under *any* circumstances - see Rule (3) above. I use it here only to illustrate a particular manifestation of a violation of Rule (3) that is easy to grasp.) One of the several reasons why it is bad idea to make "major" an attribute of student is that there can be only one row for each student in the "students" table, so there is nowhere to put the second major. (To record major subjects you should, instead, have two separate tables – one called "majors", where the names of the valid majors are held, and another called "major_choices" that represents the relationship *has chosen* between *student* and *major*.)

(5) Do not use, as non-key attributes, things that are really properties of other non-key attributes, rather than of the entity itself. Attributes that, themselves, have attributes are better thought of as entities in their own right. They should be tied to the main entity via a relationship. For example, if you want to record the supplier of the paint that was used to paint a car, do not make "paint_supplier" an attribute of *car*. Instead, define an entity *paint* and a relationship *is painted with* that ties the car to a paint of a particular color and origin. The entity *paint* can then safely be given the attribute "paint_supplier".

(6) When translating the E-R model into a database design, make sure that every relationship becomes a table (as well as every entity). Do not give in to the temptation to represent a relationship by means of direct entity-to-

entity references. For example, do not use "owner_id" (the key column of the "owners" table) as a non-key column of the "cars" table in order to associate the entity *car* with the entity *owner*. In general, *it is a bad idea to turn the key column of one table into a non-key column in another table.* Instead, you should create a table called "ownership", with the two key columns "chassis_number" and "owner_id", in order to represent the relationship <u>owns</u> between *owner* and *car*.

By following these rules, and following the approach of drawing an E-R diagram (for the part of the real world that you are interested in) before you start to design the database, you should arrive at a design that is as normalized as it needs to be for most practical purposes.

The Rule Most Often Broken

In real-world database designs, the most frequently broken rule is Rule (6). You might therefore wonder whether violations of (6) are tolerable in some circumstances. The short answer to this is "sometimes, but not often".

Sometimes you will find, when you draw an E-R diagram, that one part of the diagram has a number of entities clustered around one central entity (like *customer*), and that no other entity on the diagram has a relationship to those "surrounding" entities, for example:

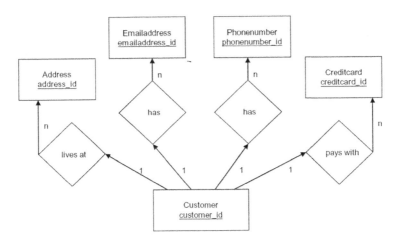

In such a case, where (a) the central entity has several close, one-to-many relationships with the surrounding entities, and (b) the surrounding entities have no relationships with any other entity, it *may* be acceptable to omit the relationship-representing tables from the database design.

As an illustration of this, we will look at just one of the sounding entities, *emailaddress*, and the central entity, *customer*. If we were to use a normalized design then we would represent the <u>has</u> relationship, between *customer* and *emailaddress*, by means of a table, such as "customer_emailaddresses". The resulting tables ("customers", "customer_emailaddresses", and "emailaddresses") are shown here with no rows of data in them:

Table name: **customers**				
customer_id	first_name	last_name	sex	date_of_birth

Table name: **emailaddresses**	
emailaddress_id	emailaddress

Table name: **customer_emailaddresses**		
customer_id	emailaddress_id	email_type_code

The key columns in this design are:

- In the "customers" table, "customer_id".

- In the "emailaddresses" table, "emailaddress_id".

- In the "customer_emailaddresses" table, "customer_id" and "emailaddress_id", taken together.

In "customer_emailaddresses", the column "email_type_code" is used to distinguish between the two or more email addresses of a single customer. For example, this type code might take values such as 'M' meaning "use this address for general messages and bulletins", 'C' meaning "use this address for confirmations of orders", or 'B' meaning "use this address for both purposes".

Now, if, instead of creating a normalized database design, we ignore Rule (6) and eliminate the relationship-representing table, we would have only two tables as follows:

Table name: **customers**				
customer_id	first_name	last_name	sex	date_of_birth

Table name: **emailaddresses**			
emailaddress_id	emailaddress	customer_id	email_type_code

The key columns in this design are:

- In the "customers" table, "customer_id".

- In the "emailaddresses" table, "emailaddress_id". (Note that the "customer_id" column is a non-key column in this table.)

Both of the above designs – the one immediately above, which is non-normalized, and the normalized one that preceded it – will satisfy most requirements. In both cases two email addresses can, if required, be associated with one customer (for example, an 'M' address and a 'C' address, distinguished by these letters in the "email_type_code" column).

The queries required to retrieve information would differ slightly between the two designs. For example, if we wanted to generate a list of the email addresses and first names of all customers who have a birthday today (so that we can send a "happy birthday" message to each of them), the two differing queries would be as follows. I assume here that I have already determined today's date (the month and day) and stored it in two temporary integer variables, @todaymonth and @todayday. I have spaced out these queries so that they are easier to read and compare:

For the normalized three-table design

```
SELECT
    customers.first_name,
    emailaddresses.emailaddress
FROM
    customers,
    emailaddresses,
    customer_emailaddresses
WHERE
    MONTH(customers.date_of_birth) = @todaymonth
    AND
    DAY(customers.date_of_birth) = @todayday
    AND
    customers.customer_id =
        customer_emailaddresses.customer_id
    AND
    customer_emailaddresses.emailaddress_id =
        emailaddresses.emailaddress_id
```

For the non-normalized two-table design

```
SELECT
    customers.first_name,
    emailaddresses.emailaddress
FROM
    customers,
    emailaddresses
WHERE
    MONTH(customers.date_of_birth) = @todaymonth
    AND
    DAY(customers.date_of_birth) = @todayday
    AND
    customers.customer_id =
        emailaddresses.customer_id
```

In the above SQL queries, the functions MONTH() and DAY() return an integer that represents just the month or just the day of the datetime value appearing in the column designated inside the parentheses.

It could be argued that the non-normalized design leads to simpler queries than the normalized design in this example. This is true here, and it is generally true of all designs. However, this slight simplification of queries, together with the reduction in number of tables, does not justify abandoning normalization rules. The non-normalized design has three drawbacks:

- The two-table design shown here can handle only a one-to-many (or one-to-one) relationship between the central entity and the "surrounding" entities. If you want to handle many-to-many relationships it will not work. For example, suppose that, in addition to allowing customers to have several email addresses, we wanted to allow one email address to be associated with several customers. (This might happen if the customers are employees of a company that requires all order-confirmation messages to go to the company's purchasing manager.) In this case we have a problem. We cannot place a single row in the "addresses" table for the purchasing manager's email address and associate several customers with that one email address. We would, instead, need to repeat the email address of the purchasing manager for each individual customer. This makes updating that email address very messy when, for instance, a new purchasing manager is hired.

- For queries to work efficiently, the Database Administrator must make sure that the DBMS generates an internal sorting index for the non-key "customer_id" columns that appear in the tables like "addresses", "emailaddresses", and so on. Because the values that appear in these columns are not unique within the table (a single customer may have several addresses or telephone numbers), this sorting index will not be as efficient as a sorting index for a key column.

- If, in a future revision of the database design, a relationship needs to be established between one or more of the surrounding entities and another entity somewhere else in the E-R model, the whole design starts to get very messy and anomaly-prone.

On the whole, it is better to follow Rule (6). However, you should not be surprised to find this kind of no-relationship-table design used in certain parts of an otherwise-normalized database design.

Practicing Normalization

One way to practice normalization is to start from scratch and design a database, starting with the E-R diagram. You could then translate this into a specific set of tables that will form your first-attempt database design (following the rules given in Chapter 2). You would then study and fine-tune the design, to identify and eliminate possible causes of modification anomalies.

However, it is hard work to start with an idea for a database exercise and a blank sheet of paper, and then draw the E-R diagram. It requires a great deal of mental effort. Without the pressure of an assignment that is due to be handed in, or a real database project deadline, it is hard to find the motivation to do even one database design, let alone, say, ten significantly different designs, just for practice.

A much less demanding form of practice for developing normalization skills is to pick holes in other people's database designs. This a lot easier than creating your own designs from scratch, and then trying to find fault with them. (Also, it can be fun.) My suggestion is therefore that you seize every opportunity to get print-outs of other people's database designs (with their permission, of course). Then take them away and study them and try to find all the problematic non-key columns. Think about how you would split up the tables (into two or more tables with fewer columns) in order to make the design more normalized.

Important note: *do your analysis in private* and keep your findings to yourself (unless you are really sure that whoever let you have a copy of his or her design would welcome a critique of the design). If you develop a reputation for being a smartass, you may soon find that nobody else will show you their database designs.

CHAPTER 5

SOME PRACTICAL ASPECTS OF USING A DBMS

Introduction

I said, in the introduction to Chapter 1, that I intend this book to complement the reference manuals of whatever DBMS you are going to be working with, and that I would therefore avoid duplication of the contents of those manuals. However, I believe that you may find it useful to read the following brief overview of a few of the practical aspects of using a DBMS. If you are reading this book to gain a general understanding of database design, rather than as a complement to a detailed study of SQL and a particular DBMS, then the information presented in this chapter will help prepare you to work with, or manage, colleagues who are working directly with the DBMS.

Classes of Database User

Although you may occasionally come across small relational databases that have been set up by an expert user for his or her exclusive use, most real-world databases are shared databases. Their value lies in the fact that the data contained in them (a) is the result of the actions of many users, and (b) is made available to many users. In practice, most database "users" are unaware that they are interacting with a shared database, because they interact with application software, which in turn interacts with the database. In this case, the database operates behind the scenes, without the user needing to know how the data is stored in various tables in the database, and without the user needing to know SQL. It is the application software that "talks" to the database using SQL.

Because databases can have many users, one important characteristic of all the major DBMSs is that they have a means of recognizing users and granting to those users the rights that are appropriate for their roles. This is typically done by means of a system of usernames and passwords. When the DBMS is first set up, a master (or "superuser") account of some sort is created. The person who adopts this account's username and password then has the ability to create any number of other accounts, each with the appropriate rights (or "privileges"). The most-privileged users will be able to issue any SQL command to the database, including commands like DROP TABLE, which deletes a table and all its contents. Obviously such rights would be dangerous in the wrong hands; and so only a very small number of users would be given them.

Users who access the database directly would typically be given the right to read, add, delete, and update the rows in the tables of the database – but not to delete entire tables, or add new columns to existing tables. Users who interact *indirectly* with the database, via application software, will typically not have individual accounts on the DBMS. More commonly, a generic account is created for the application software. The username and password for this account are available to the application software, and the application software uses these to sign on to the DBMS. One way of making the username and password available to the application software is to place them in a file on a shared server that is accessible only to application software. This is not a particularly secure method, but it at least makes it easy for the password to be changed occasionally. Another method is to "hard-code" the common username and password into the application software. This is not very secure either and has the disadvantage that it makes it hard to change the password – because new copies of executable software (with the updated password) have to be created and deployed. Even so, hard-coding of database usernames and passwords in application software is a common practice. (I am not about to embark on a tutorial on information security practices here. I simply want to prepare you for the real-world practices that you are likely to come across.)

The lowest level of privilege that can be given to a database user or application software is read-only access to the database, whereby the user can read the contents of some or all tables, but not make any changes. This level of access would typically be given to users who do not perform actions that result in changes to the contents of the database, for example, in an enquiries-only application.

Because most users of databases interact with the database through application software, only a small number of people who interact directly with the database need to concern themselves with the design of the database and its operation. These hands-on users include the following:

- The *database designer*, or design team, responsible for creating the database in the first place. Such database designers may be called upon to make changes to the database design from time to time – adding new columns to existing tables, and adding new tables. Such changes are always undertaken with great care and a lot of testing, first on a "development" copy of the database, and then on a "test" or "quality assurance" copy of the database, before the new design is moved into the "production" version of the database. This is because it is very easy to inadvertently create incompatibilities between the database design and the application software that interacts with the database. Database designers are typically given individual accounts on the development database, with a fairly high level of privilege. However, they may be given a reduced level of privilege on the production version of the database, so that only the Database Administrators (see below) can implement, in production, the changes that the database designers have developed and tested.

- The *Database Administrator* (DBA), or DBA team, responsible for keeping the database in good working order. These experts are responsible for making sure that the database performs well. They are also responsible for making sure that the various files that constitute the database, plus other files that support the operation of the database, do not exceed the space reserved for them on the system's hard drives. They accomplish these goals by (a) making adjustments to the indices that are used internally by the DBMS to efficiently locate rows in tables, based on the contents of the key columns or, in some tables, the non-key columns as well, and (b) performing various "housekeeping" functions on the database, usually at night and/or during weekends.

DBAs are typically given the highest level of privilege, and one of them is often holder of the master account.

- *Application programmers* who write and maintain application software that interacts with the database. In most large organizations these programmers, like the database designers, do their work using the development copy of the database for initial testing and debugging, prior to a formal test using the test copy of the database. Only after passing the formal tests would the application software be deployed on application servers that interact with the production database. This is because there is always a risk that the programmers will accidentally add SQL commands that delete or overwrite large numbers of rows of data. If this were to happen to the production database it would disrupt business operations. Application programmers may be given medium-privilege accounts on the DBMS, or they may simply make use of the common account that is used by the application software.

Stored Procedures

An important enhancement to DBMSs was introduced around 1993, namely, the ability to create "stored procedures". A **stored procedure** is like a small program, consisting mainly of standard SQL commands, which is stored in the database and given a unique name, such as "sp_GetSalesResults". Once a stored procedure has been stored in the database, a user (or a user's application software) can execute the stored procedure simply by using an SQL command such as:

EXECUTE sp_GetSalesResults @year=2007

What this means to the DBMS is "execute the set of SQL commands contained in the stored procedure known as 'sp_GetSalesResult', assigning the value '2007' to that stored procedure's input parameter, known within the stored procedure as @year". In most DBMSs, simplified forms of such a command are allowed. For example, EXECUTE may be shortened to EXEC. Also, the names of the input parameters (like "@year") may be omitted, provided that the input-parameter values (placed after the stored procedure name) appear in exactly the order in which they are declared inside the stored procedure. (With only a single input parameter this will always be true.) So, we could type the following simplified command to execute the stored procedure:

EXEC sp_GetSalesResults 2007

The idea behind stored procedures is to allow frequently-used sequences of SQL commands to be made available to the application software that uses the database, thus avoiding the need to incorporate these SQL command sequences into the application software itself. Stored procedures are written in an extended version of SQL that incorporates some basic elements of normal programming languages. (Each DBMS has its own slightly different extended version of SQL for use in stored procedures.) The additional features, beyond normal SQL, allow a stored procedure to include branching conditions and other program-type logic within the stored procedure, so that the stored procedure can be written to execute slightly different sequences of SQL commands depending on a variety of conditions.

There are several advantages to using stored procedures, as follows:

- The sequence of SQL commands in a stored procedure can be thoroughly tested and debugged, in one place and at one time. This avoids having to include the sequence of SQL commands in each piece of application software that needs to perform the operation in question. It does away with the need to test each instance of the sequence (or, at least, it does away with the need to check for errors in copying it from a library of already-debugged SQL command sequences).

- The use of stored procedures avoids any need to transmit intermediate results back to the server or other device on which the application software is running and then send further SQL commands back to the DBMS from that device in order to complete the operation. The activity stays within the DBMS until every step contained in the stored procedure has been performed. The final results are then returned to the device.

- If changes are made to the database design, these can be masked from the application software (and from any expert users who interact directly with the database using the stored procedures) by modifying the stored procedures that are affected by the design changes – and by doing so in such a way that their input parameters and results remain unchanged. This avoids time-consuming re-writes of application software in order to cope with a changed database design.

- By "knowing" exactly what SQL commands a stored procedure contains before the stored procedure is used for the first time, the DBMS can optimize the way that it will execute the stored procedure. It can also perform adaptive optimization, as it monitors the stored procedure in action, thus progressively improving the efficiency of execution during the first few times the stored procedure is used. (Whether or not these benefits are real in modern DBMSs has been disputed by some experts. DBMS vendors have tried to minimize the differences between the way that a series of ordinary SQL commands is executed and the way that a stored procedure is executed. As a result, some DBMSs now keep track of the ordinary SQL commands that are executed repeatedly and apply the same optimization algorithms to these as they do to stored procedures. This weakens the case for using stored procedures purely on performance grounds.)

Since the introduction of stored procedures, a new class of DBMS user has thus been created:

- The *stored-procedure programmer*, who writes, tests, and de-bugs generally-useful stored procedures, then add them to the database. Stored-procedure programmers also update the stored procedures whenever changes are made to the database design.

I will have more to say about stored procedures in Chapter 6.

Interacting with a DBMS

As a user of a DBMS, you might be offered more than one way to interact with the DBMS. The simplest method of interacting with a DBMS is via a command-line interface (a method that dates back to the early days of relational DBMSs). This is this type of interface that is typically used by Database Administrators when working with a DBMS like Oracle. One advantage of such an interface is simplicity: you simply type an SQL command, or string of commands, followed by a final command like 'GO' or 'RUN', and the DBMS immediately does what you told it to do. Also, you are talking directly to the DBMS, so there is no go-between software to slow down the execution. The disadvantage of the command-line interface is that it is easy to make a mistake when typing a command; and a simple mistake may have devastating consequences (if the user has high-level privileges).

In order to make administration and management of databases easier, applications with graphical user interfaces (GUIs) have been created for most DBMSs. Such GUI applications either run on a PC that interacts with the DBMS via a network connection or on an application server that the user interacts with via a browser. (During initial set-up of the DBMS, the GUI application may also be run on the server that the DBMS resides on.)

When application software interacts with a DBMS, there are two main ways in which the software can send commands to the DBMS and receive the results of queries. One is by means of "client" or "agent" software. This is typically provided by the DBMS vendor and can be integrated into the application software. The other is via a form of the command-line interface that operates behind the scenes, between the application software and the DBMS. The command-line interface can be used where the query results will be treated purely as text by the application. This simpler method sometimes gives a faster response time, because it eliminates the handshakes between the application software and the agent, and between the agent and the DBMS. However, use of an agent (or an equivalent method) is essential when the application needs to be able to map the data values, received from the database, into program variables of equivalent type. For example, if a result from the database includes a value like '122945.67', with format "decimal(8,2)", the application needs to be able to receive this into a variable of type "real" or "float" (depending on what programming language is used). Without such a datatype-preserving interface, the application would have to receive all query results as text strings and then parse them to extract numerical values, currency amounts, dates, and so on.

If you have not used a DBMS before, a GUI is probably the best way to start interacting with a DBMS, because you get a far better feel for what is going on in the database when you can see the tables represented in a graphical display. Such GUIs often include useful tools, such as a syntax-checker, which you can use to check SQL commands and stored procedures for syntactic errors (but not, however, for logical errors) before you try to send them to the DBMS.

Creating Tables

When you use either a GUI or a command-line interface to build a new database, for each table that you create you must do the first four of the following things (and you will almost always want to do the last two as well):

- Give the table the name that you intend it to have.

- Give the table the number of columns that you intend it to have.

- Give each column the name that you intend it to have.

- Define the format of each column.

- Mark the key column or columns of the table as key columns.

- Designate non-key columns as NULL or NOT NULL columns.

The exact means of doing these things will depend on which DBMS you are using, so I will not attempt to describe in detail the various ways in which they might be done. However, I want to briefly review what we covered in earlier chapters about the last three items, and take a quick look at how they tend to be done in most DBMSs.

Column format:

I use the term "format" in this book (rather than "datatype" or "type") in order to avoid confusion for readers who are used to talking about "type" in the mathematical sense. The "type" of a variable is strictly a mathematical characteristic such as "real number", "integer", "boolean", or "text string". (This kind of "type" is used in programming languages, like Pascal or Java.) By contrast, the descriptions used for columns in a relational database (and also in highly-format-oriented programming languages like COBOL) are much more specific than the mathematical "type", for example:

- "varchar(40)", meaning "a character string of variable length, up to a maximum of 40 characters".

- "decimal(8,2)", meaning "a real number represented as up to eight digits, with two of those digits after the decimal point".

This is why I prefer to call these descriptors "formats". (In COBOL they are called "data descriptions".) However, you should expect to find them referred to as "datatypes" or "types" in most DBMS manuals and GUIs.

When creating a table using a command-line interface, the formats of the columns are included as part of the CREATE TABLE command (as we saw in Chapter 2), for example:

```
CREATE TABLE students
  (student_id varchar(9),
   first_name varchar(40),
   last_name varchar(40),
   sex char(1),
   date_of_birth datetime
  )
```

In this example the meanings of the format descriptors are as follows:

- "varchar(9)" = variable-length character string up to nine characters maximum

- "varchar(40)" = variable-length character string up to forty characters maximum

- "char(1)" = fixed-length character string of length exactly one character

- "datetime" = a date plus (optionally) a time

Note that when a simple date, such as date of birth, is designated as having the format "datetime", the time element of the datetime variable is ignored. The time element defaults to midnight (00:00:00) in most DBMSs.

When using a GUI, the choice of format is typically done using a pull-down list, combined with an input field for the number of characters or decimal places, where appropriate.

You should always make sure that columns of different tables that represent the same attribute are created with exactly the same format. If you use one format for the column in one table, and another format for the equivalent column in another table, things will go badly wrong when users start performing queries involving the two tables. Some format mismatches, such as defining an attribute as "int" in one table and "varchar(10)" in another table, are easy to spot. However, another a common error, which is easily overlooked, is setting different limits on the length of a character string, for example "varchar(20)" in one table and "varchar(30)" the other table. This can go unnoticed until a character string is entered into these columns that exceeds the twenty-character limit of varchar(20), and is thus truncated in one table but stored in full in other.

It is also a good idea to use the same formats for columns that represent attributes that are attributes of different entities but are of a similar nature, for example, "zipcode" in the "customer_addresses" table and "zipcode" in the "supplier_addresses" table; or "last_name" in the "customers" table and "last_name" in the "employees" table. At some point in the future a situation may arise where users want to perform queries that look for equalities between such columns. These queries are more likely to work as users intend them to work if the columns are of exactly the same format.

Key columns:

As mentioned in Chapter 3, when interacting directly with the DBMS via a command-line interface, you can designate a column as a key column by including PRIMARY KEY in the CREATE TABLE command, for example:

```
CREATE TABLE students
  (student_id varchar(9) PRIMARY KEY,
   first_name varchar(40),
   last_name varchar(40),
   sex char(1),
   date_of_birth datetime
  )
```

When you are creating tables with two or more key columns, things get a little more complicated. It may be easier to do the CREATE TABLE command first, and then designate the key columns afterwards. (This can also be done for a single key column.) Because there are various different ways of designating multi-column keys, you should refer to the manual of the DBMS that you will be using in order to find out how this is done.

If you are using a GUI, then marking a column as a key column is typically done by simply checking a checkbox. A multi-column key can typically be designated by checking the checkboxes for two or more columns.

Non-key columns sometimes contain candidate keys, like Social Security Number. These are columns that could have been used as keys, because their values are unique. In most DBMSs you can designate candidate-key columns as having the property UNIQUE. (The UNIQUE function was mentioned in Chapter 3 when we were looking at the enforcement of cardinality rules.) If a non-key column is designated as UNIQUE, this means that the DBMS must check for duplicates in that column whenever a new row is added to the table and must give an error message if an attempt is made to insert a row containing a duplicate value in that column. This can be useful; but it should be used with care.

Note that the Entity-Relationship modeling process does not normally pay much attention to candidate keys, once you have made your choice of keys; so you would not normally expect to be worrying about candidate keys by the time you get to the point of creating the database. If you find that candidate keys are occurring in a lot of tables in your database design then you should start to worry that you might not have done a good job at the E-R modeling stage.

NULL constraints:

If you are using a command-line interface to create the tables, then, as mentioned in Chapter 3, you can designate the non-key columns as NULL or NOT NULL within the CREATE TABLE command, for example:

```
CREATE TABLE students
  (student_id varchar(9) PRIMARY KEY,
   first_name varchar(40) NOT NULL,
   last_name varchar(40) NOT NULL,
   sex char(1) NOT NULL,
   date_of_birth datetime NOT NULL
  )
```

If you are using a GUI, then marking a column as NULL or NOT NULL is typically done simply by checking a checkbox.

In general, it is best to make as many columns as possible NOT NULL. This is because the way that NULLs are treated in various arithmetic and logical operations varies depending on which DBMS you are using and how its basic set-up options have been configured. Whenever NULLs are allowed you have to constantly worry about how particular queries will behave if a NULL is present in a particular row.

Foreign Keys

The next feature of many DBMSs that I am going to cover in this chapter is the foreign key feature. The concept of foreign keys was introduced into relational DBMSs in order to help preserve what is called **referential integrity**. This is a tricky concept, best explained by an example.

Consider the following three tables, containing a few example rows of data. (Note that, to keep this example simple, I have slightly simplified the way that teachers are dealt here, compared with the example in Chapter 2. I now have simply a "teachers" table, rather than a design allowing both faculty members and graduate students to be assigned as teachers.)

Table name: **teachers**

teacher_id	first_name	last_name	sex	date_of_birth	date_of_hire
T19780042	Ada	Lovelace	F	1948-11-12	1978-01-02
T19790002	Mileva	Maric	F	1949-05-08	1979-05-01
T19870024	Rosalind	Franklin	F	1960-07-01	1987-10-01

Table name: **courses**

course_number	course_title	credits
P101	Philosophy	4.5
M101	Mathematics	4.5
M342	Database Design	3.0

Table name: **course_teachers**

teacher_id	course_number
T19790002	P101
T19870024	M101
T19780042	M342

As far as we can see, this part of the design is normalized. It does not suffer from insertion anomalies or deletion anomalies, that is:

- Courses can be added to the "courses" table without a teacher having to be first assigned to teach each course.

- Teachers can be hired and added to the "teachers" table without any teaching duties having to be assigned to them.

- Courses can be deleted from the "courses" table without teachers being lost from the database.

- Teachers can be deleted from the "teachers" table without courses being lost from the database.

However, if we delete course 'M342' from the "courses" table, without first deleting the associated row from the "course_teachers" table, the row in the "course_teachers" table that refers to course 'M342' is left with only its "teacher_id" value ('T19780042') being capable of being associated with another table. (There is no longer a row in the "courses" table that 'M342', in the "course_teachers" table, can refer to.)

Similarly, if we delete teacher 'T19780042' from the "teachers" table, without first deleting the associated row from the "course_teachers" table, the row in the "course_teachers" table that refers to teacher 'T19780042' is left with only its "course_number" value ('M342') being capable of being associated with another table. (There is no longer a row in the "teachers" table that 'T19780042', in the "course_teachers" table, can refer to.)

In both of these cases, the row in the "course_teachers" table is semi-marooned. (I say "semi-marooned" because the row still contains one value that can be associated with a row in another table. Only if both entities are deleted – teacher 'T19780042' and course 'M342' – does the row in "course_teachers" become completely marooned.)

Such semi-marooned or completely-marooned rows in a relationship-representing table clutter up the table with useless rows; but are they harmful? Provided that we use queries that operate on the entity-representing tables, as well as on the relationship-representing tables, the marooned rows do no harm. For example, if we wanted to create a list teachers and the courses that they are teaching, without the risk of marooned rows in the "course_teachers" table giving rise to erroneous results, we would use the following query:

```
SELECT
    teachers.first_name,
    teachers.last_name,
    courses.course_number,
    courses.course_title
FROM
    courses,
    course_teachers,
    teachers
WHERE
    courses.course_number = course_teachers.course_number AND
    teachers.teacher_id = course_teachers.teacher_id
```

Note that there are three tables mentioned in the FROM clause: two entity-representing tables ("courses" and "teachers") and one relationship-representing table ("course_teachers"). As a result, teacher/course pairings will appear in the results only if the teacher appears in the "teachers" table *and* the course appears in the "courses" table *and* the two are associated with one another via a row in "course_teachers". (Teachers not assigned to courses, and courses without teachers, will not appear in the results.) This query works correctly, even if there are semi-marooned or completely-marooned rows in the "course_teachers" table. For example, suppose that course 'M342' (Database Design) has been deleted from the "courses" table, but the third row in the "course_teachers" table is still there. The above query will, in spite of the presence of the semi-marooned row in "course_teachers", give the correct list of teachers and the courses that they are teaching:

```
first_name    last_name    course_number    course_title
----------    ----------   -------------    ------------
Mileva        Maric        P101             Philosophy
Rosalind      Franklin     M101             Mathematics
```

The WHERE clause, by requiring associations between "course_teachers" and both of the entity-representing tables ("courses" and "teachers"), ignores the semi-marooned row.

We could write queries, if required, to identify teachers not assigned to courses and teacherless courses. These queries would also give correct results, in spite of the semi-marooned row in "course_teachers", provided that all three tables are retained in the FROM clause – and provided, of course, that the queries were written correctly.

Although semi-marooned (or completely-marooned) rows in relationship-representing tables need not give rise to erroneous results (if queries are written correctly), they still represent a potential source of trouble. Users who write their own SQL queries, and application programmers who write SQL queries in their programs, may try to cut corners. For example, if a user does not need to know the names of courses, and wants a report containing only teachers and course numbers, the user might write the following query:

```
SELECT
  teachers.first_name,
  teachers.last_name,
  course_teachers.course_number
FROM
  course_teachers,
  teachers
WHERE
  teachers.teacher_id = course_teachers.teacher_id
```

This query makes no reference to the "courses" table. As a result, if the course 'M342' had been deleted from the "courses" table, but the row referring to that course remained semi-marooned in the "course_teachers" table, then the result of this query would incorrectly show course 'M342' as still on offer (with an assigned teacher):

```
first_name    last_name      course_number
----------    ----------     -------------
Mileva        Maric          P101
Rosalind      Franklin       M101
Ada           Lovelace       M342
```

The semi-marooning or complete-marooning of rows in a table (such as in a relationship-representing table like "course_teachers") is described as a **breakdown of referential integrity**: the marooned rows contain references to rows that no longer exist in other tables.

Note that the semi-marooning of rows is not a deletion anomaly. A deletion anomaly occurs only when the deletion of one piece of information leads to the unintended deletion of another piece of information.

There are several ways in which such semi-marooned and completely-marooned rows could be dealt with in a database:

- If the user is interacting with the database via application software, we could make sure that the SQL commands that are sent to the database, when deleting a row from an entity-representing table, will also delete any associated rows from the relationship-representing tables. This would prevent semi-marooned rows being left in the relationship-representing tables.

- We could write a program, and incorporate it in the nightly or weekly "housekeeping" functions that the Database Administrator performs on the database, to identify and delete all rows in relationship-representing tables that have been semi-marooned or marooned. This would clean up these tables after the fact.

- We could make sure that all queries are carefully written so as to always make reference to the appropriate entity-representing tables, as well as to relationship-representing tables, thus causing them to ignore the rows that have been semi-marooned. We would allow the semi-marooned rows to accumulate in the tables over time, but the carefully-written queries would mask their presence.

- We could arrange for the DBMS to automatically delete rows in relationship-representing tables whenever an associated row in an entity-representing table is deleted. This is the so-called **foreign key** approach.

To put a foreign key arrangement (or "foreign key reference") into effect, you tell the DBMS which columns in one table correspond to a key column in another table. For example, to establish a foreign key reference for "teacher_id" between the "course_teachers" table and the "teachers" table, we would tell the DBMS that the "teacher_id" column in the "course_teachers" table is a foreign key that references the "teacher_id" column in the "teachers" table. In this case the "master" end of the reference is in "teachers" and the "slave" end of the reference is in "course_teachers". (We could also do a similar thing for the "course_number" columns, between the "course_teachers" table and the "courses" table.)

What the DBMS will then do is to perform what is called a **cascading delete** whenever the row at the "master" end of the foreign key reference is deleted – deleting the row or rows at the "slave" end of the reference. For example, if a teacher is deleted from the "teachers" table then the DBMS will automatically delete any rows from the "course_teachers" table that represent teaching assignments for that teacher.

You may find the whole idea of foreign keys somewhat unsettling. I certainly do. It goes against the very important principle that associations between tables in a relational database are established only within the context of queries. Also, using foreign key references is not without risks, particularly if applied to a database design that is not normalized.

To illustrate this, suppose that the database designer was suffering from a bad hangover on the day that he designed the University Administration database. (Please note: I am not suggesting that heavy alcohol consumption is in any way associated with being a database designer, although you may very well be thinking that by now.) As a result of his condition, the database designer included a "teacher_id" column in the "enrollments" table, and he designated this column as a foreign key, referencing "teacher_id" in the "teachers" table (not shown on this page).

The resulting table, which I have labeled "enrollments_hangover" (in order to identify it as a don't-do-this example), would then look like the following (after a few rows have been inserted into the table):

Table name: **enrollments_hangover**

student_id	term	year	course_number	teacher_id
200800101	1	2008	M101	T19870024
200600001	1	2008	P101	T19790002
200600002	1	2008	M342	T19780042
200600017	1	2008	M342	T19780042
200600108	1	2008	M342	T19780042
200600982	1	2008	M342	T19780042
200701753	1	2008	M342	T19780042
200702722	1	2008	M342	T19780042

Now, suppose that teacher 'T19780042' dies in the middle of the term. A replacement teacher is quickly found. A database user deletes 'T19780042' from the "teachers" table and this automatically causes a cascading delete, which wipes out all the rows in the "enrollments_hangover" table relating to the course 'M342' which the late 'T19780042' was teaching. The database user now inserts the replacement teacher into the "teachers" table and assigns him to teach course 'M342' – hoping, no doubt, that everything in the database is now as it should be. But it is not. All the information about which students were enrolled in 'M342' has been deleted. The database user is now faced with the tedious task of finding the original sign-up sheets and re-entering all the enrollments for 'M342'. (Alternatively, if course-enrollment is done on-line, the new teacher will have to ask his students, during the next class or lecture, to re-enroll in the course.)

I could come up with other examples of this problem, but I do not want to needlessly expose you to non-normalized database designs. If you were to consider such examples you would quickly arrive at the following conclusion:

The less normalized a database design is, the more devastating the unintended consequences of a cascading delete can be.

In particular, if the database designer has represented a relationship by means of a direct association between one entity-representing table and another entity-representing table (rather than by using a relationship-representing table) then cascading deletes can do an enormous amount of damage. (Unfortunately, as mentioned in Chapter 4, this particular kind of non-normalized design is quite common in real-world databases.) So, if you plan to use foreign key arrangements, you should use them with extreme care. In particular:

- Make sure that the database design is fully normalized before considering the possibility of defining foreign key references.

- Use foreign keys only between entity-representing tables and relationship-representing tables (where the relationship-representing table is at the slave end of the reference and the entity-representing table is at the master end). Never use them between two entity-representing tables.

- Carefully weigh the benefits of automatically cleaning out semi-marooned rows (using the foreign key feature) against the potential problems that a cascading delete might cause. (In assessing the benefits of using the foreign key feature, determine how many commonly used queries would give incorrect results if the rows were left semi-marooned. If very few queries are affected then the benefits of clearing out the semi-marooned rows are small.)

- Consider how long the rows will be left semi-marooned before some other action causes them to be deleted, for instance, the deletion of all course-enrollment information at the end of the term.

There are other ways, besides cascading deletes, in which foreign key references can be configured to work. For example, in some DBMSs you can configure foreign key references to prevent the deletion of the row that is at the master end of the reference (the "teachers" table in the above example) until the rows at the slave end of the reference have first been deleted. If the user tries to delete the row at the master end, then the DBMS gives an error message. It is then up to the user to delete the rows at the slave end of the reference (the "enrollments_hangover" table in the above example), before deleting the row at the master end (or decide that the deletion was a bad idea in the first place). This prevent-the-deletion mode of operation makes the foreign key a fairly useless feature, because we are then back to manually cleaning up rows that have been left semi-marooned – which is exactly what the foreign key was mean to take care of for us.

Before we leave this topic, I want to warn you about a misunderstanding that you may come across (hopefully, not very often). A few database designers (who were perhaps not paying attention in their database classes), believe that a relational database will not work properly unless you link the tables together via foreign key references. They believe that this is how you tell the DBMS that, for example, "student_id" in the "students" table is the same thing as "student_id" in the "enrollments" table.

Clearly this is nonsense. If foreign key references were really necessary for a relational database to function, then it would not be necessary to include join conditions in WHERE clauses: the DBMS would already "know" about all possible associations between tables. (Whether or not this would be a good thing is not worth debating: it is not how present-day relational DBMSs work.) Foreign key references are strictly optional and are intended only as a way of enforcing referential integrity from within the database (as opposed to by other means).

So, if you come across a database design that is festooned with foreign key references, it might be a good idea to ask the person who designed it, "You do know, don't you, that across-the-board use of foreign keys is not a requirement when creating a database?"

Table Aliases

A **table alias** is a name (typically a very short one) that a user, or a stored procedure programmer, assigns to a table within a query or stored procedure. This allows the user or programmer to use the alias in place of the table name. For example, in the following query I have assigned the aliases 'c', 'ct', and 't' to the tables "courses", "course_teachers", and "teachers". I have done this by placing the letters 'c', 'ct', and 't' after the table names in the FROM clause. With these aliases declared in the FROM clause, I can use them in place of the actual table names when I write the SELECT and WHERE clauses, as follows:

```
SELECT
  t.first_name,
  t.last_name,
  c.course_number,
  c.course_title
FROM
  courses c,
  course_teachers ct,
  teachers t
WHERE
  c.course_number = ct.course_number AND
  t.teacher_id = ct.teacher_id
```

The table alias feature has been available in query languages since the early days of query languages. The original aim of table aliases was to reduce the number of characters that the user has to type when typing an SQL command directly into a DBMS. The table alias feature has remained part of SQL, and the feature has continued to be used, even though most SQL commands are now incorporated into application software and stored procedures. In creating application software and stored procedures, the person writing the SQL statements is typically using some kind of text editor. Use of a text editor allows the programmer to easily "copy and paste" table names, so that these do not have to be typed each time they are used. Alternatively, the programmer could use conspicuous abbreviations like 'zzc', 'zzct', and 'zzt' when drafting the program. He or she could then use the "find and replace" feature of the text editor to replace these temporary abbreviations with the full table names, before starting to debug the software or stored procedure. In other words, there is no reason why table aliases should ever need to be used today.

Nevertheless, table aliases continue to be used by many programmers, either out of laziness or habit. This is unfortunate, because tables aliases make it needlessly hard for someone else to follow how an SQL command or stored procedure works, making maintenance work unnecessarily difficult. The use of table aliases is particularly confusing when different programmers use different aliases for the same table. For example, one programmer may use 'c' for "customer and 'co' for "contact" and another programmer may use 'c' for "contact" and 'cu' for "customer".

I have even come across stored procedures where programmers have used different table aliases for the same tables in different parts of the same stored procedure. I can only conclude that the programmers in these cases were either insane or deliberately trying to make their stored procedures hard for others to understand. (In one particular case I think it was both.)

You have probably guessed what I am about to say:

Don't use table aliases.

If you are worried about mistyping the actual table names, then use the "copy and paste" feature of your text editor to paste them into each SQL clause. If you cannot master the "copy and paste" feature of your text editor, get help.

CHAPTER 6

WELCOME TO THE REAL WORLD

Introduction

In the previous five chapters I have concentrated on the "right way", or at least the better ways, of doing things. I have made occasional references to some less-than-ideal practices that are followed in the real world, mainly to make a point about a better way of doing something. Also, like most writers of textbooks about databases, I have used examples with only a handful of tables in order to make the examples fairly easy to follow.

In this chapter I am going to try to paint a more realistic picture of the real world of database design, where things are bigger and uglier than in the examples that appear in most textbooks and database courses.

Number of Tables

It is rare to find textbook examples of databases that extend beyond ten tables. Many examples (including most of mine) stick to three or four tables, so as not to overwhelm the reader. However, the real world is not so kind. A very simple database covering customers, their contact information, credit card information, and purchasing history, could easily consist of around 30 tables, without any product information. Once you start to look at databases that cover all aspects of a sales and distribution organization, including products, prices, orders, invoices, and so on, you will find that the number of tables climbs to around 70. If you then look at any kind of basic financial services company, such as a bank, you should expect to find database designs with over 100 tables. And if you are looking at anything to do with securities, such as brokerage or securities custody, 200 tables would not be unusual. Some generic business application suites have databases with close to 1,000 tables.

Many of these databases have evolved over time, with database designers progressively adding tables to them. If you are expecting to start working as a database designer in the near future, don't panic: nobody is going to ask you to design a one-hundred-table database on your first day as a full-time database designer. Some of the most impressive database designs (in terms of scale, rather than quality) have been started in one company and then acquired by another company as the result of the sale of part or all of that company. In a few cases I suspect that database designs have been taken from company to company without the first company's permission, for example, when a database designer has changed jobs. (It is even harder to protect the intellectual property inherent in a database design than in a computer program.)

Lookup Tables

When you examine real-world database designs, you will probably come across tables that are referred to as "lookup tables". If you are lucky, the database designer may have given these tables names that clearly indicate that they are lookup tables, for example, "faculties_lookup". Even if the tables have not been given distinctive names, you may hear application software developers (who write programs that utilize the database) talking about lookup tables. In such cases you could ask them which tables they consider to be lookup tables.

A **lookup table**, sometimes also called a reference table, is a table that is treated as an adjunct to the main database. Its contents change infrequently and can be changed only by privileged users. Information in the main database can be successfully retrieved or updated without any reference to a lookup table. However, lookup tables are used – mainly by application programs – to control the accuracy of data inserted into the database and to enhance information retrieved from the main database when presenting it to users. The key column of a lookup table represents an attribute that, in the main database, is a non-key column of one or several tables in the main database.

As an example of a lookup table, consider the following:

Table name: **faculties_lookup**		
faculty_code	**faculty_full_name**	**valid_now**
ART	Arts	Y
EDU	Education	N
MAT	Mathematics	Y
SCI	Science	Y
MUS	Music	Y
PHI	Philosophy	Y

The key column of this table is "faculty_code". The values that appear in this column are abbreviations for the names of the faculties in the university. These abbreviations are used in non-key "faculty_code" columns of tables in the main database. For example, in the "teachers" table, a "faculty_code" column would record the faculty that a teacher belongs to. Tables representing other entities (courses, non-teaching staff, buildings, and so on) may also have non-key "faculty_code" columns.

The "faculties_lookup" table records the following things:

- In the first column, it records the complete list of faculties and the abbreviations that must be used for those faculties when they appear as non-key columns in the main database.

- In the second column, it records the full name by which each faculty is known.

- In the third column, it records whether or not ('Y' or 'N') the faculty abbreviation is an allowed value for a new or updated entry in the main database. (In the case of the Education faculty you can see that this is no longer to be used in new entries into the database, although it may be found in the data that is already contained in the database.)

There are two categories of use to which a lookup table like this can be put. The first is the validation of data entry by application programs. When an application user provides information to be inserted into the database, the application will typically perform validity checks on the information as supplied by the user. For information that can take only one of a number of values, the application will check that the information typed by the user matches one of those allowed values. If the allowed values are unlikely to change, such as 'M' or 'F' for 'male' or 'female', they can be coded into the application. However, if the allowed values may change over the life of the application, it is better to place them in a lookup table in the database. This makes it possible to change the behavior of all copies of the application simply by updating the database, rather than by distributing new versions of the application software to all users' devices or to all application servers. Whenever a user is to be presented with an input screen, the application executes an SQL command that retrieves the contents of the lookup table. Most commonly, the application uses these contents to create a pull-down menu from which the user selects one item. In the "faculties_lookup" example, the pull-down menu would show the values that appear in the "faculty_full_name" column (excluding those where there is an 'N' in the "valid_now" column). When the user selects a particular faculty from the pull-down menu, the application takes the corresponding value from the "faculty_code" column and inserts this into the database. Thus, every time a value for "faculty_code" is inserted into the database it will be one of the values stored in the lookup table.

Another, less-satisfactory way of validating user input is to let the user type the faculty code (assuming that the user is familiar with the abbreviations) and then compare what the user has typed with the values from the lookup table. If there is no match then the application tells the user that the faculty code is not recognized and asks the user to try again.

The second category of use of lookup tables is in enhancing information retrieved from the database – making it easier for users to understand. For example, the "faculty_lookup" table could be used to replace faculty codes with full faculty names in a screen display or in a printed report. The application would do this by including the lookup table in the SQL command that retrieves information from the main database. The first of the following two SQL commands shows the retrieval of information about all female teaching staff (first name, last name, and faculty) *without* enhancing the faculty information (that is, presenting the faculty information in the form of the faculty code). The second shows the inclusion of the lookup table in the command in order to provide the full faculty name.

The first SQL command, which operates on only the "teachers" table, is as follows:

```
SELECT
  teachers.first_name,
  teachers last_name,
  teachers.faculty_code
FROM
  teachers
WHERE
  teachers.sex = 'F'
```

The result of this query would look something like this:

```
first_name          last_name           faculty_code
----------          ----------          ------------
Ada                 Lovelace            MAT
Mileva              Maric               PHI
Rosalind            Franklin            SCI
```

The second SQL command operates on the "faculties_lookup" table, as well as the "teachers" table. The command includes a join condition between "teachers" and "faculty_lookup" in the WHERE clause:

```
SELECT
  teachers.first_name,
  teachers.last_name,
  faculties_lookup.faculty_full_name
FROM
  teachers,
  faculties_lookup
WHERE
  teachers.faculty_code = faculties_lookup.faculty_code AND
  teachers.sex = 'F'
```

The result of this query would look something like this:

```
first_name          last_name           faculty_full_name
----------          ----------          -----------------
Ada                 Lovelace            Mathematics
Mileva              Maric               Philosophy
Rosalind            Franklin            Science
```

Note that the join condition in the second SQL command operates between the non-key "faculty_code" column in the "teachers" table and the key column ("faculty_code") in the "faculties_lookup" table. In general, we would be nervous about a query that involves key and non-key versions of the same attribute: this is typically a sign of a non-normalized database design. However, in this particular situation we regard the lookup table as lying outside the main database design and therefore not needing to follow normalization rules.

The enhancement of information in this manner (within an SQL command that operates on the tables in the main database) is one of the few situations where a lookup table is allowed to appear in an SQL command along with one or more tables from the main database. By contrast, when they are used to provide information to validate data entry within an application, lookup tables are queried individually and with no reference to the main database.

In the WHERE clause of the SQL command above there is no mention of the "valid_now" column of the "faculties_lookup" table. As a result, all rows of the table can be matched with faculty codes appearing in the "teachers" table. The reason for ignoring "valid_now" in this situation is that it applies only to new entries in the database. If you study the example rows in the "faculties_lookup" table shown earlier you will notice that the row for the Education Faculty contains an 'N' in the "valid_now" column. This indicates that the university has phased out (or is about to phase out) the Education Faculty. When the "valid_now" value for a faculty is changed from 'Y' to 'N' like this, it has the immediate effect of removing that faculty as a choice in faculty-selection pull-down menus. However, the information about the faculty is still retained in the table so that it can continue to be used to enhance retrieved information relating to entities that retain the "faculty_code" value 'EDU' (for example, faculty staff who are still considered to be part of the faculty until they retire).

In summary:

- A lookup table is an adjunct to the main database. Lookup tables could be removed from the database without destroying the integrity of the database and without any loss of important information. (A lookup table provides an alternative representation of information, such as 'Education' instead of 'EDU'. It does not supply any real additional information.)

- A lookup table is updated infrequently and may be updated only by a small number of privileged users.

- A lookup table is exempt from normalization rules. Specifically, the non-key columns of other tables become the key column of the lookup table (which would normally be a sign of a non-normalized design).

- Lookup tables are used (a) to ensure that data being inserted into non-key columns of the main database tables is valid, and (b) to convert non-key information from the main database tables into an alternative form, without changing its meaning (for example, from a short code to a full name).

- A lookup table often has two or more columns. However, it need have only one column if it is used simply to validate correct data entry. An example of a single-column lookup table is a "NA_state_codes" table that holds all the valid two-letter state codes for the USA and Canada (NJ, NM, NV, NY, and so on).

- A lookup table should be given a name that clearly identifies it as a lookup table.

Although lookup tables may be added to a database for the purposes just described, a lookup table is unnecessary and undesirable for the key attributes of entities, for example, "course_number" for the entity *course*. The entity-representing table (such as "courses") can, and should, be used by applications as a lookup table. Information, such as "course_name", which may be needed in generating easily-readable reports and in building pull-down menus, should be included in non-key columns in the entity-representing table. It would be redundant, and potentially troublesome, to create a separate "courses_lookup" table.

It follows that the need for a lookup table can be avoided if, in creating the E-R diagram, we treat things like faculties and majors as entities rather than attributes of other entities. If we choose to recognize *faculty* as an entity when drawing the E-R diagram, we then have a relationship *teacher belongs to faculty*, rather than a requirement to treat "faculty_code" as an attribute *teacher*. This is generally a much better way of modeling the real world. It allows for the possibility that, later on, a real attribute of the entity (rather than an alternative form of its name) might need to be represented in the database. This cannot be done if the faculty is regarded only as an attribute of another entity like *teacher*. In the E-R model, an attribute cannot have an attribute.

Once *faculty* is recognized as an entity, the resulting database design will include the following tables (in which I have shown a few example rows). The "faculty_assignments" table represents the relationship *teacher belongs to faculty*. Its key consists of the "teacher_id" and "faculty_code" columns, taken together. The "faculties" table represents the entity *faculty*. Its key is "faculty_code". This is the table that, in this much-better design, can be used as a lookup table whenever necessary – as well as serving its main purpose as an integral part of the database.

Table name: **faculties**

faculty_code	faculty_full_name	valid_now
ART	Arts	Y
EDU	Education	N
MAT	Mathematics	Y
SCI	Science	Y
MUS	Music	Y
PHI	Philosophy	Y

Table name: **faculty_assignments**

teacher_id	faculty_code	faculty_head_flag
T19780042	MAT	Y
T19790002	PHI	Y
T19870024	SCI	N
T19920001	EDU	Y
T19960017	SCI	N

Table name: **teachers**

teacher_id	first_name	last_name	sex	date_of_birth	date_of_hire
T19780042	Ada	Lovelace	F	1948/11/12	1978/01/02
T19790002	Mileva	Maric	F	1949/05/08	1979/05/01
T19870024	Rosalind	Franklin	F	1960/07/01	1987/10/01
T19920001	Andrew	Payne	M	1945/04/01	1992/12/15
T19960017	Fred	Baker	M	1955/08/12	1996/01/02

Note that the entity-representing "faculties" table has the same columns as the earlier "faculties_lookup" table, and differs only in its name. The "valid_now" column has been retained to allow the table to be used exactly as before in the generation of pull-down menus. By treating faculty as an *entity* it is now possible to represent attributes of the *belongs to* relationship. For example, in the above design I have included a "faculty_head_flag" in the "faculty_assignments" table. This holds the value 'Y' if the teacher is the Faculty Head of the faculty to which he or she is assigned, or 'N' otherwise.

I have taken the time to explain all this in order to (a) prepare you to understand other people's database designs as regards lookup tables, and (b) give some suggestions for how to handle requests from application programmers for lookup tables when you are designing your own database. I will deal with (a) first.

When you examine someone else's database design you may or may not find tables with names that indicate that they are lookup tables. The absence of lookup-related names does not mean that there are no lookup tables. The designer may simply not have bothered to name them in a helpful way. Conversely, even though a designer has given a table a name that indicates that it is a lookup table, you cannot be sure that it is really a lookup table until you take a closer look. The best approach is therefore to examine all tables that might be lookup tables and decide whether they really are lookup tables or not. Possible lookup tables are tables that have a single key column and a total number of columns not exceeding four. The following guidelines should help you differentiate between entity-representing tables (which form part of the main database) and lookup tables:

- Regardless of how it is named, and regardless of whether or not applications are using it as a lookup table (for example, in generating pull-down menus), a table whose single key column also appears in another table as a single key column, or one of a pair of key columns, is *not* a true lookup table. It is an integral part of the main database. The database would be incomplete, and data would be lost, if the table in question were deleted.

- Regardless of how it is named, a table whose single key column appears only as a non-key column in one or more other tables and is used by applications as a lookup table *may* be a true lookup table. However, it may in fact be an entity-representing table in a non-normalized database design. As explained in Chapter 4 under "The Rule Most Often Broken", database designers sometimes represent one-to-one or one-to-many relationships between two entities without taking the trouble to use a relationship-representing table. Instead, they make the key column of one entity-representing table a non-key column the other entity-representing table. Because of this possibility, you need to look more closely at the table and how it is used.

- A table that appears to be a lookup table is *not*, in fact, a lookup table if any of its non-key columns contains information that goes beyond what is required for lookup purposes, that is, goes beyond representing the key-column information in a longer form, or indicating which rows are to be presented to users in a pull-down menu. For example, if the "faculties_lookup" table had a column called "year_of_inception" to record the year in which the faculty was first established in the university, this would be a clear indication that it contains information of interest to database users generally, and must therefore be regarded as an entity-representing table.

- A table that appears to be a lookup table is *not*, in fact, a lookup table if it appears along with other tables in SQL commands that insert or update rows in those other tables.

- A table that appears to be a lookup table is *not*, in fact, a lookup table if it appears along with other tables in SQL commands that refer to any of its columns other than its key column in the WHERE clause.

In a few cases it may turn out to be impossible to determine whether or not a table is a lookup table. For instance, where you need to review all the SQL commands that are executed against the database in order to make a final determination as to whether a particular table is a lookup table or not, but you are unable to obtain copies of all those commands, you will be left undecided.

My second and more important objective for this section is to present some suggestions on how to handle requests from application programmers for the creation of lookup tables when you are designing your own database. In dealing with such requests, remember that an entity-representing table can always be used as a lookup table (at the same time as serving its main purpose). If you have already included the appropriate entity-representing table in your database design (for example, "faculties") then you should instruct the programmer to use this. If the programmer needs columns that do not exist in your original design (for example, "full_faculty_name" or "valid_now") then you will need to update the database design by adding these columns. This will not affect how previously-created SQL commands operate; so it can be done non-disruptively. Of course, you will have to arrange for data to be inserted into the new columns that you have added. In due course you will also have to arrange for any application programs used to update the information in the table to be modified to support the input of data for those newly added columns.

If there is no entity-representing table in your database design that could act as a lookup table then you have to choose between (a) creating a lookup table, and (b) changing the main database design to recognize an additional entity and the relationships between existing entities and that new entity. The choice between these two courses of action requires careful thought:

- Consider the costs of the disruption that will be caused if you change the main database design. If you introduce a new entity-representing table and a new relationship-representing table you will need to give everyone plenty of notice about the change, allowing them time to modify all affected SQL commands. You can provide a phase-in period by adding and populating the new tables; telling everyone about the change; and then waiting few a few weeks. Once all the SQL commands have been modified, you can start to delete the affected non-key column from the old tables. For example, you would delete the non-key "faculty_code" column from the "teachers" table. During the transition period you may need to run a series of SQL commands periodically to synchronize the information between the old and new parts of the database. The programmer who asked you to create a lookup table can start using the new entity-representing table (for example, "faculties") right away; so at least he or she will be happy. But other programmers may not be pleased by the change. Even with a phased approach, the amount of disruption that the change causes may be considerable.

- Consider possible future benefits from recognizing the non-key attribute as an entity. For example, there may already be things that cannot be done with the existing database design, such as (a) recording which teacher is the Faculty Head, (b) allowing a teacher to belong to two faculties, or (c) recording information about a faculty such as its inception date. Such benefits may make the disruption worthwhile.

- Consider how frequently the information in the new table will change. If it will change only rarely then it is much less likely that there will be any benefits from recognizing the attribute as an entity. For example, the two-letter North American state codes are better placed in a lookup table than in an entity-representing table.

If you decide to create a lookup table, rather than modify the existing main database design, you should give the lookup table a name that clearly identities it as a lookup table, such as "faculties_lookup".

One option I did not consider in the above example is to create an entity-representing table such as "faculties", and incorporate it into the design by breaking the most-often-broken normalization rule (that is, not bothering to include a relationship-representing table in the design). I did not mention this option because I do not want to encourage bad habits. In any case (as should be clear from the discussion of how hard it can be to distinguish between a true lookup table and an entity-representing table in a non-normalized design), the columns of a lookup table may, initially at least, be the same as those in an entity-representing table in a non-normalized design. Any differences would emerge only when database users started to ask for additional columns to be added to the entity-representing table (for example, "inception_date"), thus clearly establishing the table's role as representing an entity. So, aside from the name that you give to the table, and the future possibility of adding new non-key columns to the table, the option of adding an entity-representing table using a non-normalized design is not really a fundamentally different option. So, faced with the request from a programmer for the creation of lookup for a non-key attribute like "faculty_code", if you do not want to face the upheaval of adding two new tables to the database design ("faculties" and "faculty_assignments"), the safest approach is to add "faculties_lookup". If, at a later date, someone requests that additional information be recorded in the database about faculties, you can use this request as justification for a potentially disruptive change to the database design – particularly if the request can be met only with a normalized design, for example, when a many-to-many relationship needs to be represented between *faculty* and another entity. (Remember that the most-often-broken normalization rule can only be broken for one-to-one and one-to-many relationships, not for many-to-many.)

One dreadfully bad idea that I once came across, in the database design of an organization that should have known better, was to consolidate all lookup tables into a single super-lookup table. This had two key columns – "attribute_type" and "attribute_value". Attribute type was a stand-in for what should have been the name of each separate lookup table; and "attribute_value" was any value that was being looked up. Applying this to our University Administration example, "attribute_type" would take the value 'FAC' for the rows in the table that deal with faculties; and faculty codes would go in the "attribute_value" column. The other columns of this super-lookup monstrosity were given generic names such as "result1", "result2", and so on. In our example, the full name of each faculty would go in "result1" and the "valid_now" value of 'Y' or 'N' would go in "result2". The other columns, such as "result3", would be NULL. In order to be able to use this table, it was necessary to have two non-key columns in the entity-representing tables where the to-be-looked-up attributes appeared – one for the attribute value and one for "attribute_type". For example, the "teachers" table in our example would need to have an "attribute_type" column containing 'FAC' in every row, and a "faculty_code" column to contain the actual faculty codes.

While the designer of this arrangement probably thought he was being very clever by putting all the lookup information in one place, he created a nightmare for users who wanted to use the super-lookup table to generate headings in a printed report. For example, the SQL command that retrieves the full faculty names would require two join conditions in the WHERE clause – one equating "attribute_type" between the "teachers" table and the super-lookup table, and one to equating "faculty_code" in the "teachers" table with "attribute_value" in the super-lookup table. Also, when using the super-lookup table to generate a pull-down menu, the programmer has to remember to retrieve only the appropriate rows (for example, those with 'FAC' in the "attribute_type" column). Other bad things about this arrangement are:

- The names of columns in the main database tables (for example, "faculty_code") do not match the "attribute_value" column name in the super-lookup table. This violates an important principle of good design. Alternatively, if you try to correct this by using "attribute_value" as the column name in the main database tables, you violate another important principle, namely, that column names should be meaningful.

- The names of the columns in the super-lookup table do not provide any information about what information is contained in them. (They cannot, since the information is different for each type of attribute that is looked up.) This also violates the principle that column names should be meaningful.

- The format chosen for the non-key columns of the super-lookup table (for instance, an alphanumeric string of up to 30 characters) is imposed on all lookup results. Thus, if you had wanted to obtain an integer from the lookup process you would be out of luck. You could find ways of working around this, for instance, giving one of the columns (for instance, "result4") the integer format and requiring that any integer information be placed only in that column. However, this would be very confusing for everyone.

I am sure that you can guess what my advice is about super-lookup tables:

Never use super-lookup tables in your own database designs; but don't be surprised if you come across them.

Normalization

What is interesting, and may be puzzling to you the first time you encounter it, is that experienced database designers, when asked to explain why they have not normalized their database designs, will tell you something along the following lines: "Normalization is all very well in theory, but it increases the number of tables in the database and causes users to have to include more tables in their FROM clauses, leading to lousy performance".

While it is true that normalizing a database leads to more tables being used in many SQL commands, and it is true that this slows down the execution of queries, the difference between a three-table query and a six-table query is not significant today. In the early 1990s, when the query optimizers in most DBMSs could not optimize queries with more than three tables in the FROM clause, there was certainly a need to keep a close eye on the number of tables used in a single query. This may have been a valid reason for creating a non-normalized database design at that time. However, DBMS vendors have greatly improved their query optimizers since then. Today, query optimizers work well with up to ten tables in a FROM clause. Also, the power of computer hardware has increased tremendously since the early 1990s. Companies upgrade the hardware platform on which their databases run at regular intervals. Thus, the reasons for deliberately not normalizing a database design have, except in very special situations, largely vanished.

In spite of all these changes, if you ask an experienced database designer why he or she has not normalized a particular database design, you will often get a reply like the one I just quoted.

There are several possible reasons for such an answer. For instance:

- The database designer read about performance issues with fully-normalized database designs in a textbook written in the 1980s or early-1990s. Since then, he or she has not talked to anyone who has challenged this idea.

- Performance was a genuine concern when the database was first designed a few years ago and so it was not normalized. Given that so many application programs and stored procedures have been written around the original design, it would now be too disruptive and costly to change it.

- The database designer is too lazy to normalize the database design, and hopes that you will go away and stop asking annoying questions.

You may encounter even more puzzling things. For example, you may hear statements like "Every night we run a stored procedure that de-normalizes the database before we generate the nightly reports." What this probably means is that one or more temporary tables are created that represent self-contained records of transaction data, derived from a combination of raw transaction-history tables and several entity-representing tables. By the time that you get to the end of this book you will, I hope, see that so-called de-normalization in this context is not a violation of the normalized state of a database design. Rather, transaction-history tables are tables to which the standard rules of normalization do not apply. If you design these tables properly, you should not need to run "de-normalization" queries in order to prepare them for use in after-the-fact analyses of transaction-history data.

I mention this here not as a preview to the rest of this book but rather to alert you to the fact that you should not take any of these negative references to normalization as an indication that the body of expert opinion in database design has come out against normalization. It has not.

Number of Tables in a Query

In spite of the improvement in query optimizers in recent years, it is still true that the more tables an SQL command contains in its FROM clause, the more load it places on the computer on which the DBMS is running, and therefore the longer it takes to execute. If you ever have to write SQL commands or stored procedures, you should therefore exercise a little restraint when it comes to how many tables appear in a FROM clause. If you start to worry that there are too many, then you can probably find a way to reduce them. For instance, you could split the query into two steps and place the results of the first step in a temporary table: the second step in the query would then operate on the temporary table plus the remaining tables.

Having said that, I should prepare you for the real world by telling you that, if you look at some of the queries that are used today, particularly those incorporated in stored procedures, you will find that any caution that database users might have exhibited in the early 1990s (regarding the number of tables in a query) has now been cast aside. Queries that operate on six tables are common, and queries that operate on as many as ten tables no longer raise eyebrows.

There are two reasons for this trend. The first reason is that database users know that, with better query optimizers and more powerful hardware, queries with more than three tables in the FROM clause are no longer taboo. So, in situations where a stored procedure programmer might once have broken down an operation into several steps (storing intermediate results in temporary tables so as to minimize the number of tables operated on in each step), today he or she will cram all the tables into one terrifying query. The other reason is that companies do things with databases that are increasingly complex each year, some of which are hard to do without queries that operate on many tables.

It is interesting to observe that, for the reasons mentioned earlier, database designers do not seem to be exploiting the better query optimizers and more powerful hardware by moving towards fully-normalized database designs; meanwhile, the leeway given by these improvements is being consumed by stored procedure programmers, who exercise little or no restraint in how many tables their queries use.

Uses and Abuses of Stored Procedures

The first time that you read about stored procedures, and look through a few examples in a DBMS vendor's manual, you will probably form the impression that practical stored procedures should range from about twenty lines of SQL statements to a full page of SQL statements (for a really complex procedure). There are, in fact, many stored procedures in use today which fit on a single sheet of paper. However, since stored procedures were introduced, there has been a steady increase in the size of the largest stored procedures. You should not be shocked if you come across stored procedures as long as ten pages. I am sure there are stored procedures as long as twenty pages in use in some systems (although, luckily, I have not yet needed to read any that are that long).

The trend towards larger stored procedures has been driven by the recognition of the fact that, in some situations, it is easier to manipulate data entirely within the DBMS than to transmit large amounts of data (representing intermediate results) backwards and forwards between the DBMS and the application software – particularly given that most programming languages are not very well suited to manipulation of large data arrays. Manipulating data within the database, using a stored procedure, also minimizes the number of times that data has to be mapped between the formats used in the database (such as "decimal(8,2)") and the data types used in the application programming language (such as "float" or "real").

So, large stored procedures are not necessarily a bad thing. If it takes ten pages of code to take, for instance, six input parameters, look up some data, perform a few calculations, and generate a result consisting of twelve columns of data, then that is what it takes. Things are as complex as they are. However, what is worrying is that fundamental business logic is, little by little, migrating from the application software to stored procedures. In many organizations this is happening without anyone clearly thinking through what this means in terms of how the system as a whole will be maintained. (In a few extreme cases, system architects have *deliberately* approached the job of designing a new system by putting almost all the business logic into stored procedures.) Because this is a fairly recent trend, it will be some time before its full effects are felt. I believe that some (but by no means all) organizations that have allowed fundamental business logic to migrate into stored procedures will start to see that this has increased the costs of maintaining the system as a whole (that is, the application software plus the database and its stored procedures).

I do not have an answer to the problems that the migration of business logic to stored procedures is creating. I simply want to alert you to this trend.

If you are accustomed to fairly high standards in application software, in terms of overall neatness of the code and extensive use of program comments, then you may be shocked when you start looking at typical stored procedures. This is not necessarily true in all organizations; but I have seen it in several companies that aspire to high standards in software development. What you may find is that many stored procedures look awful. Specifically:

- The code contains few comments. In some stored procedures there are no comments at all.

- The practice of indenting lines of SQL, to improve readability, is not followed.

- Gratuitous use is made of the table alias feature, making it harder for someone other than the author to get to grips with how the stored procedure works. In some cases different table aliases are used for the same tables within a single stored procedure.

- Some reserved words are uppercase and some are lowercase: no standard is adopted or followed.

I hope your observations are more encouraging than this. But if they aren't, please speak up. What organizations that use stored procedures should be aiming for, and what I hope you will promote, are the following practices:

- Stored procedures should contain adequate comments. In particular, there should be a clear explanation of what the stored procedure does, what exactly each input parameter means, what the expected result is, and what the limits of applicability of the stored procedure are. There should be copious comments throughout the code, and comments at the start of each major section of code explaining what it does.

- Stored procedures should be structured in a way that makes them easy to understand.

- Table-name aliases should be avoided. (Programmers should learn to use their text editors.)

- SQL statements should be split across multiple lines, using one line for each element and indenting the lines to improve readability (as illustrated in all the examples in this book). Where nested blocks of code are used (each enclosed by the reserved words BEGIN and END), indenting should be used to make it clear at what level within the nest each statement sits.

- Reserved words should be written consistently in either uppercase or lowercase. (It does not matter which. My personal preference is lowercase.)

Recording Things That Happen

Almost all of the examples that you will find in database textbooks, and all the examples that I have used so far, are to do with recording the present state of things, for example:

- Which students are enrolled in which courses.

- Which teachers are teaching which courses.

- Which students are living in which dorm rooms.

- Which library books are on loan to which students.

However, once you start to look at the real world of business and professional databases, you will soon realize that, although a fair amount of "present-time" information is contained in these databases, a larger part of the content is concerned with "things that happen". For example:

- An order, containing ten items, was shipped to a customer yesterday.

- Mr. Smith withdrew two hundred dollars from his account at 10:15am today at a particular cash machine.

- Mr. Jones sold 100 shares of IBM stock yesterday at 2:46 p.m. at a price of $91.50.

- Alice was promoted to division head, effective the first of the month, and her salary was increased by 10%.

In other words, real-world databases are used to record events which, when represented in a database, have at least one time-related characteristic. The representation of time in databases was not a pressing requirement during the first decade of the history of pre-relational databases (1961 to 1970). As a result, at the time that Codd defined the relational model (1970), not much attention was paid to how to represent time in a relational database, or indeed in any type of database. About twelve years later, as relational databases began to be used in the business world, database designers started to recognize the need to use relational databases to record business transactions and events. They developed a number of approaches and solutions (not all of them good ones), which are now found throughout the world of business and professional databases.

As a result, as soon as you start to look at a real-world database you will find that you have left the safe territory of the University Administration database example and entered the very different territory of "tables that record things that happen".

The rest of this book escorts you gently, one step at a time, into this potentially frightening but, I hope, interesting and ultimately not-so-frightening territory.

CHAPTER 7

REPRESENTING TIME IN DATABASE DESIGNS

Datetime

Any relational database used in a business or professional application (particularly one used in accounting, banking, or brokerage operations) will consist of many tables with columns that contain dates or dates-plus-times. When such a database is created, these time-related columns are typically created with a **datetime** format. (A datetime format may also be referred to as a datetime type or datetime datatype.)

The way in which the DBMS actually stores a datetime may be very different from the way it is entered and displayed. Most DBMSs allow the user to enter and display dates in any one of several familiar formats; however, the internally stored datetime used by the DBMS (and hidden from the user) will be the same in all cases. This means that comparisons, and other mathematical operations, performed on two or more datetime values that have been entered by different users are not affected by the input/display format chosen by each user.

SQL provides a wide range of functions that can be used to construct commands involving the values of datetime data elements. These functions can be used in the WHERE part of an SQL command in order to compare the values of datetimes with one another, or with fixed values.

As a simple example, the following query will return information about all students born in 1989 and 1990:

```
SELECT
  students.student_id,
  students.first_name,
  students.last_name,
  students.date_of_birth
FROM students
WHERE
  YEAR(students.date_of_birth) = 1989 OR
  YEAR(students.date_of_birth) = 1990
```

In the above example, the function YEAR() returns an integer that represents just the year of the datetime value placed in the parentheses. With the example contents of the "students" table shown in Chapter 1, this query would give the result:

```
student_id        first_name        last_name         date_of_birth
----------        -----------       ---------         -------------
200600001         Sally             Sparrow           1990-05-28
200600002         John              Liu               1989-12-26
```

Most implementations of SQL provide for the extraction (and comparison with another datetime) of any part, or combination of parts, of a datetime (for example, just the year, just the month, just the day, or just the time). The datetime format can be used to store a date by omitting the time information. In this case the time part of the data element (the hours, minutes, seconds part) will default to midnight (00:00:00).

Other representations of time, besides the datetime format, may appear in some tables. For example, a university term/semester may be represented by an integer (1, 2, or 3, for Term 1, Term 2, and Term 3), or by a letter. Also, the database designer may decide to use an integer to represent a year or month, instead of using a datetime data element.

Typical uses of datetime (and other representations of time) are:

- Recording when an event or transaction occurred.

- Recording the date of a future event or transaction.

- Recording a period (using a start datetime and end datetime) during which a situation will apply (such as the effective period of a magazine subscription or a service contract).

- Recording when a particular piece of information was entered or updated in the database.

Although databases in the real world make extensive use of time, database examples in textbooks tend to shy away from anything involving time (apart from very simple examples, like the one above using students' dates of birth). The reason for avoiding discussion of time is that dealing with time in data models and in database designs is much more complex than dealing with other types of data attributes.

The Problem with Time

Why is time so tricky to handle in databases? There are several reasons; but the most fundamental reason is that the concepts underlying the relational model (and also the earlier hierarchical and network models) were based primarily on the idea of storing data about the world *as it is in the present,* not how it was yesterday or last month or last year.

In the University Administration database example (which I introduced in Chapter 1 and which is used in many textbooks and database courses), the table "enrollment" is used to record which students are enrolled in which courses for the current year/term/semester. In the same example, a table such as "room_use" might be used to record which lecture rooms and classrooms are being used for which courses in the present year/term/semester.

At the start of a new year/term/semester, when updates are made to the "room_use" table, the entries for the previous period are overwritten. This does not matter (unless the database user is, for some reason, interested in the history of room assignments). However, the overwriting of information about which courses a student has taken could cause the database to fail to meet the needs of its users.

If the database is to be used to record the courses that students have completed, as well as to manage the sizes of classes and the assignment of teachers to classes, the overwriting of information about course enrollments causes information about the courses that students were taking in the previous year/term/semester to be lost.   To preserve "historical" information (such as courses that a student has completed), it is necessary for the database designer to make provision in the database design for the storage of information about completed actions or events.

There are various ways of arranging to store information about completed actions or events.   One way is to include, in the data model, a relationship such as the relationship *has completed* between the entity *student* and the entity *course*. This relationship would have time-related non-key attributes, such as "year" and "term" or "semester", as well as other important non-key attributes such as "grade". (As mentioned in Chapter 2, I will use the term "entity" where, strictly speaking, I should say "entity set", because to keep saying "entity set" is tedious. I will use the term "entity set" only where I need to make a clear distinction between a particular instance of an entity and the entity set.)

Note that the relationship *has completed* operates between the same two entities as the relationship *is enrolled in*, namely, *student* and *course*. In effect, the two relationships operate "in parallel" with one another between these two entities. The relationship *has completed* would be represented in the database design by a table called, for example, "grades", with key columns "student_id" and "course_number". (The tables "students", "courses", and "enrollments" remain exactly as they were before.)   The "grades" table, with a few example rows added to it, might look like the following example:

Table name: **grades**				
student_id	course_numbe	grade	year	term
200800101	M101	A	2008	1
200800102	P101	A	2008	1
200800103	M101	B+	2008	1
200800104	M101	D	2008	1
200700198	M101	B+	2007	1
200700198	P101	A	2007	2
200700198	M207	B-	2007	3
200700198	M211	C+	2007	3
200700198	M342	A	2008	1

Although the method of recording historical information illustrated in this example is consistent with all good practices for creating a normalized database design, it can nevertheless give rise to modification anomalies. (Note: here, and in all that follows, I use the generic term "modification anomalies" as shorthand for "anomalies arising from data insertions, deletions, and/or updates". When I am describing a specific type of anomaly, such as a deletion anomaly, I will refer to it as such.)

Suppose that the university decides to stop offering a particular course.   A database user therefore deletes that course from the "courses" table.   If the database design is normalized, this should not give rise to a deletion anomaly *as regards the present state of affairs*: nobody can be taking, or teaching, a course that no longer exists. However, the deletion of the course does, in fact, give rise to a special kind of deletion anomaly as regards the "grades" table: all rows in the "grades" table that contain, in the "course_number" column, the number of the deleted course are now left with nothing to refer to in the "courses" table.

For example, suppose that the course numbered 'M211' was taken off the curriculum in 2008 and deleted from the "courses" table. Consider what will happen if the database user later attempts to print a report of the course history of a particular student (the student with student_id = 200700198, who has completed the now-deleted M211), using the following query:

```
SELECT
  grades.course_number,
  courses.course_title,
  grades.grade,
  courses.credits,
  grades.year,
  grades.term
FROM
  grades,
  courses
WHERE
  grades.course_number = courses.course_number AND
  grades.student_id = '200700198'
```

The result of this query will look something like this:

```
course_number  course_title                  grade  credits  year   term
-------------  ----------------------------  -----  -------  -----  ----
M101           Mathematics                   B+     4.5      2007   1
P101           Philosophy                    A      4.5      2007   2
M207           Introduction to Programming   B-     3        2007   3
M342           Database Design               A      3        2008   1
```

Although the student has taken the deleted course (M211), there is no mention of that course in the resulting report, because the condition that ties together the "grades" table and the "courses" table:

```
grades.course_number = courses.course_number
```

cannot be true for the deleted course.

Masking the Problem using an Outer Join

There is, in fact, a way of constructing the query so that the deleted course will at least be mentioned, even though some of its details will be missing. This involves modifying the first part of the WHERE condition to make it operate as what is called an **outer join**. (This is a special case of a "join" which, as explained in Chapter 1, is a term that dates back to the days of relational-algebra-based DBMSs.)

The above query, modified to use an outer join, would contain the following modified WHERE clause:

    WHERE
        grades.course_number *= courses.course_number AND
        grades.student_id = '200700198'

The asterisk is used here as a "wildcard" symbol, meaning "any value" or "all values", which is consistent with many different programming languages. A test of equality between any value and a wildcard will always be true. (By the way, some DBMSs support alternative ways of writing down an outer join condition, such as using the reserved words LEFT OUTER JOIN.)

The easiest way to picture how an outer join operates is to imagine that writing this modified WHERE clause adds a "wildcard row" to the table named on the right-hand side of the condition (that is, the "courses" table). This imaginary wildcard row would be as shown in the last entry of the table in the example below. The wildcard row has NULL in all the non-key columns. (NULL means that the cell is empty.) Note that the table does not actually contain such a row. This is just the easiest way of picturing how the query using the outer join will behave.

Table name: **courses**

course_number	course_title	credits
M101	Mathematics	4.5
P101	Philosophy	4.5
M207	Introduction to Programming	3.0
P321	Life, the Universe, and Everything	3.0
M342	Database Design	3.0
*	NULL	NULL

When the query attempts to match, for the deleted course, the value of "course_number" (M211) in the "grades" table with the contents of the "course_number" column in the "courses" table, and finds no proper match, it will, as a last resort, select the wildcard row. Thus, it will use the value NULL for "course_title" and "credits" when returning the results of the query. (Note that the above example shows only a few example rows in the "courses" table. In practice there would obviously be many more courses in this table.)

I repeat: there is no actual wildcard row placed in the "courses" table. This is just an easy way to explain how the outer join operates. Another way of explaining it is to say that the outer join condition tells the DBMS: "If there is a match for 'course_number' between the 'grades' table and the 'courses' table then display the information from the 'courses' table. However, if there is no match, display the information contained in the selected row in the 'grades' table, and display the value NULL for the non-existent items you were hoping to extract from the 'courses' table".

The careful construction of certain queries, using outer joins, can allow us to use a table like "grades" to record historical information, without suffering the worst effects of this type of deletion anomaly (that is, avoiding the perceived disappearance of certain pieces of historical information when a query is performed). However, it still does not solve the problem that the information for "course_title" and "credits" can no longer be found for the deleted "course".

The student will hardly be impressed by the efficiency of the University Administration office when he receives a grade report looking something like this:

```
              Report for student: 200700198

Course    Course Title                  Grade  Credits  Year   Term
M101      Mathematics                   B+     4.5      2007   1
P101      Philosophy                    A      4.5      2007   2
M207      Introduction to Programming   B-     3        2007   3
M211      NULL                          C+     NULL     2007   3
M342      Database Design               A      3        2008   1
```

The query, using the outer join, has resulted in one row of the report showing a NULL in the "course_title" column and in the "credits" column. If the query were to contain a summation of the credits that the student has accumulated, the result would, depending on how the DBMS treats NULLs in summations, be either an error condition or a total that excludes the credits for M211 (that is, a total of 15 credits, instead of 18).

The inability to correctly determine how many credits the student has accumulated is clearly a very serious problem. We will now look at an approach to the design of historical tables, like the "grades" table, that addresses the problem of time-related deletion anomalies – in a simple and reliable manner.

A Pragmatic Approach to Preserving Historical Information

A simple and effective way of recording the historical information about the courses that students have completed, without problems of this sort, is to create an expanded "grades" table – that is, a "grades" table with a greater number of columns and that forms a self-contained record of the historical information.

For instance, an expanded "grades" table containing a few example rows might look like the following example. Here, the extra columns, "course_title" and "credits", have been added to the original table. (The key columns are still "student_id" and "course_number", taken together.)

Table name: **grades**						
student_id	**course_number**	**grade**	**year**	**term**	**course_title**	**credits**
200800101	M101	A	2008	1	Mathematics	4.5
200800102	P101	A	2008	1	Philosophy	4.5
200800103	M101	B+	2008	1	Mathematics	4.5
200800104	M101	D	2008	1	Mathematics	4.5
200700198	M101	B+	2007	1	Mathematics	4.5
200700198	P101	A	2007	2	Philosophy	4.5
200700198	M207	B-	2007	3	Introduction to Programming	3
200700198	M211	C+	2007	3	Programming in Pascal	3
200700198	M342	A	2008	1	Database Design	3

When examined from the point of view of traditional database normalization, this table clearly breaks the rules. The non-key attributes "course_title" and "credits" are not functionally dependent on "the key, the whole key, and nothing but the key". They depend only on the value of "course_number". Also, they are already stored in a separate "courses" table (where they really belong in a normalized database design). However, for a table that holds historical data, breaking the normalization rules does not matter. In fact, it eliminates the possibility of the kind of deletion anomaly that we were worried about.

With this version of the "grades" table, the query to create a report of a particular student's course history can now be constructed as follows, using data only from the "grades" table:

```
SELECT
    grades.course_number,
    grades.course_title,
    grades.grade,
    grades.credits,
    grades.year,
    grades.term
FROM
    grades
WHERE
    grades.student_id = '200700198'
```

This will return a result as follows, with no missing data:

```
course_number  course_title                    grade  credits  year  term
-------------   ------------                    -----  -------  ----  ----
M101           Mathematics                      B+     4.5      2007  1
P101           Philosophy                       A      4.5      2007  2
M207           Introduction to Programming      B-     3        2007  3
M211           Programming in Pascal            C+     3        2007  3
M342           Database Design                  A      3        2008  1
```

A Second Problem with Time

A second kind of modification anomaly can occur when trying to record historical information using a traditional normalized database design, namely, an update anomaly. An **update anomaly** arises from the effects of updates to, rather than deletions of, the data that records the present state of affairs. As an example, consider a table called "order_details" in a company's Order and Invoice Management database. The "order_details" table records the details of customers' orders – details that will be used in preparing the packages of goods to be shipped, and in preparing invoices to be sent to customers. (This example is, I hope, a welcome change from the University Administration database example.) The "order_details" table, with a few example rows, might look something like this:

Table name: **order_details**			
order_number	line_number	quantity	product_code
2008-000199	1	12	A71298
2008-000199	2	1	G42938
2008-000199	3	1000	N91827R
2008-000200	1	36	A71298
2008-000200	2	6	B63524
2008-000201	1	100	N91828R
2008-000201	2	50	G42938
2008-000201	3	10	C23638
2008-000201	4	5	D12345

This table represents the relationship _contains_ between the entity _order_ and the entity _product_. The key for this table consists of the columns "order_number" and "product_code", taken together. The value of "line_number" represents the position in which the item should appear on documents (packing lists, invoices, and so on), and is not an absolutely essential attribute. Another approach to the organization of products in each order would be to adopt a convention that items are always listed in alphanumerical order of their product codes.

This "order_details" table is used in the database in combination with at least four other tables whenever orders are entered into the database; and also when information is retrieved from the database to create packing lists, mailing labels, invoices, and so on. The use of five separate tables is in keeping with standard normalization practices. The other four tables are:

- An "orders" table, whose columns represent various attributes of the order _as a whole:_ "status", "purchase_order_number", "date_of_order", "shipping_date", and so on. The key for this table is "order_number".

- A "products" table, which holds the details of each product that the company offers for sale, such as "product_description" and "price". The key for this table is "product_code".

- A "customers" table, which holds basic details of customers, such as company name, together with other details such as credit status, line-of-

93

business, and so on. Addresses may be included in this table or, for reasons of normalization, in yet another table. (In this example, for simplicity, I will put the address in the "customers" table.) The key for the "customers" table is "customer_id".

- An "orders_placed" table, which has three columns: "order_number", "customer_id", and "sales_channel_code" (which records how the order was received, for example, by telephone, mail, or email). The key for this table consists of "order_number" and "customer_id", taken together. This table represents the relationship *has placed* between *customers* and *orders*.

Rather than clutter up this example by including, in the various tables, example rows related to many orders, products, and customers, I will show only the rows that are directly involved in a single example order – order number 2008-000201:

Table name: **customers**

customer_ id	customer_name	line_of_ business	credit_ status	address_ line1	address_ line2	address_ line3
37666	Initech Inc.	TECH	OK	99 Sloe Lane	San Jose	CA 95134

Table name: **orders_placed**

customer_ id	order_number	sales_channel_ code
37666	2008-000201	PHONE

Table name: **orders**

order_ number	status	purchase_ order_ number	date_of_ order	shipping_ date	invoice_ date	payment_ due_date	branch_ code
2008-000201	C	S-2008-547	2008-02-27	2008-02-28	2008-03-14	2008-04-14	SFO

Table name: **order_details**

order_ number	line_number	quantity	product_code
2008-000201	1	100	N91828R
2008-000201	2	50	G42938
2008-000201	3	10	C23638
2008-000201	4	5	D12345

Table name: **products**

product_code	product_description	price
N91828R	Pocket protector	1.00
G42938	Four-color pen set	3.50
C23638	CD-RW, ten-pack	8.95
D12345	Stapling machine, red	10.50

Without going in to the details of the SQL command that would be used, we can see that an appropriate SQL command, directed at these five tables, would generate an invoice something like the following. (For simplicity I have assumed that the order number is also used as the invoice number. In practice these numbers might be different.)

```
Invoice to:
Initech Inc.
99 Sloe Lane
San Jose                              Invoice number: 2008-000201
CA 95134                              Your P.O. No.:  S-2008-547

       Product Code    Product Description   Quantity   Unit Price   Extended Price
1      N91828R         Pocket protector        100         1.00          100.00
2      G42938          Four-color pen set       50         3.50          175.00
3      C23638          CD-RW, ten-pack          10         8.95           89.50
4      D12345          Stapling machine, red     5        10.50           52.50

                                               Total:                    417.00
```

In this example we are going to focus on the "order_details" table and how it interacts with the "products" table. Suppose that, a few months after the goods were shipped, and the invoice printed and mailed, the customer has a question about the invoice. Suppose, also, that the price of product D12345 (the red stapling machine) has been increased from $10.50 to $11.50. The row in the "products" table for the stapling machine now reads:

Table name: **products**		
product_code	**product_description**	**price**
D12345	Stapling machine, red	11.50

If the same query that was used to generate the original invoice is now used to re-create the invoice, the re-created invoice will no longer match the original one that was mailed to the customer. It will now show the 5 stapling machines costing a total of $57.50, not $52.50, and the invoice total will be $422.00, not $417.00, as follows:

```
Invoice to:
Initech Inc.
99 Sloe Lane
San Jose                              Invoice number: 2008-000201
CA 95134                              Your P.O. No.:  S-2008-547

       Product Code    Product Description   Quantity   Unit Price   Extended Price
1      N91828R         Pocket protector        100         1.00          100.00
2      G42938          Four-color pen set       50         3.50          175.00
3      C23638          CD-RW, ten-pack          10         8.95           89.50
4      D12345          Stapling machine, red     5        11.50           57.50

                                               Total:                    422.00
```

This problem is caused by the fact that the "order_details" table describes a situation in the past, while the "products" table, from which the price is taken, describes the situation in the present.

Solving the Second Problem

This problem can be solved by breaking the rules of normalization and expanding the "order_details" table, in the same way that we earlier expanded the "grades" table. In this case we can solve the problem by adding the column "price" to the "order_details" table. In order to make the "order_details" table completely independent of the "products" table it is also a good idea to add the column "product_description" as well, which is what I have done here:

Table name: **order_details**

order_number	line_number	quantity	product_code	product_description	price
2008-000199	1	12	A71298	Dry erase marker, black	2.35
2008-000199	2	1	G42938	Four-color pen set	3.50
2008-000199	3	1000	N91827R	Pocket protector	1.00
2008-000200	1	36	A71298	Dry erase marker, black	2.35
2008-000200	2	6	B63524	Highlighter, yellow	2.20
2008-000201	1	100	N91828R	Pocket protector	1.00
2008-000201	2	50	G42938	Four-color pen set	3.50
2008-000201	3	10	C23638	CD-RW, ten-pack	8.95
2008-000201	4	1	D12345	Stapling machine, red	10.50

This table now represents a self-contained record of the details of orders, with the "product_description" and "price" data values "frozen" at the values that applied at the time that customers placed their orders.

An invoice-generation query, similar to the one used before, but taking the product descriptions and prices from the expanded "order_details" table (instead of from the "products" table) will produce an invoice exactly like the original invoice. Thus, the modification anomaly with respect to the price of the red stapling machine has been eliminated.

The Pragmatic Approach Summarized

This approach can be generalized as follows:

> *To create, in a relational database, a record of events, transactions, or past situations, without the risk of modification anomalies arising in the future, it is necessary to copy the current values of potentially-changeable data elements from the normalized present-time tables into one or several "historical" tables, which do not follow the rules of normalization.*

Not all potentially-changeable attributes need be treated in this way. Some common sense is called for. For example, the address of a customer might change; and it could be argued that the address, as it appeared on the original invoice, ought to be preserved in a historical table. But in practice it might make more sense to keep the address information within the present-time tables. In this way, if a customer, who has recently moved, says that he or she has lost the original invoice, and requests a duplicate, the new copy will be mailed to the correct (new) address.

There are several important points to note about the contents of an expanded historical table (such as the expanded "order_details" table, which has the additional columns such as "price" and "product_description"):

- The table is, as far as users are concerned, a "read-only" table. Once a row has been entered into the table, that row may not be updated by a user. It represents a record of the past. It is therefore not updateable data.

- Similarly, no row can be deleted from such a table because this would cause valuable historical data to be lost. (Obviously there may come a point when the information is so old that it need no longer be retained. But at this point it would be the Database Administrator, not the ordinary user, who would purge the old rows from the table.)

- The addition of rows to historical tables should be an automatic process, controlled by a "trigger" process within the DBMS, or by a program that is attached to the database. This will take care of adding rows to historical tables when the appropriate triggering events occur.

- The additional non-key columns (like "product_description" and "price"), which hold point-in-time copies of the contents of other tables, are logically different from their present-time equivalents (the columns "product_description" and "price" in the "products" table). Users should be careful not to accidentally use the historical-table versions when they are composing queries about the present.

Column Naming in Extended Historical Tables

Regarding this last point, it is a good idea to give the additional columns in historical tables a slightly different name from their equivalents in the present-time tables. It is also a good idea to adopt a naming convention for this. For example, in the "order_details" table you could use column names like "product_description_aiwt" and "price_aiwt". The suffix "aiwt" is an abbreviation for "as it was then".

If you don't like "aiwt" then use a different suffix, but try to keep it short. Avoid words or abbreviations that may occur in normal column names; and do not use a suffix like "old", which creates the impression that the information in the table is no longer valid and that better information exists elsewhere in the database. In fact, the historical data *is* valid: it is valid for the time to which it relates. Whatever suffix you decide to use, use it consistently across all historical tables. Note that a suffix is much better than a prefix: use of a suffix ensures that the present-time versions of the column names and the historical versions of the column names will be adjacent in a catalog of column names (or in a data dictionary).

Adopting this convention, the final versions of the extended historical tables in the two examples will be created as follows.

For the University Administration Database example, the "grades" table will look like this:

97

Table name: **grades**						
student_id	course_numbe	grade	year	term	course_title_aiwt	credits_aiwt

For the Order and Invoice Management Database example, the "order_details" table will look like this:

Table name: **order_details**					
order_number	line_number	quantity	product_code	product_description_aiwt	price_aiwt

Pure Historical Tables and Dual-Use Tables

In the above example, the "order_details" table is not a purely historical table. Both the "order_details" table and the "orders" table are treated as present-time tables when the database is being used to support the day-to-day business of recording, preparing, and dispatching customers' orders, and in generating invoices and packing lists for those orders. For these purposes they are used in conjunction with present-time tables such as "products", "orders_placed", and "customers". It is only after the order has been processed that we start to view them as historical tables. We can describe a table like this as a **dual-use historical table**. Such a table is used day to day as a present-time table, but it is also used as an historical table when rows relating to completed orders or transactions are used in queries later on.

We could, if we wanted to, design the database with separate present-time and historical versions of tables like these. If we did this then work in progress – like orders that are being processed – would be represented by rows in the "orders" and "order_details" tables; but completed orders would be represented by rows in the historical tables. (We might call the historical tables something like "completed_orders" and "completed_order_details".) If we used this approach then it would be necessary, when an order is completed, to arrange for copies of rows from the present-time tables to be inserted into the historical tables; and for the corresponding rows to be deleted from the present-time tables. This could be done by an automatically-triggered SQL command associated with the application through which the users interact with the database. Alternatively, it could be done by means of triggers within the database itself. The columns used to preserve as-it-was-then values of data elements (like "price_aiwt") would then appear only in the historical tables, and not the present-time tables. The values inserted into these columns would be determined by the SQL command that copies the rows from the present-time tables to the historical tables.

There may be situations where separate present-time and historical versions of tables represent a better approach than dual-use tables. However, in many database designs this approach has no benefits, while making life more complicated for users. In some cases dual-use tables have significant advantages over separate tables. This is the case in the example above. By copying information like "price" from the present-time "products" table into the "price_aiwt" column in "order_details" at the time an order is placed, and thus treating "order_details" as, in some respects, historical right away, we prevent modification anomalies arising during the processing of an order. For example, if the price of a product is changed between the time a customer places an order and the time the packing list or invoice is generated, the customer needs to be charged the price at which the product was offered for sale when the order was placed. The copying of the price from the "products" table to the "price_aiwt" column in "order_details" makes sure of this by preserving the information about the price as it was at the time of the order – information that would otherwise be lost as soon as the row in "products" is updated.

The first example of a historical table that we looked at in this chapter – the "grades" table – represents a purely historical table. The rows inserted into a purely historical table relate to actions which are already completed at the time that the rows are inserted. We shall look at other examples of such tables in the next chapter.

Summary

The standard rules of normalization do not prevent time-related modification anomalies occurring with respect to tables that hold historical information. In order to prevent time-related modification anomalies, it is necessary to disregard the standard normalization rules. We must add, to tables that hold information about the past, one or more columns to hold as-it-was-then copies of potentially-changeable present-time data elements.

These additional columns are logically different from their present-time equivalents and should therefore be given a different and distinctive name, such as "price_aiwt", so that users will not confuse them with the columns in present-time tables. The rows of data in such tables are, as far as users are concerned, "read-only" information: they represent a record of the now-unchangeable past.

CHAPTER 8

OTHER TYPES OF HISTORICAL TABLE

Introduction

The previous chapter dealt with:

- The inclusion, in a database design, of historical tables (like the "grades" table), in order to record completed actions or events.

- The inclusion, in historical tables, of columns that would not be allowed under standard normalization rules (such as the "credits" column in the "grades" table, or the "price" column in the "order_details" table), in order to preserve information about the values of these attributes *as they were at the time of the completed action or event,* and thus prevent modification anomalies occurring in the future.

In this chapter we will look at some more examples of historical tables and the various issues that have to be addressed in the handling of time in these tables.

Tracking Changes in Present-Time Data

One use of historical tables, which differs from the examples given so far, is to record the changes that have been made, over time, to non-key attributes in present-time tables. This might be required in order to produce reports of trends in a particular attribute over time, or to retain historical information in compliance with laws or industry regulations. For example, if we wanted to keep track of the prices at which products have been offered for sale in the past, we would include, in the database design, a table like the following:

Table name: **prices_history**

product_code	price	valid_from	valid_to
A71298	2.35	2005-07-01	NULL
G42938	3.50	2005-07-01	NULL
N91827R	1.00	2005-07-01	NULL
B63524	2.20	2005-07-01	NULL
C23638	7.95	2005-07-01	2007-08-31
C23638	8.95	2007-09-01	NULL
D12345	10.50	2005-07-01	2008-03-31
D12345	11.50	2008-04-01	2008-05-31
D12345	10.50	2008-06-01	NULL

In this table the date at which a particular price was put into effect is shown in the "valid_from" column, which has datetime format. (In this example July 1, 2005 was the date on which all the original prices were entered into the database was set up.) Where there is no date in the "valid_to" column this means that the price is still in effect. When a price is changed, the last day of validity of the old price is entered in the "valid_to" column and a new row is added to the table. This new row shows the new price, together with the date it came into effect in the "valid_from" column. So, for example, product D12345, originally priced at $10.50, was increased in price to $11.50 on April 1, 2008; but on June 1, 2008 the price was changed back to its original level of $10.50.

An important question about this table is: what is the key? Clearly it cannot be "product_code" and "price", taken together, because these two attributes may not uniquely identify a row – as in the case of D12345 at $10.50, which appears in two rows. In order to form a reliable key it is necessary to use the columns "product_code" and "valid_from", taken together.

Although this table was created in order to record historical price information for its own sake, it is interesting to consider how this table might be pressed into service as an alternative way of tackling the time-related problem of the original (non-expanded) "order_details" table that we looked at in Chapter 7. Note that this is not the primary purpose of this table. At this point we are doing this just as an exercise – although, as I will describe in Chapter 13, this approach has been proposed as the basis of a general solution to the problem of time-related modification anomalies.

Referring to the earlier example of re-creating an invoice some time after the date of the order, and, for simplicity, ignoring any time problems arising from changes in "product_description", we can see that it would be possible to match values of "product_code" in the "order_details" table with values of "product_code" in the "prices_history" table, instead of in the "products" table. By taking price information from "prices_history", instead of from "products", the invoice-generation query would supply the correct price information for an invoice whenever the query is performed – now and at any point in the future.

However, the fact that such a query is possible does not make it elegant or easy to construct. To find the correct price for each item, the query would have to compare the date of the order, taken from the "orders" table, with the "valid_from" and "valid_to" dates in the "prices_history" table. The correct row in "prices_history" is the one for which (a) the "valid_from" date precedes the date of the order and (b) the "valid_to" date (if any) comes after the date of the order. Composing such a query is not easy. By comparison, the approach that we looked at in the last chapter – expanding the "order_details" table by adding extra columns to record the as-it-was-then price and product description – is a lot simpler.

In summary, a table like "prices_history" is an example of a historical table that is used to keep a record of the history of the changeable non-key attributes of entities whose present-time values are held in a present-time table. A table like "prices_history" is useful for analyzing trends over time, or for storing data which must be retained for legal or regulatory reasons. Such tables could also, *in theory*, be used as a way to deal with the time-related problems of other historical tables (like "order_details"); but this necessitates hard-to-construct queries.

Recording Transactions

One of the most common uses of historical tables is to record data about transactions or events. We have already looked at an example of this with the "grades" table, where the "transaction" that is recorded is the completion of a course by a student. In that example, a row was added to the "grades" table at the end of the year/term/semester. This would typically be done automatically by the application software that users the database, not directly by the database user. The user would be prompted for data by an "Enter Course Results" program. Once the user has confirmed that a particular student has completed a particular course, and the user has entered the grade that the student achieved, the application software would add the new row to the "grades" table. At the same time, it would delete, from the "enrollments" table, the row that recorded the fact that the student was taking the course.

Another slightly different approach to recording transactions is to add a row to a historical table (like "grades") at the start of the transaction (for example, at the time the student first enrolls in the course), but leave one or more of the data elements (such as "grade") with a value of NULL. Then, at the end of the transaction, the row would be updated to complete the record of the transaction. The row then becomes final (for example, "grade" is changed from NULL to the actual grade achieved). In this approach, the entire act of taking the course is regarded as a transaction, which has a start and an end separated by a period of time (many weeks in this example). This approach would be needlessly complicated for the "grades" table. It is far simpler to treat course-completion as an instantaneous transaction. But in some uses of historical tables it is important to track the progress of a transaction over a period of time, adding data to the row as various intermediate points in the transaction are reached. This can be done by designating as "NULL-allowed" those columns whose contents will not be available at the start of the transaction.

A variant of this approach is to use two tables instead of one: a transactions-in-progress table, which has the NULL-allowed columns; and a transactions-completed table, in which all columns are NOT NULL. Once a transaction is completed, a row is written into the transactions-completed version of the table to record the completed transaction and the corresponding row is deleted from the transactions-in-progress version of the table. This approach has the advantage of guarding against an incomplete row being left as the final record of the transaction. It also clearly separates the phase during which the transaction details are updateable and the point at which they become "read-only" (that is, when the row becomes a true historical record that should never be altered).

Before looking at other examples of recording transactions, we will first try to develop a good definition of a transaction.

Defining Transactional Data

Some database designers talk about "transactional data" as being fundamentally different from data about real-world objects (such as students, employees, customers, and products), which they describe as "entity data". However, while drawing a distinction between transactional and non-transactional data may be useful, defining "entity data" as the antithesis of transactional data is confusing and wrong. It seems to imply that entities must be tangible objects and that transactions therefore cannot be entities, which is not the case. Chen's definition of an entity clearly includes intangible things. An airplane flight, a customer's order, a patent, a television program, a telephone call, and a doctor's appointment can all be regarded as entities, because they exist and can be distinguished from other similar things. They continue to be entities after they are completed, provided that they are remembered or recorded. It should also be noted that dead entities, which have ceased to have a physical existence, are also still considered to be entities. Someone designing a database for an art gallery would find life difficult if he or she were told that Vincent van Gogh could not be considered to be an entity because he is no longer in tangible form.

So, rather than talk about "transactional data" and "entity data", it is better, and more useful, to talk about (a) **transactional entities** (whose attributes represent **transactional data**) and (b) **non-transactional entities** (whose attributes represent **non-transactional data**).

However, this does not complete the description of transactions. While it is true that transactions can be described as entities, other transactions are better described as relationships. The "grades" table records transactions, namely, "students completing courses"; and it does so in terms of the relationship *student has completed course*. We can therefore describe the relationship *has completed* as a **transactional relationship**. By contrast, the relationship *is enrolled in*, which also operates between *student* and *course*, is a present-state **non-transactional relationship**.

Some transactions may be described as either an entity or a relationship, depending on which we find more convenient. There is no hard-and-fast rule about when a transaction should be represented as an entity and when it should be represented as a relationship. It just depends on what fits best into the Entity-Relationship model. For instance, it would be difficult to represent an order, in the Order and Invoice Management Database example, as a relationship because the entity *order* needs to take participate in two relationships: *customer has placed order* and *order contains product*. (These two relationships were represented, respectively, by the tables "orders_placed" and "order_details".) If we had tried to represent an order as a relationship then things would have become very complicated. However, in a different situation it might be both easier and better to represent an order as a relationship, for instance, where customers are making one-at-a-time purchases of individually identifiable items. In *customer has ordered airplane*, the order is represented by the relationship *has ordered* and this is a transactional relationship.

In summary, when we look carefully at the subject of transactions, we find that "transactional data", is very much part of the Entity-Relationship model. What constitutes transactional data is the values of the attributes of transactional entities and transactional relationships.

What, then, distinguishes transactional entities and relationships from non-transactional entities and relationships? One important characteristic of transactional entities and relationships is that their attributes cannot change after they are completed, although their attributes can change between the time they are initiated and the time they are completed. The rows in the database that represent a *completed* transaction must therefore be regarded as *read-only data*.

However, this is not a defining characteristic of a transactional entity or relationship. Data about non-transactional entities that have ceased to interact with the real world (such as dead artists) should also be treated as read-only, since this data represents the now-unchangeable past. In fact, the more you think about this topic, the more it becomes apparent that there is no clear-cut distinction between transactional and non-transactional entities, or between transactional relationships and non-transactional relationships: it really depends on the how the information in the database is going to be used. For example, a homeowner may personally view his or her thirty-year mortgage as a non-transactional entity; but the homeowner's bank may view it as a transaction that takes thirty years to complete. (Such very long transactions are more common that you might expect. Other examples of transactions that may have long execution times are bonds and trials.)

In short, transactionlikeness is very much in the eye of the beholder.

Although a clear-cut definition of a "transaction" is hard to arrive at, the following guidelines are useful in trying to distinguish between transactional entities and relationships (which have a clear effective date or an end date) and non-transactional entities and relationships (that have a less-clear end date of some sort):

- Transactional entities and relationships have an end datetime that is either (a) already in the past, or (b) scheduled for, or very likely to occur at, a specific datetime in the future. By contrast, those non-transactional entities and relationships that have some sort of end date tend to have an end date that is unpredictable (such as a presently-living person's date of death) or revisable.

- Transactional entities and relationships, once they are completed and have thus acquired an end datetime, are of continuing operational importance in the activity for which the database is to be used. By contrast, non-transactional entities and relationships that have acquired an end datetime (through defection, retirement, closure, divorce, or death) tend to be of interest only for occasional reference purposes, if at all. For example, when you take money from a cash machine, your bank is going to be using the record of that *transaction* perhaps dozens of times after it is "completed", at least up until the preparation of your next monthly bank statement. But if you close your account, the *non-transactional* record that is retained (for legal and other reasons) of you as a former customer may never be referred to again.

By the way, even though many non-transactional entities have some sort of real-world "start" datetime (just as many transactional entities do), in practical database designs these "start" datetimes may not be included as columns in the tables that represent those entities: this information may be of no importance to the enterprise for which the database was created. For example, the date on which a course was first included in the curriculum was not included as a column in the "courses" table. Examples of "start" datetimes that *are* often included in entity-representing tables are date of birth, date of registration, date of opening, and date of construction.

Datetimes in Transactions

We will now look in more detail at the datetime attributes of transactional entities and transactional relationships.

A transaction will always have at least one datetime attribute, for example, one that defines when it took place. Most real-world transactions are not instantaneous and therefore have both a measurable start datetime and a measurable end datetime. However, many transactions are completed in such a short time that they can be treated as instantaneous. In this case the start and end datetimes may be recorded as a single datetime. In the table that represents the transactional entity or relationship there is then a single datetime column. However, you should always remember to think of these tables as containing distinct start and end datetimes that happen to have the same value, and that are therefore recorded in the same column. This concept becomes important when you construct queries that compare the datetimes of two transactions, one of which has explicit start and end datetimes and the other of which has a single, combined datetime.

Other transactions may take sufficiently long to complete that it is useful to explicitly record the start datetime and end datetime. As mentioned earlier, some transactions may have important intermediate stages in their execution that need to be recorded. In these cases there may be a third, or even a fourth, datetime column in the table that represents the transaction.

Transactions That Just Happen

In the earlier examples of transactional entities and transactional relationships, the database designs included tables that represented present-time entities and present-time relationships that are recognized prior to the point at which we recognize that a transaction has taken place or has been completed. For example, in the case of students taking courses, there was a present-time relationship *student is enrolled in course*, preceding the recognition of the transactional relationship *student has completed course*. When we think about how we might draw this on an E-R diagram, the relationship *has completed* can be seen to operate "in parallel" with the relationship *is enrolled in*. Similarly, the entity *order* is involved in the present-time relationship *customer has placed order,* from the time that the order is placed to the time that the order has been completed (that is, the order has been assembled, shipped, received, and invoiced). At that point in time we start to regard the order as a "completed transaction". Before that point, it is a transaction in progress.

In contrast to these two examples involving courses and orders completed over time, it is possible to have real-world transactions (or events) that "just happen". That is to say, they are immediately recognized as transactions when they occur, without having passed through a phase of being involved in, or represented as, a present-time relationship. Such nearly-instantaneous transactions are usually better described as entities than relationships. This is because, if we try to view them as relationships, we find that we have to struggle to find suitable entities for them to operate between. For example, consider the transaction "telephone call to the Customer Service desk". If we try to describe this transaction as the relationship *customer _telephones_ customer-service-desk*, we find that the entity set *customer-service-desk* is not a very good entity set to use for this. In fact, there is only one Customer Service desk, so the entity set has only a single member. If we try, instead, to describe the transaction as the relationship *customer _telephones_ customer-service-agent*, we at least have an entity, at the other end of the relationship, of which there is more than one. But this entity is still not a good choice. The customer did not select the particular agent to talk to. Instead, the first available agent answered the call. The identity of the agent is better thought of as a non-key attribute of the call, not the target of the call. In summary, trying to describe, as a relationship, a transaction like this that "just happens" does not seem to work very well; and this is often the case with such transactions. By contrast, when we view such a transaction as an entity, things seem to make more sense. For example, we can say *customer _made a_ customer-service-call*, and represent the entity *customer-service-call* by the table "customer_service_calls". This table can have, as non-key attributes, all the things that we might be interested in recording about the call, such as the datetime at which it occurred, why the customer was calling, which agent handled the call, and so on.

Before we look at an example of such a table, it is useful to first think about how we would represent the relationship _made a_ in the database design. If we were designing a present-time part of the database then we would follow the standard normalization rules and represent the _made a_ relationship by a two-column table. This table would have "customer_id" as one column and the other column would contain the key attribute of the "customer_service_calls" table (for example, "csvc_call_id"). However, as we saw in Chapter 7, once we are dealing with historical tables we no longer benefit from following the standard normalization rules.

Therefore, what we can do instead is to is dispense with the _made a_ relationship table and use "customer_id" as a non-key column of "customer_service_calls". This gives us a table like the following, into which I have inserted a few example rows:

Table name: **customer_service_calls**				
csvc_call_id	**customer_id**	**call_starttime**	**agent_id**	**problem_description**
23821	100-091	2008-04-04 09:17:30	42101	The overnight shipment from yesterday did not arrive this morning.
23822	100-091	2008-04-04 09:45:37	39102	Sorry, we found the package. Ignore earlier call.
23823	200-007	2008-04-04 10:05:15	42101	Are the red stapling machines back in stock yet? – No.
23824	100-091	2008-04-04 10:22:01	42101	On opening the package it was found that the pocket protectors had been omitted.
23825	300-223	2008-04-04 10:29:24	42101	There was an error in this month's invoice. (Call transferred to Billing Dept.)

For this table the key is "csvc_call_id", a unique number generated programmatically for each new call that is recorded. The "customer_id" information might, in some systems, be supplied by the Customer Service Agent who enters it on his or her keyboard after answering the call. More commonly, the "customer_id" is supplied by a program that retrieves the Customer ID from the "customers" table, based on all or part of the customer's name (typed by the agent). The date and time of the call is entered into the "call_starttime" column programmatically. The "agent_id" column records which Customer Service Agent took the call. This might be the Agent's Employee Number. It would typically be entered programmatically, based on which agent had signed on to the workstation on which the call details are being entered. The contents of "problem_description" are entered by the agent. These contents are in the form of a single, long character string. (For example, the column may be of format "varchar(300)", meaning that it can contain up to 300 alphanumeric characters.)

In some ways this table is similar to the earlier example of the "orders" table. However, unlike the "orders" table, "customer_service_calls" is less likely to exhibit any serious time-related modification anomalies, either directly or indirectly, for the following reasons:

- Two of the non-key columns ("call_starttime" and "problem_description") represent fixed, self-contained data about each call. This data is not affected by changes elsewhere in the database.

- The columns "customer_id" and "agent_id" are *potential* sources of deletion anomalies. It could be argued that we should place a copy of essential information about the customer and the agent in as-it-was-then columns in the "customer_service_calls" table. This would prevent information such as the customer's name and the agent's name becoming unavailable when customers have been deleted from the "customers" table; or when employees, who work as customer service agents, have been deleted from an "employees" table. However, this information may not be regarded as "essential" information in the context of customer-service calls. For the purposes of analyzing calls to the customer service helpdesk, it is probably not necessary to know the names of customers who are no longer customers and the names of agents who are no longer employees.

So, I am going to leave the design of this table as it stands.

Characteristics of Transactions that Just Happen

The kind of transaction-history table illustrated by "customer_service_calls" is common throughout the business world (but rare in database textbooks). Such tables have the following common features:

- Like the other examples of transaction-history tables that we looked at earlier, this type of transaction-history table always includes at least one column that holds a date or datetime. Where the information in the table is fixed at the time the row is added to the table (as in the above example, where the row is written into the table at the end of the call) there may be a single datetime value, acting as a single "timestamp". In other cases there may be separate "start" and "end" timestamps. (In a few special cases there may be additional, intermediate timestamps.) Separate start and end timestamps may be used where the duration of the transaction needs to be measured. In the "customer_calls" table I could have included a "call_endtime" column if I had wanted to be able to perform queries about how long it takes agents to handle calls. Alternatively, the end time could have been represented implicitly by having a "call_duration" column that records the difference between the end time and start time.

- This type of transaction-history table typically has a key (like "csvc_call_id") that is defined solely for the purpose of recording the transaction, and for which values are generated programmatically at the time of recording the transaction. This type of key is used, instead of a combination of other already-existing or available data elements (such as "customer_id" and "call_starttime"), because (a) a combination of other data elements may sometimes fail to create a unique key, and (b) use of a key like "csvc_call_id" guards against the data in the transaction table becoming "marooned" in the database when a row is deleted from another table (such as "accounts"). It is generally a worse thing to lose the ability to know that a transaction has occurred than to lose part of the information about the transaction, particularly where the transaction involves money. For example, it is worse for a bank not to know that it has received a million dollars than to know that it has received the million dollars but be unable to tell which account it belongs to. In the latter case someone can at least be alerted to the need for a manual investigation of whose million dollars it is. Records of transactions are the most fundamental business records – hence the need for a completely reliable, programmatically-generated key that does not depend on anything else in the database.

- This type of transaction-history table typically represents a transactional entity (in this example, *customer-service-call*) that is closely associated with one principal entity (such as *customer* or *account*). It may also be associated with other, less-important entities. In the above example, besides being associated with *customer*, the *customer-service-call* is also associated with *customer-service-agent*. Another example of such a secondary association, taken from a retail banking database design, is the association of the transactional entity *cash-machine-debit* (whose main association is with the entity *account*) with the secondary entity *cash-machine*. This association records which particular cash machine was used to withdraw cash from the bank account.

- The two different associations, between a transactional entity and (a) its principal associated entity (such as *customer* or *account*) and (b) a secondary associated entity (such as *customer-service-agent* or *cash-machine*), can both be represented by including, in the transaction-history table, non-key columns that represent the key attributes of these principal and secondary associated entities. For example, the principal associated entity can be represented by a non-key column such as "customer_id" or "account_id"; and the secondary associated entity (or entities) can be represented by one or more non-key columns such as "agent_id" or "cashmachine_number". It is neither necessary nor useful to include relationship-representing tables in the database design in order to establish these associations: following the standard normalization rules is of no benefit when dealing with historical tables. No harm will come, in this situation, from turning the key attributes of the associated entities (such as "customer_id" and "agent_id") into non-key columns of a transaction-history table.

Summary

From the examples in this chapter and in Chapter 7, it is clear that there are several different kinds of historical table that may be included in a database design. We have looked at six kinds:

(1) *Single-use transactional-relationship tables.* These are relationship-representing tables that describe a relationship, established by a past action or situation, a record of which is of continuing importance in the enterprise for which the database was created, for example, the "grades" table, which represents the relationship *student has completed course.* Such relationships often operate "in parallel" with present-time relationships and have different attributes to the present-time relationships: in this example the relationship *has completed* has the attribute "grade", which the relationship *is enrolled in* does not. Rows are added to historical tables like "grades" at the time of the appropriate event or conclusion of action. These rows then represent a unchangeable record of the past; they are therefore regarded as read-only data once they are added to such a table.

(2) *Dual-use transactional-entity tables.* These are entity-representing tables that serve the dual purpose of being (a) present-time tables for actions or work in progress, and (b) historical tables for completed actions or work. For example, the "orders" table contains information about orders that have been placed but are not yet completed (that is, they have not been shipped or invoiced). Once orders are completed, the corresponding rows in the "orders" table become unchangeable historical records of completed orders. These rows are then regarded as read-only data.

(3) *Single-use transactional-entity tables derived from present-time situations.* These are entity-representing tables that record only completed actions or work, and serve no present-time purpose. For example, if we move information about completed orders from the "orders" table to an "orders_completed" table, thus avoiding the need to treat "orders" as a dual-use table, the resulting "orders_completed" table would be a purely historical transactional-entity-representing table. The rows inserted into "orders_completed" are regarded as read-only data as soon as they are added to the table.

(4) *Single-use transactional-entity tables with no present-time precedent.* These are tables that represent transactions or events which, while associated with an entity (for example, *customer* or *account*), do not derive from the conclusion of a present-time situation. Instead, this type of table represents transactions or events that "just happen" and are recorded as they happen (for example, telephone calls to the Customer Service desk, or debits to a customer's bank account). The rows in such tables are regarded as read-only data as soon as they are added to the table.

(5) *Dual-use transactional-detail-relationship tables.* These are relationship-representing tables (like "order_details") that operate between dual-use transactional-entity tables (like "orders") and present-time entity-representing tables (like "products"). In this example, the "order_details" table represents the relationship *order contains product.* We saw in Chapter 7 that, for such tables to be used in their historical roles without the risk of time-related modification anomalies, it is necessary to isolate them from present-time tables by including columns that hold as-it-was-then values, taken from the present-time table. The rows in a table like "order_details" start to be regarded as read-only data at the point where revisions cease to be possible, for example, as soon as the order is shipped.

(6) *Entity-history tables.* These are tables, like "prices_history", that keep a record of the history of changeable non-key attributes of entities. Such tables would generally be used to supplement, rather than replace, normal present-time tables. This is because complex queries would be required to extract present-time values from such tables. Although these tables represent entities, they represent information that falls outside the Entity-Relationship model: the model does not consider the history of attribute values. Rows in such tables are regarded as read-only data once an end date has been entered in the "valid_to" column.

CHAPTER 9

AGGREGATE DATA

The Aggregation of Data

It is a common requirement, in many types of business, to generate aggregated transactional information. Some types of aggregated transactional information are used in day-to-day business operations. They are therefore generated throughout the business day, as the information is needed. Other types are used only after the fact – perhaps days or weeks later – in order to provide support for business decision-making. (The types of aggregated transactional information used in day-to-day business operations may also be used after the fact to support business decision-making; but this is generally a secondary use of this information.)

Some examples of aggregate data are:

- Account balance

- Securities portfolio holdings

- Inventory by product by branch

- Total sales by product

- Total revenue by customer

- Total profits by region

The first three examples are "balance-type" or **point-in-time** aggregates. This is the type of aggregated transactional information that is used primarily in day-to-day business operations (and only secondarily in after-the-fact analyses). The last three examples are **time-period** aggregates, consisting of totals calculated for a particular time period, such as a year. This is the type of aggregated transactional information that is used in after-the-fact analyses.

Aggregated transactional information, often referred to simply as **aggregate data**, can be produced, when needed, by means of SQL commands. These data-aggregating commands include *mathematical functions* that operate on *sets of values* of a *data element of interest*. A **data element of interest** is a quantity, such as "amount of an account debit or credit" or "total invoiced amount of an order", that the person requesting the aggregate data is interested in. A "set of values" (of a data element of interest) is chosen by selecting, from a transaction-history table, the transactions that occurred within a particular time period.

The data element of interest is sometimes found in a single column in the transaction-history table, for example, the number of units of a particular product in an order. In other cases it may be derived from two or more columns in the table, for example, number of units sold multiplied by price, to give the invoiced amount of the order.

There are several different "mathematical functions" that can be used in data aggregation. The most common is the SUM() function, which adds together the values of the data element of interest. Less commonly, other functions may be used, such as AVG(), which calculates the average value, or MAX(), which selects the maximum value.

Time-period aggregate data may consist of a single value, such as "total sales for the year 2007". Alternatively, and more commonly, it may be generated in the form of a report in which the mathematical function has been applied to *groups of values* within the total set of values for the time period (in effect, generating subtotals for each group of values). The grouping of values is carried out according to one or several variables that are characteristics of the transactions (that is, other characteristics aside from the data element of interest). For example, the aggregate "total sales *by product* for the year 2007" is an aggregate in which values of the data element of interest (in this case, "total sales") have been grouped by the variable "product" for the time period "the year 2007". In this example, "product" is an example of what is called a **grouping variable**. There may be one or several grouping variables used in the generation of aggregate data. For example, we use two grouping variables if we generate "total sales *by product by customer* for the year 2007".

Grouping variables are typically the attributes of entities. Most commonly, they are the key attribute of an entity, such as "product_code" or "customer_id". However, non-key attributes of entities, such as the color of a product, can also be used as grouping variables. When grouping is based on "the entity itself", that is, on its key attribute (rather than a non-key attribute like color), the entity is referred to as the **grouping entity**. We can therefore say that product and customer are *grouping entities*, for which "product_code" and "customer_id" are the *grouping variables*.

Another way in which aggregate data can be organized is *by time periods within a* **time span**, for example, "total sales *by year* for the years 1998 to 2007". In this case the "time period" is a year, and the "time span" is the ten-year period 1998 to 2007. Here, the time period is being used in a similar way to a standard grouping variable (such as "product"). Grouping like this, by time period, can be combined with grouping by standard grouping variables, as in the aggregate "total sales *by product by year* for the years 1998 to 2007".

In summary, for any given mathematical function like SUM(), there are six different kinds of aggregate data that can be generated by means of the appropriate SQL command, operating on the raw transactional information contained in historical tables:

A.   Single-valued point-in-time (or "balance-type") aggregates, for example, "account balance".

B. Multi-valued point-in-time aggregates (that is, reports containing several values of the data element of interest), for example, "total inventory *by product by branch*", where point-in-time balances are calculated corresponding to the values of one or more grouping variables.

C. Single-valued time-period aggregates, for example, "total sales for the year 2007" (with no grouping by a standard grouping variable).

D. Multi-valued time-period aggregates based on grouping of the transactions by one or more grouping variables within a single time-period, for example, "total sales *by product by customer* for the year 2007".

E. Multi-valued time-period aggregates based on grouping of the transactions by time period within an overall time span (but with no grouping by a standard grouping variable), for example "total sales *by year* for the years 1999 to 2007".

F. Multi-valued time-period aggregates based on grouping of the transactions by one or more grouping variables *and* by time periods within an overall time span, for example "total sales *by product by customer by year* for the years 1998 to 2007".

Type F is the most general case of a time-period aggregate. Aggregates of types C, D, and E can be thought of as special cases of type F – where there is, respectively, no grouping at all (type C), grouping only grouping variables (type D), or grouping only by time periods within a time span (type E).

Generation of Aggregate Data

As an example of a query that generates aggregate data, consider the SQL command that generates the type-D aggregate "total sales by product for the year 2007", using information from the two historical tables, "order_details" and "orders":

```
SELECT
    order_details.product_code,
    SUM((order_details.price_aiwt) * (order_details.quantity)) AS total_sales
FROM
    order_details,
    orders
WHERE
    YEAR(orders.date_of_order) = 2007 AND
    orders.order_number = order_details.order_number
GROUP BY
    order_details.product_code
```

The results of this query (if there were just six products in the database for which sales had occurred in 2007) might look something like the following:

```
product_code              total_sales
------------              -----------
A71298                      59504.35
B63524                      99290.40
C23638                     136040.00
D12345                      56700.00
G42938                      67550.00
N91828R                     65324.00
```

For every product of which at least one item has been sold in 2007, the above query sums the value of "price_aiwt" (price as it was then) multiplied by "quantity" for all rows in the "order_details" table related to orders dated within the year 2007. The YEAR() function, which operates on "date_of_order", extracts just the year from the datetime. Note that "date_of_order" is found in the "orders" table, while the "quantity" (of items sold) and the as-it-was-then value of "price" are found in the "order_details" table. The second line of the WHERE clause joins these two tables for the query.

The operator SUM() works together with the GROUP BY clause, which is required in order to tell SUM() over what groups of rows it is to perform the summations. (Note that this query does not include the calculation of a grand total for all products, although it would be easy to modify it to include a grand total.) The asterisk that appears inside the SUM() function is a multiplication operator. (Note that, in most versions of SQL, an asterisk may be a multiplication symbol or a wildcard symbol, depending on the context.) The reserved word "AS" assigns the name 'total_sales' to the results of the SUM() operation. Without "AS total_sales" in the statement, the second column of the result would appear without a title.

The above SQL command (which generates a type-D aggregate) could be modified to include additional grouping variables. Also, it could be modified to include grouping by time periods within a time span – with or without standard grouping variables (like "product"); that is, it could be modified to generate a type-F or type-E aggregate. In each case, the SELECT statement would be written so as to produce, in the resulting report, a column for each grouping variable and (where aggregation is done by time period within a time span), a column for the time period. So, the type-F aggregate "total sales *by product by customer by year*, for the years 1998 to 2007" would have four columns: "product_code", "customer_id", "year", and "total sales". It would also contain many more rows of results than the equivalent type-D aggregate (as illustrated above) because of all the possible combinations of values of grouping variables that it would cover.

I will return to the topic of multi-value aggregate results later in this chapter; but at this point I want to first look at ways of making the generation of aggregates simpler and free from modification anomalies. I am addressing this topic next because the practices I am about to describe will affect the names appearing as the headings of some of the columns in the data-aggregation results; and I want to prepare you for those names before giving further examples.

Designing Historical Tables with Aggregation in Mind

When designing the transaction-history tables in a database, it is necessary to consider not only the *primary* business purpose of these tables (in the current example – the assembly and shipping of customers' orders and the generation of invoices) but also the *secondary* requirement of allowing users to perform after-the-fact data-aggregation queries directed at those tables.

In order to be able to perform aggregation queries on one or several transaction-history tables (like "orders" and "order_details") it is a requirement that each transaction be easily associated with all potential grouping variables. By "potential grouping variable" I mean any grouping variable that a user might reasonably ask to be used in the generation of aggregate data. When constructing a data-aggregation SQL command, there are two ways in which grouping variables might be associated with transactions in the transaction-history table: (a) through an *indirect* association via another table that has a column (for example, "customer_id") that corresponds to the desired grouping variable, or (b) through use of a column in the transaction-history table itself that corresponds to the desired grouping variable (for example, "product_code").

First I will consider case (a) and why this can be problematic. As an example of case (a), if we want to create a data aggregate with values grouped by customer, we would need to obtain the values of "customer_id" by matching "order_id" in the "orders" table with "order_id" in the "orders_placed" table. (The "orders_placed" table is a relationship-representing table with key columns "customer_id" and "order_id". It represents the relationship *customer has placed order*.) This is necessary because neither of the transaction-history tables ("orders" or "order_details") contains information about which customer placed an order. Thus, the FROM clause in the data-aggregation command would need to contain the table "orders_placed", as well as the "orders" and "order_details" tables.

One disadvantage of having to include an extra table in the SQL command that performs the aggregation is that the SQL command will take longer to execute and executing it will place more load is placed on the computer system on which the DBMS is running. As explained earlier, this is not generally a concern in modern DBMSs running on modern servers. However, because data aggregation typically involves very large numbers of transactions, we need to exercise some caution in adding more tables to the SQL commands than are absolutely necessary.

Another more-serious disadvantage of having to refer to other tables (like "orders_placed") is that it introduces the possibility of modification anomalies affecting the aggregate data. For example, if a former customer has ceased to be a customer, and if the row representing that customer has been deleted from the "customers" table, it is possible that information related to that customer has also been deleted from the "orders_placed" table (for instance, by a cascading delete under a foreign key reference). In this case the aggregate data would omit, from the sales figures, the purchases made by the deleted customer in the years prior to the customer ceasing to be a customer.

In Chapter 7 we saw how we can prevent the occurrence of modification anomalies with respect to the price of products by adding the column "price_aiwt" to the "order_details" table – thus making "order_details" a self-contained historical record of the order as at the time it was completed. (We also added a "product_description_aiwt" column to address the potential issue of changes occurring to the product description.) In the example SQL command that was used in the last section to generate "total sales by product for the year 2007" we were able to use the "price_aiwt" column of the "order_details" table when calculating the total sales:

SUM((order_details.price_aiwt) * (order_details.quantity)) AS total_sales

Had it not been for the existence of the "price_aiwt" column in the "order_details" table, it would have been necessary to get the price of each item from the "products" table. The existence of the "price_aiwt" column (in the "order_details" table) was advantageous in two ways. First, it allowed us to reduce, by one, the number of tables that were operated on by the aggregating query. Second, it protected the aggregation process from potential modification anomalies arising from changes in the value of "price" in the "products" table. Such changes would distort the "total sales" information – because the value of orders would be assessed using the current prices of products, rather that the prices at which they were actually sold.

We can make broader use of the technique of adding columns, like "price_aiwt", to transaction-history tables in order to achieve two objectives: (a) making aggregation less demanding on the computer system on which the DBMS runs; and (b) preventing changes in present-time tables affecting the accuracy of the aggregate data. Specifically, we can add a number of additional as-it-was-then columns to transaction-history tables (like "orders") in order to hold values of potential grouping variables. For example:

- We can add a "customer_id_aiwt" column to the "orders" tables, to avoid the need to involve the "orders_placed" table in SQL commands that generate aggregates "by customer".

- We can add a "sales_channel_code_aiwt" column to the "orders" tables to avoid the need to involve the "orders_placed" table in SQL commands that generate aggregates "by sales channel". (The information about the sales channel through which an order is received is, for present-time purposes, contained in the non-key "sales_channel_code" column of the "orders_placed" table.)

- We can add a "salesperson_id_aiwt" column to the "orders" tables to avoid the need to include another table in SQL commands that generate aggregates "by salesperson". (Note that, in the examples given in Chapters 7 and 8, this part of the database design was not shown. The table that would associate a salesperson with an order might be a table called "sales_credits", representing the relationship *salesperson handled order*.)

In this way, we make the values of all the potential grouping variables available within the transaction-history tables themselves; and we record the value of these variables "frozen" as at the times of the transactions.

Before proceeding with further examples of aggregate-data generation, let's take a look at the even-further-expanded "orders" table, and the "order_details" table, that we have now arrived at:

Table name: **orders**							
order_ number	status	purchase_ order_number	date_of_ order	shipping_ date	invoice_ date	payment_ due_date	branch_ code
Columns, continued...		customer_ id_aiwt		sales_channel_ code_aiwt		salesperson_ id_aiwt	

Table name: **order_details**					
order_ number	line_ number	quantity	product_ code	product_ description_aiwt	price_ aiwt

To generalize what we have done here:

To make it possible for users to perform aggregation of transaction-history data by a variety of grouping variables, efficiently and without modification anomalies arising, you should add non-key columns to the transaction-history tables to hold the values as at the time of the transaction of all not-already-included potential grouping variables.

Note that this practice goes against standard normalization rules. However, as we have seen in Chapter 7, not only do the standard rules of normalization not apply to historical tables but we must go against standard normalization rules to prevent modification anomalies occurring with respect to historical tables.

It should be noted that, even with columns like "customer_id_aiwt" added to tables like "orders", the queries required to generate aggregate data still put a somewhat heavy load on the DBMS (although not as heavy as they might have done). Such queries may involve many thousands, or even millions, of rows of data in the transaction-history tables. As a result, it may take quite a long time to execute such queries (perhaps as long as twenty minutes). Also, the heavy load on the DBMS may have an adverse effect on the performance of the database as seen by other users. Because of this, it is a common practice to make arrangements to generate aggregate data outside working hours, and store it in the database in anticipation of users' queries. We will look at this practice in the next section.

Storing Aggregate Data in a Database

Although aggregate data for after-the-fact analysis can, in the last resort, be generated at the time it is needed, it is a fairly common practice to run pre-programmed automatic SQL commands, at regular intervals (typically at night), to generate aggregate data. This aggregate data is then stored in tables in the database itself, rather than being printed out. Users can then retrieve the aggregate data at a later time, by means of relatively simple SQL commands that operate on the aggregate-data tables. The storing of commonly-requested aggregate data in tables in the database also makes it easy for users to execute, during working hours, queries that carry out *further* mathematical operations on the aggregate data, in order to produce "superaggregated" information. **Superaggregation** is the application of aggregating operations to data that is already aggregate data (as opposed to "raw" transaction-history data).

Aggregate data, stored in a relational database, is regarded as a separate class of historical information, distinct from the basic transactional data from which it is derived. Aggregate data lies outside the Entity-Relationship model, whereas basic transactional data falls within the Entity-Relationship model (but outside the standard rules for normalization). Note, in particular, that (when considering aggregate data) you should avoid any temptation to think of aggregate data as an attribute of the entity that it may, at first sight, appear to describe. Aggregate data, such as "total sales by product", "total revenue by customer", "total inventory by branch", "total profits by region", and "account balance", may sound vaguely like attributes of *product, customer, branch, region,* and *account.* However, they are not attributes in the way that things like color, date-of-birth, and account type are. Under the Entity-Relationship model, *attributes must be strictly single-valued data elements.* By contrast, aggregate data is not single-valued. Aggregate data of types B, D, E, and F consists of collections of values; and so it is clearly not single-valued. Aggregate data of types A and C, although single-valued for, respectively, a specific datetime or a specific time period, are not truly single-valued: they may have one of many possible values, *depending on the datetime or time period that is chosen.*

Of course, the fact that aggregate data lies outside the Entity-Relationship model does not prevent us placing tables of aggregate data in a relational database. However, what it does mean is that we cannot include aggregate data in the end-to-end database design process (the process that starts at the E-R modeling stage and ends with a completed database design). Instead, we have to tack on the design of the aggregate-data tables at the end of the database design process, once the basic design is complete.

Point-In-Time Aggregate Data

In this section I am going to briefly describe a number of important characteristics of point-in-time aggregates (type-A and type-B aggregates) that distinguish them from time-period aggregates. At the start of this chapter I gave three examples of point-in-time aggregates, which we will now look at in more detail:

- Account balance

- Securities portfolio holdings

- Inventory by product by branch

First, it should be noted that point-in-time aggregate data is, in practice, almost always based on the mathematical function SUM(). Second, it should be noted that point-in-time aggregate data is a function of a *single* datetime – the point in time for which the "balance" is calculated. We can determine the balance of an account only if we are told what datetime is to be used. For example, we can calculate a balance for the present moment (the current balance), for the close of business yesterday, or for the start of the current month. For any specified point in time, a value like "account balance" represents, *in concept*, the aggregation of all transactions from the time the account was opened to the datetime for which the balance is to be calculated. *In practice*, a balance is calculated by starting with the balance that has been stored in the database for an earlier point in time (such as the end of the prior month, or the end of the prior business day). All the subsequent debit and credit transactions are then applied to this baseline balance, up to the datetime for which the balance is to be calculated (such as right now, or the end of the month just ended).

The value of aggregates like "securities portfolio holdings" and "inventory" are calculated along the same lines as "account balance". However, unlike "account balance", which can be represented by a single number, the "balance" in these other two examples consists of a collection of pairs of values, each pair representing an item and the quantity of that item. In the inventory example, the "items" are represented by a product code. In the securities portfolio example, the "items" are represented by an identification code for each security. For example, the securities held in a brokerage account might be represented as follows:

```
security_id              quantity_held
-----------              -------------
IBM                            1000
ORCL                           1500
MSFT                           2500
F                               100
AMZN                           3000
```

When generating the aggregate "securities portfolio holdings", the quantities of each stock or other security must be dealt with separately, by grouping transactions according to "security_id". The number of a particular security held in the portfolio, such as IBM, is analogous to "account balance" in the bank account example; and the way that this number is calculated follows similar principles: starting with a baseline, such as the number of shares at the start of the month, all subsequent "debits" (IBM stock sales) and "credits" (IBM stock purchases) are applied to this baseline, up to the datetime for which the portfolio holdings are to be calculated.

Note that, for the aggregates "securities portfolio holdings" and "inventory by product by branch", it is possible derive a single data element from these "balances" by valuing the portfolio or inventory as of a particular datetime. For example, the portfolio holdings could be valued using today's stock prices. However, the portfolio *value* should not be confused with the portfolio *holdings*. The holdings at a particular point in time (such as at the end of the day, last Friday) were what they were. No matter how many times we perform a query to calculate the portfolio holdings as at that datetime, we always get the same result. By contrast, the *current market value* of last Friday's portfolio holdings will be different each time it is calculated, as stock prices move up and down. The comments that follow, about type-A and type-B aggregates, apply to the basic balance information, like "portfolio holdings", *not* to single values like "portfolio value" derived from the basic balance by applying market values.

The general rule for generating point-in-time aggregates (including single-value type-A aggregates like "account balance" and multi-value type-B aggregates like "securities portfolio holdings") can be expressed as follows:

(1) For each entity to which the balance relates (for example, for each account), take the value (or set of values) that constitute the most recent baseline balance. Make a note of the datetime at which the balance was calculated.

(2) Calculate the appropriate time-period aggregate for the *data element of interest* (for example, the amount of the transaction or the number of shares bought or sold). In cases like the securities portfolio, where the quantities of several different items constitute the "balance", the aggregation involves a grouping by that item, for instance, a grouping *by security*. The time period for the aggregation is the period from the datetime of the baseline balance to the datetime for which a new balance is required.

(3) Add the aggregation results from Step (2) to the baseline value (or values) as in Step (1), to obtain the required new balance.

Look carefully at Step (2). For a single account, Step (2) is, *in itself*, either a type-C time-period aggregation (in, for instance, the case of a bank account) or a type-D time-period aggregation (in, for instance, the case of a securities portfolio, where the transactions are grouped "by security"). Since Steps (1) and (3) are very simple, it follows that any principles that we derive from studying type-C and type-D *time-period* aggregation can easily be applied to *point-in-time* aggregation. I will therefore concentrate on time-period aggregation in the rest of this chapter and the next two chapters. (I will return to the subject of point-in-time aggregate data in Chapter 12.)

The Three Factors of Time-Period Aggregation

As mentioned earlier, aggregate data of types C, D, and E can be thought of as special cases type-F aggregate data (which is based on grouping by grouping variables *and* by time periods within an overall time span). In the rest of this chapter we will therefore focus on type-F aggregates. This will give us the broadest possible view of the problem of creating aggregates. Also, as mentioned above, type-A and type-B "balance" aggregates are derived by adding the result of type-C or type-D aggregates to baselines, stored in the database. Therefore, by focusing on type-F aggregates (of which type C and type D are special cases) we adequately cover type-A and type-B aggregates as well.

For simplicity, unless I state otherwise, I will use a time span (for the type-F aggregate examples) consisting of the total time for which the database has existed. Also, I will use aggregates based on the mathematical function SUM(), which is the most-frequently used basis of data aggregation.

When generating a particular type-F aggregate, there are three factors that characterize the required SQL commands:

- The *data element of interest* (for example "sales" or "profits").

- The *time periods* (within the overall time span) by which the transactions are grouped (for example, by day, month, or year). Note that, although the time periods must fall within the time span, the time periods, taken together, do not necessarily add up to the entire time span. For example, we may use a time period of "every Monday" and a time span of "the last ten years", thus ignoring all transactions that took place within the last ten years on other days of the week. In this case the sum of the time periods (all the Mondays) is only one seventh of the time span (ten years).

- The *choice or choices of grouping variables*, that is, the other variables by which results will be grouped (for example "by product", or "by product by branch").

For any collection of transactions (such as "orders" or "calls to the Customer Service desk") there are thus many possible aggregates that can be formed – by making different choices for each of these three factors.

Before looking at how the choices for each of these three factors affects the resulting aggregate, we will first look at a simple example of aggregate data which could be stored in the database. We saw earlier how a query could generate the type-D aggregate "sales by product for the year 2007", giving a two-column result like the following:

```
product_code   total_sales
------------   -----------
A71298          59504.35
B63524          99290.40
C23638         136040.00
D12345          56700.00
G42938          67550.00
N91828R         65324.00
```

If these values are inserted into a two-column table", with columns "product_code" and "total_sales", then this table becomes an aggregate-data table. Alternatively, and more usefully, if we want to use a single table to hold annual sales information for *every* year of the company's history, we would use a slightly different query to create the type-F aggregate "sales by product by year", which has three columns of data. We would then insert the three columns of data into a table like the following:

Table name: **sales_by_product_annual**		
product_code	total_sales	sales_year
A71298	34291.00	2005
B63524	45291.50	2005
C23638	69463.00	2005
D12345	17926.00	2005
G42938	55821.00	2005
N91828R	38917.00	2005
A71298	43020.35	2006
B63524	65432.40	2006
C23638	80730.00	2006
D12345	24098.00	2006
G42938	67550.00	2006
N91828R	36292.00	2006
A71298	59504.35	2007
B63524	99290.40	2007
C23638	136040.00	2007
D12345	56700.00	2007
G42938	67550.00	2007
N91828R	65324.00	2007

To keep this example simple I have assumed that the company has been in business for only the years 2005, 2006, and 2007. Having created this table in the database we would then create an automatically-triggered SQL command in the DBMS that runs at the end of every year, outside business hours, and which updates this table by adding rows for the year just finished.

With such a table in the database (and the automatically-triggered command that updates it annually), a user can quickly and easily retrieve data for any year and any product, without putting a heavy load on the DBMS during business hours. For example, if you wanted to know the total sales of red stapling machines for the 24-month period from January 2006 to December 2007, you would use the query:

```
SELECT
    sales_by_product_annual.product_code,
    SUM(sales_by_product_annual.total_sales) AS total_sales_2006_2007
FROM
    sales_by_product_annual
WHERE
    sales_by_product_annual.product_code = 'D12345' AND
    (sales_by_product_annual .sales_year = 2006 OR sales_by_product_annual .sales_year = 2007)
GROUP BY
    sales_by_product_annual.product_code
```

The results of this query, based on the above example aggregate-data table, would be:

```
product_code      total_sales_2006_2007
------------      ---------------------
D12345            80798.00
```

123

The contents of the aggregate-data table "sales_by_product_annual" is just one example of the aggregate data that could be derived from transaction history stored in the tables "orders" and "order_details". There are many other possible aggregations. The range of results that can be obtained by users at a later time, using queries directed at aggregate-data tables (or directed at a combination of aggregate-data tables and other tables), is limited by the contents of those aggregate-data tables. For example, if the person who created the tables had included aggregates only for full calendar years (as in the above example), a query directed at these tables could not produce results for a single month. It would be necessary, in this situation, to resort to a query that operates on the "raw" transaction data in the "orders" and "order_details" tables. As explained earlier, this could adversely affect the performance of the database for other users. It is therefore important that the range of queries that users will want to perform be anticipated by the database designer who creates the aggregate-data tables and who writes the automatic-update queries.

In order to make the database ready to handle all possible aggregate-data queries that users might want to perform, there would, ideally, be tables covering every possible aggregation of the historical data stored in the database. However, in most real-world databases, this would lead to a very large number of tables (and associated automatic-update queries to keep these tables up-to-date).

The Number of Possible Aggregate-Data Tables

Let's take a look at just how many aggregate-data tables might be required in order to allow users to generate a wide range of possible reports. In a database like the one in the Order and Invoice Management example, coverage of all reasonable aggregate-data requests might require aggregate-data tables for every combination of choices of the following three factors:

(1) The data element of interest, selected from (for example) the four choices: sales (in dollars), unit sales (number of items sold), profits, customer calls

(2) The time period over which the aggregation is to be calculated, selected from the following six choices: days, weeks, weeks (weekdays only), months, quarters, years

(3) Single or multiple choices for the other potential grouping variables, selected from (for example) this list of six: product, customer, sales channel, salesperson, department, branch

Let us consider how many different data aggregates these choices give rise to (and, for simplicity, include even those that are not very meaningful or useful).

The total number of possible aggregates is the product of the numbers of choices for each of these factors. Factors (1) and (2) present simple choices of one item from four and six variables respectively. Factor (3) is more complicated, because we can choose one variable from the list; or a combination of two, three, four, or five variables; or we can choose all six variables. This gives a total number of possibilities for the six grouping variables of Factor (3) of:

$$^6C_1 + {}^6C_2 + {}^6C_3 + {}^6C_4 + {}^6C_5 + {}^6C_6 = 6 + 15 + 20 + 15 + 6 + 1 = 63 \text{ possibilities.}$$

In the above calculation, the function ^nC_r represents the number of ways that you can make a choice of 'r' items from 'n' items, where order does not matter. (^nC_r = n!/r!(n-r)! where n! is the product of the integers from 'n' down to 1.) In addition to these 63 combinations, there is one more possibility: we could also choose to have no grouping variable (resulting in a type-E aggregate). So, the total number of choices for Factor (3) is 64. This means that, taking into account the choices that can be made across (1), (2), and (3), the total number of different aggregates that can be arrived at is 4 x 6 x 64 = 1,536.

The creation of 1,536 tables, and associated automatic-update queries, is not a practical proposition. Instead, the database designer will need to poll the users and determine what queries of aggregate data are actually going to be performed regularly; or, at the very least, he or she will need to make informed guesses about what aggregate-data tables will be required by users. Even with a tailored selection of popular aggregates, the creation of the tables, plus the writing of table-updating queries, puts a strain on the staff who are responsible for supporting the database. Clearly this approach has its limitations.

Recognizing this, you might be inclined to give up on the idea of generating, and storing in the database, all these tables of aggregate data and, instead, just tell users to do their aggregation queries whenever they need to – and live with complaints about queries taking too long and the performance of the database deteriorating for all users when individual users are running their aggregate queries. In fact, other solutions to the problem of making aggregate data readily available to users have been developed and these generally involve exporting historical data to other kinds of database, where users can query the data using graphical user interfaces (GUIs). More will be said about such solutions later. However, the problem of creating and storing aggregate data in the main relational database is not quite as bad as it might at first appear. There are ways in which the proliferation of aggregate-data tables can be contained.

Minimizing the Number of Aggregate-Data Tables

Although there may be many thousands of possible type-F data aggregates that users might be interested in, there are pragmatic approaches that can be followed in order to minimize the number of aggregate data tables that need to be stored in the database. The best of these approaches seeks to eliminate the largest of the three numbers from the calculation of the total number of aggregates to be stored in the database (the number 64 in the calculation 4 x 6 x 64 = 1536 in the above example). This approach involves collapsing the results of all the aggregates for a particular combination of the first two factors into a single aggregate-data table. In the above example this would reduce the number of aggregate-data tables to 4 x 6 = 24 (which is a manageable number of tables).

The way that this is done is as follows:

- For each combination of the first two factors (that is, for each of the 24 combinations in the above example) a table is created that has a column for the data element of interest (such as "unit_sales"), a column for the aggregation period (such as "sales_year"), and columns for all the possible grouping variables: "product_code", "customer_id", "sales_channel_code", "salesperson_id", "department_code", and "branch_code". For the case where Factor (1) is "unit sales" and Factor (2) is "years", the empty table would look something like this:

Table name: **unit_sales_annual_multifactor**							
unit_ sales	sales_ year	product_ code	customer_ id	sales_channel_ code	salesperson_ id	department_ code	branch_ code

- Next, an aggregating query is performed using *all* the possible grouping variables. The results are inserted into the table.

- Finally, a fairly complicated multi-part query is performed on these initial table contents in order to perform superaggregation of its contents (that is, to apply aggregating operations to data which is already aggregate data). The superaggregation proceeds in a number of phases. In each phase, all possible choices of a certain number of grouping variables from the six possible grouping variables are used. In this example, the first phase would use the six possible choices of five grouping variables from the six. The second phase would use the fifteen possible choices of four grouping variables from the six. The third phase would use the twenty possible choices of three grouping variables from the six. The fourth phase would use the fifteen possible choices of two grouping variables from the six. The fifth phase would use the six possible choices of one grouping variable from the six. The final phase would use none of the grouping variables: the total sales for each year would be calculated without any breakdown by any grouping variable. The results for every combination of grouping variables, at each of these phases of the superaggregation, are inserted into the table, with the value 'ALL' entered in the column or columns for which the variables have been omitted from the GROUP BY clause.

Note that it is necessary, in order to avoid ambiguity, that none of the grouping variables have the text-string 'ALL' as an actual data element in the raw transaction-history tables on which the aggregation is performed. This could be ensured programmatically at the time of data entry.

An example, based on the six grouping variables shown above, would take up too much space and be very hard to follow. So, instead, I am going to use a simplified version of the example, with only three possible grouping variables: "product_code", "customer_id", and "salesperson" (rather than "salesperson_id", in order to make the results easier to read). To keep the size of the example manageable, I will assume that the company has been in business for only two full years (2006 and 2007); sells only two products (with product codes A71298 and D12345); has only three customers (with customer IDs 37666, 49123, and 72401); and has only two salespersons (Alice and Bob).

The table that I am going to populate with aggregate data is the one for the data element of interest "number_sold" and a time period of one year – "unit_sales_annual_multifactor". I will assume that this five-column table has been created, ready to hold the results. The first step is the first aggregation, with a GROUP BY clause that includes all three variables ("product_code", "customer_id", and "salesperson"), performed on the transaction-history tables. This query might look something like the following. Note that I have used the reserved word AS to assign column names in the resulting table that omit the "aiwt" suffix, in order to keep the column names shirt (which will avoid the need to use an unreadably-small font):

```
INSERT INTO unit_sales_annual_multifactor
SELECT
    SUM(order_details.quantity) AS number_sold,
    YEAR(orders.date_of_order) AS sales_year,
    order_details.product_code,
    orders.customer_id_aiwt AS customer_id,
    orders.salesperson_aiwt AS salesperson
FROM
    order_details,
    orders
WHERE
    orders.order_number = order_details.order_number
GROUP BY
    YEAR(orders.date_of_order),
    order_details.product_code,
    orders.customer_id_aiwt,
    orders.salesperson_aiwt
```

The results of executing this first SQL command might be seventeen rows of data like the following:

Table name: **unit_sales_annual_multifactor**

number_sold	sales_year	product_code	customer_id	salesperson
24	2003	A71298	37666	Alice
32	2003	A71298	37666	Bob
16	2003	D12345	37666	Alice
15	2003	D12345	37666	Bob
22	2003	D12345	72401	Alice
198	2007	A71298	37666	Alice
163	2007	A71298	49123	Alice
182	2007	A71298	72401	Alice
137	2007	A71298	37666	Bob
143	2007	A71298	49123	Bob
132	2007	A71298	72401	Bob
45	2007	D12345	37666	Alice
49	2007	D12345	49123	Alice
33	2007	D12345	72401	Alice
26	2007	D12345	37666	Bob
65	2007	D12345	49123	Bob
21	2007	D12345	72401	Bob

Note that the table contains no zero values in the "number_sold" column. This is because the SQL command was constructed so as not to add any rows to the table for combinations of values for which no items have been sold. Such entries would serve no useful purpose and would cause the table to become needlessly large.

Now we come to the complicated part, in which *superaggregation* occurs in a *combinatorial* manner on subsets of these three possible grouping variables, that is:

- Grouping by the three possible choices of two grouping variables from the three.
- Grouping by the three possible choices of one grouping variable from the three.
- Elimination of all grouping variables.

Rather than show the multi-step SQL command that does all this, I will go straight to the resulting table contents (shown on the next page), from which it is fairly easy to see what has happened. The three superaggregating steps have added a further 41 row to the original 17, making 58 rows in total. In the newly added rows, the word 'ALL' appears in one, two, or all three of the grouping-variable columns (as a result of the first, second, and third superaggregating phases).

There are various names that have been used to describe the kind of table shown in this example. None of them is entirely satisfactory, and so I am going to describe it in full as a **combinatorially-superaggregated transaction-history table**, which I am going to abbreviate to **C-table**.

This technique is a very useful one. In this simplified example it has allowed us to replace a number of tables (eight, in fact) by a single table. In the full example, with six possible grouping variables, a single C-table would replace 64 tables. Thus, in the full example, we reduce the total number of aggregate-data tables that need to be stored in the database from 1,536 tables to only 24 C-tables – one for each pair of choices for Factor (1) and Factor (2). The task of creating 24 C-tables, and the queries that periodically update them, is a manageable one (whereas doing this for 1,536 tables is not).

Obviously, the number of rows in the above simplified example of a C-table (58 rows) is very much less than the number you would find in a real-world database. The need for users to perform queries directed at this table, in order to retrieve only the information that is of interest, is not apparent in this example: a user could print out the whole table (as below) and visually locate the rows of interest to him or her. However, in the real world, a C-table would typically contain a huge number of rows. With six or more grouping variables, a business that has been operating for ten years or more, thousands of products offered for sale, hundreds of thousands of customers, and hundreds of salespeople, the results of the first aggregation step might be a table with tens of millions of rows. The superaggregation steps would then expand the size of the table even further. (In the simplified example you can see that the superaggregation steps have more than tripled the number of rows in the table, from 17 to 58.) Clearly, it would not be useful to print out the contents of a table with tens of millions of rows and try to find the rows that you are interest in by visual inspection. A real-world C-table is only useful as the target of specific end-user queries to extract the particular set of aggregate data that the user is interested in.

Table name: **unit_sales_annual_multifactor**

number_sold	sales_year	product_code	customer_id	salesperson
24	2003	A71298	37666	Alice
32	2003	A71298	37666	Bob
16	2003	D12345	37666	Alice
15	2003	D12345	37666	Bob
22	2003	D12345	72401	Alice
198	2007	A71298	37666	Alice
163	2007	A71298	49123	Alice
182	2007	A71298	72401	Alice
137	2007	A71298	37666	Bob
143	2007	A71298	49123	Bob
132	2007	A71298	72401	Bob
45	2007	D12345	37666	Alice
49	2007	D12345	49123	Alice
33	2007	D12345	72401	Alice
26	2007	D12345	37666	Bob
65	2007	D12345	49123	Bob
21	2007	D12345	72401	Bob
40	2006	ALL	37666	Alice
47	2006	ALL	37666	Bob
22	2006	ALL	72401	Alice
24	2006	A71298	ALL	Alice
32	2006	A71298	ALL	Bob
38	2006	D12345	ALL	Alice
15	2006	D12345	ALL	Bob
56	2006	A71298	37666	ALL
31	2006	D12345	37666	ALL
22	2006	D12345	72401	ALL
62	2006	ALL	ALL	Alice
47	2006	ALL	ALL	Bob
87	2006	ALL	37666	ALL
22	2006	ALL	72401	ALL
56	2006	A71298	ALL	ALL
53	2006	D12345	ALL	ALL
109	2006	ALL	ALL	ALL
243	2007	ALL	37666	Alice
212	2007	ALL	49123	Alice
215	2007	ALL	72401	Alice
163	2007	ALL	37666	Bob
208	2007	ALL	49123	Bob
153	2007	ALL	72401	Bob
543	2007	A71298	ALL	Alice
412	2007	A71298	ALL	Bob
127	2007	D12345	ALL	Alice
112	2007	D12345	ALL	Bob
335	2007	A71298	37666	ALL
306	2007	A71298	49123	ALL
314	2007	A71298	72401	ALL
71	2007	D12345	37666	ALL
114	2007	D12345	49123	ALL
54	2007	D12345	72401	ALL
670	2007	ALL	ALL	Alice
524	2007	ALL	ALL	Bob
406	2007	ALL	37666	ALL
420	2007	ALL	49123	ALL
368	2007	ALL	72401	ALL
955	2007	A71298	ALL	ALL
239	2007	D12345	ALL	ALL
1194	2007	ALL	ALL	ALL

Querying C-tables

To see how a C-table can be used to give the specific aggregate data that a particular user is interested in, I will stay with the simplified example using three possible grouping variables (which gives the five-column C-table shown above). Suppose that a user wants to obtain "unit sales by salesperson for all items sold in 2007". The user would use the following query, directed at the C-table "unit_sales_annual_multifactor":

```
SELECT
    unit_sales_annual_multifactor.number_sold,
    unit_sales_annual_multifactor.salesperson
FROM
    unit_sales_annual_multifactor
WHERE
    unit_sales_annual_multifactor.sales_year = 2007 AND
    unit_sales_annual_multifactor.product_code = 'ALL' AND
    unit_sales_annual_multifactor.customer_id = 'ALL' AND
    unit_sales_annual_multifactor.salesperson <> 'ALL'
```

In this query the comparison operator "<>" means "not equal to". This query will result in the following report:

```
number_sold      salesperson
-----------      -----------
670              Alice
524              Bob
```

You can see that this query has simply selected the appropriate two rows from the table (the eighth-from-the-bottom and seventh-from-the-bottom rows). Thus, the query performs a very simple action and will execute quickly, placing minimal load on the DBMS. I repeat my earlier comment: this is a trivial task for a C-table with only 58 rows; but use of a query to locate the required rows is essential for a real-world C-table with tens of millions of rows.

A quick reminder before I continue: in the above examples I used "salesperson" and "salesperson_aiwt", each taking a single-name value like 'Alice', in order to simplify the examples. The actual database design would use "salesperson_id" and "salesperson_id_aiwt" in these roles. The names of salespeople would be found (whenever required) from the table "salespeople":

Table name: **salespeople**		
salesperson_id	**first_name**	**last_name**

When I summarize this example in Chapter 17, I will use the non-simplified design.

Further Reducing the Number of Aggregate-Data Tables

The C-table approach turns an almost impossible task (creating and keeping updated thousands of aggregate-data tables) into a manageable one (creating and keeping updated a few tens of aggregate-data tables). Even so, some database designers might find it tedious to deal with tens of aggregate-data tables and the writing of the queries required to keep these updated. In the next two chapters we will therefore continue to look for ways in which a database designer can further reduce the number of aggregate-data tables to be stored in a database.

Before ending this chapter, I want to point out one fairly simple way in which the number of tables can be reduced somewhat. This is by handing back some of the aggregation work to the user – by cutting down the number of different time periods for which aggregates are generated. This can be done if users are told that they will sometimes have to do some timewise aggregation in the queries that they direct at the C-tables.

For example, rather than having C-tables containing aggregations by day, by week, by month, by quarter, and by year, we could decide to have C-tables covering only by day, by month, and by year. In this case:

- If a user wants by-day, by-month, or by-year information, a simple query of the by-day C-table is all that is required.

- If a user wants by-week information then he or she will need to write a query that aggregates the results from the by-day C-table into weekly results.

- If the user wants by-quarter information then he or she will need to write a query that aggregates the results from the by-month C-table into quarterly results.

The last two queries, which perform the additional timewise aggregation, will put a heavier load on the system than the other queries. However, these are relatively simply aggregation queries that could be tolerated during business hours (whereas the queries that are used to build the C-tables in the first place must be run outside business hours).

It is thus possible to keep the number of C-tables down to as few as two or three per data element of interest. However, there is a better way than burdening the user with a modest amount of timewise aggregation, as you will see in Chapter 11.

Summary

Aggregate data of various kinds can be produced by SQL commands that operate on transaction-history tables. The efficient generation of aggregate data is aided by the inclusion, in the design of the historical tables, of columns that hold as-it-was-then values of potential grouping variables.

Data aggregation is an operation which places a heavy load on the computer system on which the DBMS is running. It is therefore better done outside business hours. To make aggregate data accessible to users, without placing a heavy load on the system, aggregate data can be generated outside business hours and placed in tables in the database. Once this is done, users can get the aggregate data, when they need it, by means of simple SQL commands directed at those tables.

Aggregate data, stored in a database, is outside the scope of the Entity-Relationship model.

Aggregate data of types C, D, and E can be thought of as special cases of the most-general type, type F. Also, point-in-time (balance-type) aggregate data (type A and B) can be thought of as derivative of types C or D, and hence another special case of type F.

A given set of type-F aggregate data is characterized by three factors: the data element of interest, the time period for the aggregation (within the overall time span), and the grouping variables (that is, the other variables by which users want to see the results grouped). There may be many thousands of possible combinations of choices for these three factors, making storage of all possible aggregates in the database impractical. To overcome this problem, it is possible to create C-tables, that is, tables containing superaggregated data that covers all possible combinations of the grouping variables. This greatly reduces the number of tables needed to store the aggregate data: a C-table is needed only for each combination of the data element of interest and the time period.

CHAPTER 10

DATA AGGREGATION WITH NESTED GROUPING VARIABLES

Generalization Relationships

In the examples of data aggregation in the previous chapter, the entities (such as *product, customer, salesperson*), whose key attributes form the grouping variables, were independent of one another. However, it is sometimes the case that users want to generate aggregates based on *related* entities – entities such as *branch, area, region*, and *country*. Entities like this are related by means of *generalization relationships* (introduced in Chapter 2).

The generalization relationships that exist between these kinds of entities are sometimes *is a* relationships, as in the relationship *product is a product-group-member*. Two instances of this relationship might be "D12345 is a stationery item" and "K48263 is a computer item". More commonly, in the context of data aggregation, the generalization relationships between the grouping entities are *is part of* relationships, as in *branch is part of area*. An instance of this relationship might be "Stamford is part of New-York-Tri-State-Area".

Both types of generalization relationships (*is a* and *is part of*) behave in the same way when it comes to possession of attributes, that is, the less general entity set "inherits" all the attributes of the more general entity set; but the less general entity set may have additional attributes that cannot be possessed by the more general entity set. (This rule will *not* be illustrated in the first example that follows; but I will return to this point in the next chapter.)

In this chapter we will look at the implications of using grouping entities that are related by generalization relationships.

Nested Entities

Consider the set of related entities *branch, area, region*, and *country*. These related entities may be described as a set of **nested entities**, because each entity is contained in the next (more-general) entity. When they are used as grouping variables in data aggregation, we can describe them as a set of **nested grouping entities**, and their key attributes ("branch_code", "area_code", "region_code", and "country_code") as a set of **nested grouping variables**. In an E-R diagram, the nesting of these entities would be represented by a chain of relationships, as follows:

(By the way, I am using the term "area code" here to mean a code like 'NYTRI' that represents a geographical area, not an area code in the telephonic sense.) If the four geographical entities and three relationships shown in the above diagram were translated into a normalized database design, they would be represented by, in total, seven tables – one for each of the four entities, and one for each of the three relationships. These seven tables, with a small number of example rows inserted into them, would look something like the following:

Table name: **branches**

branch_code	branch_name
NYC	New York
PNY	Parsippany
STM	Stamford

Table name: **branches_by_area**

branch_code	area_code
NYC	NYTRI
PNY	NYTRI
STM	NYTRI

Table name: **areas**

area_code	area_name
NYTRI	NY-Tri-State
FLWST	Florida-West
SIVAL	Silicon-Valley

Table name: **areas_by_region**

area_code	region_code
NYTRI	USNE
FLWST	USSE
SIVAL	USSW

Table name: **regions**

region_code	region_name
USNE	US-Northeast
USSE	US-Southeast
USSW	US-Southwest

Table name: **regions_by_country**

region_code	country_code
USNE	US
USSE	US
USSW	US

Table name: **countries**

country_code	country_name
US	USA
FR	France
DE	Germany

These tables can be used, as they stand, in aggregation queries – although this has the drawback of adding two or more extra tables to the aggregating queries. (Later we will look at ways of reducing the number of geographic tables that need to be included in these queries.) As an example of how these tables could be used in an aggregation query, consider the query that would be required to find "sales *by product by area* for the year 2006". We will assume that geographical information has been included in the "orders" table at the finest level of detail, that is, according to the branch at which each order was placed. This is done by means of a "branch_code" column in the "orders" table. The query to find "sales by product by area for the year 2006" would be:

```
SELECT
    SUM((order_details.price_aiwt) * (order_details.quantity)) AS total_sales,
    order_details.product_code,
    areas.area_name
FROM
    order_details,
    orders,
    branches_by_area,
    areas
WHERE
    YEAR(orders.date_of_order) = 2006 AND
    orders.order_number = order_details.order_number AND
    orders.branch_code = branches_by_area.branch_code AND
    branches_by_area.area_code = areas.area_code
GROUP BY
    order_details.product_code,
    areas.area_name
```

This will produce a report something like the following. To keep this example simple, I have assumed that, in 2006, the company was operating in only three areas of the USA.

```
total_sales    product_code   area_name
-----------    ------------   ---------
  12762.85     A71298         Florida-West
  38359.05     A71298         NY-Tri-State
   8382.45     A71298         Silicon-Valley
  25130.60     B63524         Florida-West
  62513.00     B63524         NY-Tri-State
  11649.00     B63524         Silicon-Valley
  47130.70     C23638         Florida-West
  79261.20     C23638         NY-Tri-State
   9657.05     C23638         Silicon-Valley
   4525.50     D12345         Florida-West
   3664.50     D12345         NY-Tri-State
  48520.50     D12345         Silicon-Valley
  26390.00     G42938         Florida-West
  30534.00     G42938         NY-Tri-State
  10629.50     G42938         Silicon-Valley
  35234.00     N91828R        Florida-West
  13203.00     N91828R        NY-Tri-State
  16887.00     N91828R        Silicon-Valley
```

If we wanted to populate aggregate-data tables with data like this showing sales by year (for a time span covering all the data in the database), we would (a) remove the year condition from the WHERE clause, so that transactions for all years would be included, and (b) include, in both the SELECT and GROUP BY clauses, the YEAR() function that extracts the year from the date of each order. The resulting query would be:

```
SELECT
    SUM((order_details.price_aiwt) * (order_details.quantity)) AS total_sales,
    order_details.product_code,
    areas.area_name,
    YEAR(orders.date_of_order) AS sales_year
FROM
    order_details,
    orders,
    branches_by_area,
    areas
WHERE
    orders.order_number = order_details.order_number AND
    orders.branch_code = branches_by_area.branch_code AND
    branches_by_area.area_code = areas.area_code
GROUP BY
    order_details.product_code,
    areas.area_name,
    YEAR(orders.date_of_order)
```

We could place the four-column result of this query into a "sales_by_product_by_area_annual" table. Similarly, we could produce variations of the above query to generate aggregates with different choices (other than *area*) for the geographic grouping entity, for example, "sales by customer *by region* by year". We could combine these different geographical choices with different choices for the non-geographic grouping variable or variables, for example, "sales *by product by customer by country by year*".

By creating aggregates "by area", "by region", and "by country", as well as "by branch", we have now quadrupled the number of aggregate-data tables that need to be stored in the database. As we saw in Chapter 9, trying to cover all possible choices for grouping variables, as well as choices for (1) the data element of interest, and (2) the time period (year, quarter, month, week, day), leads to extremely large numbers of aggregate-data tables. By introducing the nested entities *branch→area→region→country* we have exacerbated this problem. However, as we also saw in Chapter 9, we can significantly reduce the number of aggregate-data tables by generating a single C-table for each combination of data element of interest and time period, thus covering all the grouping variables in each C-table. We will now look how this approach is extended to nested grouping variables.

Minimizing the Number of Aggregate-Data Tables

In Chapter 9 we looked at the example C-table "unit_sales_annual_multifactor". In that example I did not include "branch_code" because I wanted to keep the example small enough to fit on one page. However, if I had included "branch_code" then the C-table would have looked like the following. (Note that I have named this table "unit_sales_annual_multifactor_v2" in order to avoid confusion with the C-table in Chapter 9):

Table name: **unit_sales_annual_multifactor_v2**

number_ sold	sales_ year	product_ code	customer_ id	salesperson	branch_ code

Now, let's suppose that we further modify the C-table-generation query to include the four nested grouping variables: "branch_code", "area_code", "region_code", and "country_code". The resulting C-table would then have the following columns:

Table name: **unit_sales_annual_multifactor_v3**

number_ sold	sales_ year	product_ code	customer_ id	salesperson	branch_ code	area_ code	region_ code	country_ code

This table is similar in most respects to the original C-table, except that it now has nine columns. When we create the SQL query needed to populate this C-table with aggregate data, we need to take account of something very important: *the geographic columns are not independent of one another.* This means that, during the superaggregation steps of the query, the SQL must be written such that it will not create nonsensical rows of data, for example, a row which has 'ALL' in the "area_code" column but a normal value like 'NYC' in the "branch_code" column. The fact that the grouping variables are nested means that 'ALL' can appear in one of the three columns "area_code", "region_code", or "country_code" *if, and only if,* there is an 'ALL' in *all* the geographical columns to the left of it.

I will return to this point in a moment. First we will look at how users would direct queries at a C-table like "unit_sales_annual_multifactor_v3" in order to get the specific aggregate data that they need.

Querying a Nested-Grouping-Variable C-table

As in the Chapter 9 example, once a full set of C-tables is stored in the database, users can quickly retrieve aggregate data at the level of detail that they are interested in. To do this they use queries that look for 'ALL' in the appropriate columns.

For example, suppose that a user wants to create the report "unit sales by product by area for the year 2007" using the C-table "unit_sales_annual_multifactor_v3". The query that the user would employ would make a selection of rows using a WHERE clause that incorporates the following four conditions:

(1) For the nested variables that correspond to *a finer level of detail* than the level that is to be appear in the results, the WHERE clause should look for 'ALL' in the columns that represent those finer-detail variables. In this case, since we want results "by area", it is just the "branch_code" column that corresponds to a finer level of detail (than "area"). So, the WHERE clause should look for 'ALL' in the "branch_code" column.

(2) For the nested variables that correspond to a *more-general level* than the one that is to be appear in the results, the WHERE clause should look for rows that do *not* have 'ALL' in the columns that represent those variables. In this case, the WHERE clause should look for rows that do not have 'ALL' in the columns "region_code", and "country_code".

(3) For the particular nested grouping variable that we want to see in the results, and also for the non-nested grouping variables that we want to see in the results, the WHERE clause should look for rows that do *not* have 'ALL' in the columns that represent these variables. In this example we include the conditions that the columns "area_code" and "product_code" should not contain 'ALL'.

(4) For the other variables, like "customer_id" and "salesperson", that have columns in the C-table but are not to be featured in the results of the query, the WHERE clause should look for 'ALL' in the columns that represent those variables.

Following these four rules, we get the query shown below (to extract "unit sales by product by area for the year 2006" from the C-table):

```
SELECT
    unit_sales_annual_multifactor_v3.number_sold,
    unit_sales_annual_multifactor_v3.product_code,
    unit_sales_annual_multifactor_v3.area_code
FROM
    unit_sales_annual_multifactor_v3
WHERE
    unit_sales_annual_multifactor_v3.sales_year = 2006 AND
    unit_sales_annual_multifactor_v3.product_code <> 'ALL' AND
    unit_sales_annual_multifactor_v3.customer_id = 'ALL' AND
    unit_sales_annual_multifactor_v3.salesperson = 'ALL' AND
    unit_sales_annual_multifactor_v3.branch_code = 'ALL' AND
    unit_sales_annual_multifactor_v3.area_code <> 'ALL' AND
    unit_sales_annual_multifactor_v3.region_code <> 'ALL' AND
    unit_sales_annual_multifactor_v3.country_code <> 'ALL'
ORDER BY
    unit_sales_annual_multifactor_v3.product_code,
    unit_sales_annual_multifactor_v3.area_code
```

The results of this query would look something like this:

```
number_sold    product_code   area_code
-----------    ------------   ---------
       5431    A71298         FLWST
      16323    A71298         NYTRI
       3567    A71298         SIVAL
      11423    B63524         FLWST
      28415    B63524         NYTRI
       5295    B63524         SIVAL
       5266    C23638         FLWST
       8856    C23638         NYTRI
       1079    C23638         SIVAL
        431    D12345         FLWST
        349    D12345         NYTRI
       4621    D12345         SIVAL
       7540    G42938         FLWST
       8724    G42938         NYTRI
       3037    G42938         SIVAL
      35234    N91828R        FLWST
      13203    N91828R        NYTRI
      16887    N91828R        SIVAL
```

The ORDER BY clause in the above example query is an SQL sorting instruction. I included it simply to make sure that the results are sorted in the exact order that we want them, in case they are not in that order in the C-table.

Note that the results of this query have "area_code" in the third column, rather than "area_name". If we need the full area names to appear in the report then we have to change the above query as follows:

- Include the "areas" table in the FROM clause.
- In the SELECT clause, replace
  unit_sales_annual_multifactor_v3.area_code by area.area_name.
- In the WHERE clause, include the condition:
  unit_sales_annual_multifactor_v3.area_code = areas.area_code

Note also that the above example report is generated by a query does not produce all-areas subtotals for each product. If you want such subtotals to be included in the result of the query (that is, rows with 'ALL' in the "area_code" column), then you should omit mention of the "area_code" column from the WHERE clause. This will cause both the rows of the C-table with a normal value in the "area_code" column and the rows with 'ALL' in that column to appear in the results.

Other Examples of Nested Grouping Variables

Besides the nested group of geographic grouping entities mentioned above, branch→area→region→country, there are several other possible nested groups that may be found in a complete data model of a company's operations. For example:

- customer→customer-group
- product→product-manufacturer
- product→product-type→product-family

The entity customer-group represents a categorization of customer by size and/or type of the customer (customer, in this context, being an organization, not a person). The assignment of customers (as represented in the "customers" table) to customer groups would typically be done by means of the following tables, into which I have inserted a small number of example rows. The "customers_by_group" table represents the relationship is part of. The "customer_groups" table represents the entity customer-group.

Table name: customers_by_group	
customer_id	customer_group_code
37666	COS
39821	COS
40162	COL
44872	GOV
49123	COL
60762	COS
72401	COS

Table name: customer_groups	
customer_group_code	customer_group_description
RTL	Retail-direct
GOV	Government
COL	Commercial-large
COS	Commercial-small

The second example of nesting (product→product-manufacturer) is not fundamentally a generalization relationship. It is really the normal (non-generalization) relationship product is produced by product-manufacturer. However, when it comes to creating aggregate sales data, we can choose to regard this particular relationship as a generalization relationship. This is because we can treat the entity product-manufacturer as being equivalent to product-source-group. We can then say that the relationship between product and product-manufacturer is equivalent to the relationship product is part of product-source-group. The key attribute of product-source-group would be the same as the key attribute of product-manufacturer, namely, "product-mfr-id". In this way we can, when performing an aggregation, treat "product_mfr_id" and "product_code" as though they were nested grouping variables.

The third example (product→product-type→product-family) is a set of genuinely nested grouping entities. The assignment of products to a product type, and product types to a product family, would be done by means of two relationship-representing tables and two entity-representing tables (in addition to the "products" table). Note that the entity *product* is thus part of two separate sets of nested grouping entities (*product→product-type→product-family* and also *product→product-manufacturer*). It is not unusual to find a grouping entity that participates in two nested sets like this.

Issues in C-table Creation with Nested Grouping Variables

In this section I am going to look at two issues that arise in the creation of C-tables containing nested grouping variables: (a) database performance and (b) potential modification anomalies. These are the same problems that we looked at in Chapter 9; but they apply with even more force after we introduce nested grouping variables.

First, we will consider performance, by which I mean how demanding the SQL commands needed to create the C-tables are on the computer system on which the DBMS is running and therefore how long they take to execute. The demands that an SQL command makes on the system are a function of how many rows of information have to be processed in performing the aggregation and how many tables the SQL command operates on. The number of rows of transaction-history information is something that we can do nothing about. It is probably large; but it is what it is. However, the number of tables that the SQL command has to operate on depends on the database design; so it is something that we can control. The fewer tables that are operated on, the better the performance of the SQL command (that is, the less load it puts on the system and the faster it executes).

We will examine how many tables would be involved in the generation of an all-encompassing C-table for annual sales (in dollars), with the basic grouping entities product, customer, branch, and salesperson, and all of the four sets of nested grouping entities:

- *branch→area→region→country*
- *customer→customer-group*
- *product→product-manufacturer*
- *product→product-type→product-family*

The tables on which the SQL command would need to operate are:

- "orders" (which includes the columns "branch_code" and "customer_id_aiwt")
- "order_details" (which includes the column "product_code")
- "branches_by_area"
- "areas_by_region"
- "regions_by_country"
- "customers_by_group"
- "products_by_product_manufacturer"

- "products_by_product_type"
- "product_type_by_product_family"

This is a large number of tables. It approaches the limit that most DBMSs' query optimizers can take account of in optimizing the way a query is executed. It would be better if we could reduce this number.

The second problem – that of potential modification anomalies – also arises because of the use of historical tables like "orders" and "order_details" in combination with present-time tables like "customers_by_group" and "areas_by_region". If changes are made to these present-time tables at some point after the sales occurred then it will distort the results of data aggregations. For example, changes made to "customers_by_group" or "areas_by_region" may result in the attribution of sales to customer groups or regions that the orders were not associated with at the time of the order. (By the way, this is a very common problem in many large companies. Sales organizations are reorganized at frequent intervals. There are often heated arguments over the way that sales results are reported after a reorganization.)

We can solve both problems (performance and modification anomalies) by a single set of changes to the database design. Specifically, we can follow the same approach that we followed in Chapter 9, when we added the column "customer_id_aiwt" to the "orders" table. What we would do in this case is to add the following as-it-was-then columns to the "orders" and "order_details" tables:

- To the "orders" table we would add the columns "area_code_aiwt", "region_code_aiwt", "country_code_aiwt", and "customer_group_code_aiwt".

- To the "order_details" table we would add the columns "product_mfr_id_aiwt", "product_type_code_aiwt", and "product_family_code_aiwt".

We thus make "orders" and "order_details" self-contained records of all the values of these potential grouping variables. Once we have done this, these historical tables are insulated from changes in present-time tables. Also, the SQL commands used to generate aggregate data can now operate on just two tables ("orders" and "order_details") instead of nine. In summary:

When it is required that C-tables be generated that include columns for nested grouping variables, as well as standard grouping variables, the generation of those C-tables can be made both more efficient and free from modification anomalies if columns are added to the transaction-history tables for as-it-was-then copies of the key attributes of all members of all the sets of nested grouping entities.

Dealing with the Interdependence of Nested Grouping Variables

Earlier, I mentioned that the multi-part query required to generate a C-table like "unit_sales_annual_multifactor_v3" must be written in such a way that it will not create nonsensical rows. I will now explain this in more detail. The point that I am about to illustrate is this:

> When writing queries to create C-tables, because nested grouping variables are not independent, specific steps must be taken, during the superaggregating stage, to prevent the creation of meaningless, duplicate rows in the resulting table.

The following example will illustrate this. As in the earlier example, suppose that the resulting C-table is going to be placed in a table with the following columns:

Table name: unit_sales_annual_multifactor_v3								
number_ sold	sales_ year	product_ code	customer_ id	salesperson	branch_ code	area_ code	region_ code	country_ code

If we do *not* take account of the fact that a branch is part of an area, an area is part of a region, and a region is part of a country, and we were to treat these variables as though they were no more alike than "products" and "customers", the resulting table would include many rows that are, in reality, duplicates, even though they contain different data values in certain columns. For example, the following eight rows are, in effect, all the same row:

number_ sold	sales_ year	product_ code	customer_ id	salesperson	branch_ code	area_ code	region_ code	country_ code
49	2007	D12345	49123	Alice	NYC	NYTRI	USNE	US
49	2007	D12345	49123	Alice	NYC	NYTRI	USNE	ALL
49	2007	D12345	49123	Alice	NYC	NYTRI	ALL	US
49	2007	D12345	49123	Alice	NYC	ALL	USNE	US
49	2007	D12345	49123	Alice	NYC	NYTRI	ALL	ALL
49	2007	D12345	49123	Alice	NYC	ALL	USNE	ALL
49	2007	D12345	49123	Alice	NYC	ALL	ALL	US
49	2007	D12345	49123	Alice	NYC	ALL	ALL	ALL

The first row is how the information *should* appear; but below it there are seven nonsense rows, containing duplicated information in the first six columns. These seven rows are nonsense because the New York branch can only be in one area, region, and country, namely, the ones it is actually in. Thus, the appearance of 'ALL' in any column to the right of the "branch_code" column, when "branch_code" does not contain 'ALL', is meaningless.

Similarly, in rows that represent area-level aggregation (that is, rows that have 'ALL' in the "branch_code" column, but do not have 'ALL' in "area_code" column), there will be three nonsense rows (the second, third, and fourth rows) in addition to the correct row:

number_ sold	sales_ year	product_ code	customer_ id	salesperson	branch_ code	area_ code	region_ code	country_ code
49	2007	D12345	49123	Alice	ALL	NYTRI	USNE	US
49	2007	D12345	49123	Alice	ALL	NYTRI	USNE	ALL
49	2007	D12345	49123	Alice	ALL	NYTRI	ALL	US
49	2007	D12345	49123	Alice	ALL	NYTRI	ALL	ALL

Having all these extra, nonsense rows is a problem. Not only do the nonsense rows make the C-table quite a lot bigger than it needs to be, but also the presence of these rows will confuse users. Furthermore, if users perform queries against the C-table, without taking steps to exclude the nonsense rows from the results, any calculations of subtotals and totals performed in the users' queries will give incorrect results.

In order to prevent such nonsense rows appearing in the C-table, the multi-part query used to create the C-table must be constructed so as to exclude aggregations in which 'ALL' would appear to the right of a "real" value in any of the geographic columns. For example, if "branch_code" contains a real value like "NYC" then the columns "area_code", "region_code", and "country_code" must not contain 'ALL'.

Summary

Some grouping variables that may be used in producing aggregate data are not independent of one another. Rather, they are **the key attributes of entities that are** members of a set of nested entities. These key attributes, when used in aggregation, must be given special treatment.

The members of a set of nested grouping variables can be included in a C-table, in order to minimize the number of aggregate-data tables that need to be stored in the database. However, the fact that these variables are not independent of one another must be taken into account when writing the multi-part queries used to create the C-tables; otherwise nonsensical rows will result. Such rows would confuse users who direct queries at the C-table and cause incorrect subtotals and totals to be generated in reports.

The generation of C-tables containing nested grouping variables can be made both more efficient and free from modification anomalies if columns are added to the transaction-history tables to hold as-it-was-then copies of the key attributes of all members of all the sets of nested grouping entities.

CHAPTER 11

TIME PERIODS AS PSEUDO-ENTITIES

Time-period Aggregation

In Chapters 9 and 10, when giving examples of aggregate data, I used "one year" as the time period over which the aggregation of the transactional data was performed – for both simple time-period aggregation and aggregation by time periods within an overall time span. I chose one-year time periods in order to keep the examples simple and consistent with one another.

In this chapter we will now look more closely at grouping by time periods in data aggregation, and consider other time periods besides a year. We will look at ways of doing complex time-period aggregations and ways of minimizing the number of resulting aggregate-data tables that need to be stored in the database.

Time-Periods Aggregates: a Brief Re-cap

Chapters 9 and 10 contained a lot of information; so I will start by summarizing the key points about time-period aggregate data, as represented by the most general case of a type-F aggregate.

From a *time* point of view, time-period aggregates are described by two things:

(a) The length of the *time periods* by which aggregation is to occur (for example, days, weeks, months, or years). During the aggregation of the raw transaction-history data, the transactions are grouped into these periods according to the contents of a datetime column that appears in the transaction-history tables.

(b) The overall *time span* covered by the aggregation. The time span is often chosen as the entire history covered by the database, up to the end of the most recent time period. So, if the database went into operation in November 1997, and a time period of one year is being used, an aggregation performed in 2008 would cover the ten full years from 1998-01-01 to 2007-12-31. In some cases a shorter time span might be used, such as "the last five full years".

Before an aggregation can be performed, it is first necessary to identify the datetime column that will be used to determine which time period a transaction falls in. This requires a certain amount of careful thought. In the "orders" table, for example, we could choose "date_of_order" or "date_of_shipment". For aggregation by long time periods, like a year, the choice between these two will not significantly affect results. However, for shorter periods it might. If a lot more orders are placed on Fridays than on other days, and if most of the orders placed on Friday are shipped on the following Monday, then the choice of "date_of_shipment" as the datetime by which orders are aggregated could give a misleading picture of daily sales patterns: it would make Monday look like the busiest sales day, instead of Friday. The choice of datetime column should be based on the datetime that leads to the most useful and meaningful results from the point of view of the users of the aggregate data.

From a *non-time* point of view, time-period aggregates are characterized by:

- The data element of interest, for example, total sales (in dollars), unit sales, or profits.

- The mathematical function that will be applied to the data element of interest, for example, SUM(), AVG(), or MAX().

- The choices of one or several grouping variables, such as "product_code", "customer_id", or "branch_code".

One more point about aggregate data that I will summarize, before going on to the subject of time periods, is the technique of creating a C-table. Instead of being stored in the database in a large number of different aggregate-data tables, aggregate data can be incorporated into a much smaller number of C-tables. These provide users with aggregate data in a very flexible form. Each C-table covers:

- One particular data element of interest (for example, unit sales).

- All of the possible grouping variables (for example, product, customer, and salesperson), including nested grouping variables (for example, branch, area, region, and country).

- One particular time period (for example, years).

I will also remind you that tables containing aggregate data, and tables containing superaggregated data (in particular, C-tables), represent things that are outside the scope of the Entity-Relationship model.

Time Periods

The time periods by which data aggregation is performed are, *conceptually* at least, defined by a start datetime and an end datetime. So, when we talk about '2008' as a time period, what we really mean is "the 365 days from January 1 to December 31, 2008, inclusive". Similarly, when we talk about '2008-12-23' as a one-day time period, what we really mean is "the 24-hour period from 00:00:00 to 23:59:59, December 23, 2008".

When we perform time-period aggregation, what we are doing, *in concept*, is comparing the datetime of each individual transaction with a number of datetime ranges that define the start and end of each of the time periods covered by the aggregation, and determining which time period the transaction should be assigned to. We then apply the mathematical function, such as SUM(), to the groups of transactions that have been assigned to each time period. However, *in practice* we simplify this process by approaching the task in a different way. We first translate the datetime of each transaction into a value (typically an integer, although it could be a character string). This value defines the time period to which the transaction belongs. For example, we use the YEAR() function to extract a single integer value, such as '2008', from the transaction's datetime. By doing this we avoid the hard work of comparing the transaction's datetime with the start and end datetimes of the time periods. Once we have derived the single integer values like '2008', we then use the GROUP BY function to group the transactions according to those values.

I used "one year" as the time period for all the examples in Chapter 9 and 10 because this is the easiest time period to handle in this way. When we use other time periods we have to work a bit harder to apply this approach.

In general, what we need to do for any choice of time period is to convert the relevant datetime of the transaction (for example, "date_of_order") into a single value that identifies the specific time period within which the datetime falls. In this context, a datetime can be thought of as consisting of four parts: a year, a month, a day, and a time. (In many situations the time part of a datetime is not used: it defaults to 00:00:00. But in some cases the times of transactions may be recorded. More importantly, there is always the *possibility* that times will start to be used in datetimes after the database has been in use for some time. You should therefore, when creating data-aggregation queries, consider the repercussions of the time part of the datetime of transactions having a non-default value at some point in the future.) When we use the YEAR() function to generate a single integer value, the function is simply throwing away the other parts of the datetime and keeping the year. However, when we use other time periods things are not quite this simple.

In order to generate a value that identifies the month within which a transaction's datetime falls, it is no good to throw away the year, the day, and the time, and keep the month. If we ignore the year then we will end up grouping together all the transactions from January 2001, January 2002, January 2003, and so on. We need to represent both the year and the month in the single value that we generate.

There are various ways of approaching this. One fairly simple one is to operate on the transaction's datetime using the function:

    ((100*YEAR(orders.date_of_order)) + MONTH(orders.date_of_order))

The function MONTH() extracts the month from a datetime and represents it as an integer. The function YEAR() does the same to the year. By multiplying the year by 100 and adding the result to the month, we get a single value like '200812', which represents December 2008. The single values derived in this way uniquely identify a particular month within a particular year. (The only drawback of this approach is that these values are not contiguous. That is, there are gaps, for example, between 200812 and 200901, because the values from 200813 to 200899 are not used.)

We can adopt a similar approach for quarters, weeks, and days. Many (but not all) DBMSs support the SQL function DATEPART(), which generates integer values in the same way that MONTH() does, but with greater flexibility. For example, we can generate a single value that represents quarters using the function:

((10*YEAR(orders.date_of_order)) + DATEPART(QUARTER, orders.date_of_order))

The argument QUARTER causes DATEPART() to generate a value of 1, 2, 3, or 4 to represent the quarter within which "date_of_order" falls. By adding this to the year multiplied by 10, we create a five-digit integer, such as '20084', meaning Fourth Quarter, 2008. Similarly we can generate a six-digit integer that represents the week using:

((100*YEAR(orders.date_of_order)) + DATEPART(WEEK, orders.date_of_order))

which gives a value like '200851', meaning Week 51, 2008; and we can generate a seven-digit integer that represents the day using:

((1000*YEAR(orders.date_of_order)) + DATEPART(DAYOFYEAR, orders.date_of_order))

which gives a value like '2008357', meaning the 357th day of 2008 (December 22, 2008).

In the case of days, an alternative to the above approach would be to simply take the datetime of the transaction and perform the grouping using the datetime value itself as the grouping variable. However, this approach carries the risk that it will cease to work correctly if users start to record transaction datetimes that include the time. Each transaction whose datetime contains a time will become a one-transaction aggregate in the result, separate from all the transactions for that day whose datetimes do not contain times, and separate from the other transactions with different times. It is therefore necessary to discard the time part of the datetime before using it in the GROUP BY clause. This can be done by extracting the year, month, and day, and then "re-building" the datetime value. However, this approach then becomes rather complex: it is generally easier to convert the datetime to a seven-digit value like '2008357'.

Before moving on to the next subject, I want to alert you to some of the difficulties surrounding "weeks". Depending on whether you treat Sunday or Monday as the first day of the week, there may be differences in the assignment, to a particular year, of the last few days of one year and the first few days of the next year. There may also be differences in the number of weeks in certain years. For example, January 1, 2004 fell on a Thursday; so Week 1 of 2004 was considered to start on Sunday, January 4 according to calendars that treat weeks as starting on Sunday. (The days January 1 to 3 were counted as part of the last week of 2003.) But calendars that treat weeks as starting on Monday counted the start of Week 1 of 2004 as December 29, 2003, because the majority of days of that Monday-to-Sunday week fell within 2004. As a result of this difference, calendars where weeks were considered to start on Monday "borrowed" three days from 2003 and two days from 2005, causing 2004 to have 53 weeks. But calendars in which weeks were considered to start on Sunday showed only 52 weeks in 2004. Because of these differences, you should make sure, when using week numbers in databases, that the same convention is being followed in the database as in the business that the database supports; and that any differences between different departments (such as Sales and Accounting) are at least understood, if not resolved.

Once we have applied functions to the transactions' datetimes to generate single-integer values like '200851', the GROUP BY function can group these using those values. At this point it may be helpful to look at an SQL command that operates in this way, this time using weeks instead of years:

```
SELECT
  SUM(order_details.quantity) AS number_sold,
  ((100*YEAR(orders.date_of_order)) +
    DATEPART(WEEK, orders.date_of_order)) AS sales_week,
  order_details.product_code
FROM
  order_details,
  orders
WHERE
  orders.order_number = order_details.order_number AND
  orders.date_of_order > '2000-12-31'
GROUP BY
  sales_week,
  order_details.product_code
```

This will calculate "unit sales by week by product from the start of 2001 onwards". Note that I have placed the week number before the product code in the GROUP BY clause, so that the rows in the result will be arranged first by week, and then by product within each week. Also note that, in the GROUP BY clause, I have taken advantage of the 'AS' assignment of the name "sales_week" in the SELECT clause, so that I do not have to repeat the calculation of "sales_week".

To keep this example simple we can assume that the company has been selling only four products. In this case the results of the above SQL command would start off with the following rows:

number_sold	sales_week	product_code
20	200101	A71298
12	200101	D12345
32	200101	G42938
14	200101	N91828R
8	200102	A71298
6	200102	D12345
15	200102	G42938
9	200102	N91828R
17	200103	A71298
39	200103	D12345
4	200103	G42938
11	200103	N91828R

The approach described above deals with basic time-period aggregation. Now, suppose that we want to do something a little more complicated, such as generate aggregates "by week (weekdays only)". In this case we have to include conditions in the WHERE clause that filter out the days that we do not want to include in the aggregate, namely, Saturdays and Sundays. This can be done by including, in the WHERE clause, the condition:

```
WHERE
  DAYOFWEEK(orders.date_of_order) <> 7 AND
  DAYOFWEEK(orders.date_of_order) <> 1
```

The function DAYOFWEEK() generates an integer in the range 1 to 7. (In this example I have assumed that the DBMS is configured to treat Sunday as Day 1, so Saturday is Day 7.) If we use the same SQL command as before, but with these conditions added to the WHERE clause, the result will be "unit sales by week (weekdays only) by product from the start of 2001 onwards".

We can deal with many time-period aggregation requirements in this manner. However, we start to run into trouble if we want to create an aggregate "by week (non-holiday weekdays only)" or "by month (Sundays and holidays only)". Once we start imposing conditions like this we find that we need to somehow look up information about days: the standard SQL functions like DAYOFWEEK() are no longer adequate. Before looking at how we can do this, we will first step back and take another look at time periods from an Entity-Relationship model point of view.

Another Way of Thinking About Time Periods

What I am about to say in this section applies mainly to the generation of aggregate data for use in after-the-fact analyses. (In some situations what I describe below may be useful in the generation of point-in-time, "balance" type aggregate data, but such situations are unusual.)

As I have stated several times, once we are dealing with aggregate data, it is no longer necessary to follow the strict rules of the Entity-Relationship model. Given this, it may make things easier if, *strictly within the context of dealing with aggregate data*, we stop thinking about time periods as attributes of transactional entities or transactional relationships and, instead, start treating time periods as though they were entities in their own right. This may seem to be a strange idea when you first encounter it. However, once you get used to this idea, you will find that it has a number of advantages. To make it clear that time periods are not true entities, I will refer to time periods, viewed in this way, as **pseudo-entities**.

Once we describe time periods as pseudo-entities, the following things become possible:

- Time periods can be represented by tables.

- Time periods can have their own attributes, such as "holiday_flag", which takes the values 'Y' or 'N' to mark a day as being a public holiday or not.

- Time periods can be recognized as members of a set of nested entities, such as *days→weeks→months→quarters→years*:

Pseudo-Entity Tables

Having described time periods as pseudo-entities, we can represent each different set of time periods as a table in the database design. The following is a short extract of eight rows from the "days" table:

Table name: **days**									
day_id	year	month_number	day_number_in_month	day_number_in_year	week_id	day_of_week	weekday_flag	last_day_of_month_flag	holiday_flag
D001606	2003	5	25	145	W00229	SUN	N	N	N
D001607	2003	5	26	146	W00229	MON	Y	N	Y
D001608	2003	5	27	147	W00229	TUE	Y	N	N
D001609	2003	5	28	148	W00229	WED	Y	N	N
D001610	2003	5	29	149	W00229	THU	Y	N	N
D001611	2003	5	30	150	W00229	FRI	Y	N	N
D001612	2003	5	31	151	W00229	SAT	N	Y	N
D001613	2003	6	1	152	W00230	SUN	N	N	N

The key of this table is the "day_id" column, which holds a single value that uniquely identifies each day for every day that the database has been in use. In this table I have used a radically different scheme for assigning values to "day_id" from the one that I described earlier (which was based on integer values like '2008357'). In this table I have used text strings consisting of the letter 'D' followed by six digits. The six digits are assigned sequentially, starting at D000001 on the first day that the database went into operation. Similarly, I have assigned values to "week_id" (which is a non-key column in this table) consisting of 'W' followed by five digits. The values of "week_id" are assigned sequentially, starting at W00001 on the first week that the database went into operation.

Note that the inclusion of a "week_id" column in the "days" table goes against standard normalization rules. We have turned the key column of another pseudo-entity-representing table ("weeks") into a non-key column of the "days" table (instead of representing the relationship *is part of*, between *day* and *week*, as another table). However, since we are already outside the realm of present-time tables, there is no need to follow standard normalization rules.

The second, third, and fourth columns of the "days" table contain information that is needed to tie the values of "day_id" back to real datetimes. The sixth column, "week_id", allows us to determine which week a particular day falls in, without having to use the DATEPART(WEEK,) function. The last four columns are where we store the useful information about each day.

To see how these columns could be used, suppose that we want to exclude holidays and weekends from an aggregation. We need to be able to associate rows in the "days" table with rows in "orders". One way in which we *could* have made this possible would have been to include a "normal_datetime" column in the "days" table. This would be a non-key column that holds the date of each day in a datetime format. (Note that such a column is not shown in the above example of the "days" table.) We could then write the WHERE clause as follows:

```
WHERE
    days.holiday_flag = 'N' AND
    days.weekday_flag = 'Y' AND
    days.normal_datetime = orders.date_of_order
```

However, this approach has two disadvantages. First, the equality condition between the datetime columns in "days" and "orders" will fail if "date_of_order" includes a time as well as a date. And second, this approach will not work for the other pseudo-entity tables like "weeks" and "months": it is better if the same approach is used for all the time periods.

A Better Approach to Associating Transactions with Time Periods

A far better approach is to operate the other way round: instead of adding a datetime column to "days", we can add a column to the "orders" table to hold the value of "day_id" that corresponds to the datetime value of "date_of_order". (It is easy to arrange for the value of "day_id" to be inserted in this column when each new order is entered into the database. This can be handled programmatically, along with the insertion of the date of the order – which would typically be inserted programmatically as well, rather than typed by the user.) Once we have done this, the holiday-and-weekend-exclusion condition can be written:

```
WHERE
    days.holiday_flag = 'N' AND
    days.weekday_flag = 'Y' AND
    days.day_id = orders.day_id
```

In fact, we can go further with this approach. Suppose that we have created pseudo-entity tables called "weeks", "months", "quarters", and "years", with key columns "week_id" (which would take values like 'W00229'), "month_id" (which would take values like 'M0049'), "quarter_id" (which would take values like 'Q0017'), and "year_id" (which would take values like 'Y005'). In the same way that we added a "day_id" column to the "orders" table, we can add further columns to the "orders" table, to hold "week_id", "month_id", "quarter_id", and "year_id". (The appropriate values would be inserted into these columns programmatically, along with "day_id" and "date_of_order".) Once we have done this, we can refer directly to any of the information in any of the time-period tables when writing the WHERE clause.

For example, suppose that the "weeks" table has a "season" column, which takes the values 'SPR', 'SUM', 'AUT', 'WIN' (for Spring, Summer, Autumn, Winter). The "weeks" table, with a few example rows, might look like this:

Table name: **weeks**					
week_id	year	week_number_in_year	year_id	first_day_of_week_day_id	season
W00229	2003	22	Y005	D001606	SPR
W00230	2003	23	Y005	D001613	SPR
W00231	2003	24	Y005	D001620	SPR
W00232	2003	25	Y005	D001627	SPR
W00233	2003	26	Y005	D001634	SUM
W00234	2003	27	Y005	D001641	SUM
W00235	2003	28	Y005	D001648	SUM

If we wanted to find "total sales by year for all Fridays in Spring" we would include the following conditions in the WHERE clause:

```
WHERE
    days.day_of_week = 'FRI' AND
    weeks.season = 'SPR' AND
    days.day_id = orders.day_id AND
    weeks.week_id = orders.week_id
```

Besides giving us the ability to perform complex time-period aggregations, the addition of columns like "day_id" and "week_id" to the "orders" table has another major benefit: it allows us to simplify the basic aggregation process, reducing the load that it places on the system. For example, instead of using functions like YEAR() and MONTH() in the GROUP BY clause, we can now use the time-period key values (like "week_id") in the aggregation commands. We can rewrite the earlier example of an aggregation by week as follows:

```
SELECT
    SUM(order_details.quantity) AS number_sold,
    orders.week_id,
    order_details.product_code
FROM
    order_details,
    orders
WHERE
    orders.order_number = order_details.order_number AND
    orders.date_of_order > '2000-12-31'
GROUP BY
    orders.week_id,
    order_details.product_code
```

The "orders" table is now a completely self-contained record of all the time-related information that we might want to use in generating a basic time-period aggregate, such as "by week" or "by quarter"; so we no longer need to use "date_of_order" in data aggregation. (Note that the "weeks" table does not appear in this query. We need to include "weeks" in the FROM and WHERE clauses only if we want to apply conditions based on the characteristics of weeks.)

One slight drawback of the above query is that it gives us the values of "week_id" in the second column of the result:

```
number_sold        week_id           product_code
-----------        -------           ------------
        20         W00105                A71298
        12         W00105                D12345
        32         W00105                G42938
        14         W00105                N91828R
         8         W00106                A71298
         6         W00106                D12345
        15         W00106                G42938
         9         W00106                N91828R
```

The values of "week_id" would be meaningless to a user. If the query is being used to create a report (rather than to create values to go in a table of aggregate data, stored in the database) then we can make the report more user-friendly by including the "weeks" table in the query as follows:

```
SELECT
  SUM(order_details.quantity) AS number_sold,
  orders.week_id,
  weeks.year,
  weeks.week_number_in_year AS week,
  order_details.product_code
FROM
  order_details,
  orders,
  weeks
WHERE
  orders.order_number = order_details.order_number AND
  orders.date_of_order > '2000-12-31' AND
  orders.week_id = weeks.week_id
GROUP BY
  orders.week_id,
  order_details.product_code
```

This will give us a report that starts with the following rows:

```
number_sold        week_id       year    week    product_code
-----------        -------       ----    ----    ------------
        20         W00105        2001      1         A71298
        12         W00105        2001      1         D12345
        32         W00105        2001      1         G42938
        14         W00105        2001      1         N91828R
         8         W00106        2001      2         A71298
         6         W00106        2001      2         D12345
        15         W00106        2001      2         G42938
         9         W00106        2001      2         N91828R
```

However, if the results of the aggregation are to be stored in a table in the database, for later retrieval of selected aggregate data by users, then only the "week_id" column need be included in this table: the actual year and week number information can be retrieved (by including the "weeks" table in the queries) at the time the user directs queries at the aggregate-data table.

In summary, the addition of the columns such as "day_id" and "week_id" to the "orders" table has improved the database design in two ways. First, it has made it easier to establish the association between the "orders" table and the time-period tables. In this way, detailed information about time periods, contained in time-period tables, can be introduced into the WHERE clause in complex time-period aggregations. And second, it has simplified the time-period aspects of data aggregation (and therefore reduced the load that the queries place on the system) by removing the need for date-manipulation functions in the GROUP BY and SELECT clauses.

Adding Time Periods to C-tables

Looking again at the idea that the basic time periods can be recognized as members of the set of nested pseudo-entities *day→week→month→quarter→year*, this brings to our attention the possibility that we could apply to "time period" the same principle that we applied to the geographic nested grouping entities (*branch→area→region→country*) when creating a C-table.

Just as we added columns to the C-table for "area", "region", and "country", we could take a basic C-table like "unit_sales_daily_multifactor", and add columns for "day_id", "week_id", "month_id", "quarter_id", and "year_id". We could then populate it using a multi-part query as described in the last two chapters. The resulting table, with a small number of example rows, might look like the following. (So that this example would fit on the page, I have omitted six columns from the earlier examples – columns which would be included in the final design of this C-table – "product_family_code", "product_type_code", "product_mfr_id", "customer_group_code", "salesperson_id", and "department_code".)

Table name: unit_sales_multiperiod_multifactor

number_ sold	year_ id	quarter_ id	month_ id	week_ id	day_ id	product_ code	customer id	branch code	area_ code	region code	country_ code
198	Y004	ALL	ALL	ALL	ALL	D12345	37666	SFO	SIVAL	USSW	US
51	Y005	Q0017	ALL	ALL	ALL	D12345	37666	SFO	SIVAL	USSW	US
18	Y005	Q0017	M0049	ALL	ALL	D12345	37666	SFO	SIVAL	USSW	US
5	Y005	Q0017	M0049	W00209	ALL	D12345	37666	SFO	SIVAL	USSW	US
2	Y005	Q0017	M0049	W00209	D001464	D12345	37666	SFO	SIVAL	USSW	US
4	Y005	Q0017	M0049	W00209	D001464	D12345	72501	NYC	NYTRI	USNE	US

In this table, looking at just the five time-period columns:

year_id	quarter_id	month_id	week_id	day_id	
Y005	ALL	ALL	ALL	ALL	means that this row is an annual total
Y005	Q0017	ALL	ALL	ALL	means that this row is a quarterly total
Y005	Q0017	M0049	ALL	ALL	means that this row is a monthly total
Y005	Q0017	M0049	W00209	ALL	means that this row is a weekly total
Y005	Q0017	M0049	W00209	D001464	means that this row is a daily total

When a user selects specific rows from this C-table, in the manner described in Chapters 9 and 10, the query would make use of the time-period tables ("days", "weeks", and so on) to convert the values of "day_id", "week_id", "month_id", "quarter_id", and "year_id" to meaningful representations of the time periods. As an example, suppose that the user wants the retrieve "unit sales by month for the New York branch for 2003 and 2004" (with no breakdown by product or customer). The user's query would do the following three things:

Step 1: Look up, in the "years" table, the "year_id" values for the years of interest. (The values of "year_id" for 2003 and 2004 would be, for example, 'Y005' and 'Y006' if the database started at 'Y001' in 1999). These "year_id" values will be used to define the time span that we are interested in.

Step 2: Select the rows of interest from the C-table, taking only those with monthly figures. In order to do this the query would contain the following conditions in the WHERE clause:

```
WHERE
(unit_sales_multiperiod_multifactor.year_id = 'Y005' OR
 unit_sales_multiperiod_multifactor.year_id = 'Y006') AND

unit_sales_multiperiod_multifactor.branch_code = 'NYC'
unit_sales_multiperiod_multifactor.product_code = 'ALL'
unit_sales_multiperiod_multifactor.customer_id = 'ALL'

unit_sales_multiperiod_multifactor.month_id <> 'ALL' AND
unit_sales_multiperiod_multifactor.week_id = 'ALL' AND
unit_sales_multiperiod_multifactor.day_id = 'ALL'
```

In the above WHERE clause I have spaced out the three parts of the clause to make it easier to read. I have also shown 'Y005' and 'Y006' as literal values. In practice, Step (1) would be combined with Step (2) and the actual years ('2003' and '2004') would appear in the combined SQL command, rather than the values of "year_id" ('Y005' and 'Y006') as shown above. In the above WHERE clause:

- The first two lines select rows covering the total time span for the report ('Y005' and 'Y006').

- The third line selects only the rows with a branch code of 'NYC' (New York); and the fourth and fifth lines make sure that we select rows containing aggregates covering all products and all customers at that branch.

- The last three lines select the rows containing the monthly totals. (Look at the table above to see why this is the right combination of 'ALL' and 'not ALL'.)

Step 3: Use the "months" table to turn the values of "month_id", from the extracted rows, into the year and the month, written in a user-friendly way, to be placed in the columns of the final report that the user sees.

The user is thus able to retrieve, from this single "unit sales" C-table, aggregates based on *any* combination of grouping variables and *any* time period.

Creating C-tables with time-period columns like "day_id" and "month_id" (as well as the other grouping variables, like "branch_code") has thus significantly reduced the number of C-tables that need to be stored in the database. If you think back to the calculation of how many aggregate data tables we might have needed in this example, we saw that it could be as many as 4 x 6 x 64 = 1,536. In Chapter 9 we saw how the creation of C-tables can eliminate the third number from this calculation, giving us the need for only 4 x 6 = 24 C-tables. In Chapter 10 we saw how we could stay with this number, even when nested grouping variables are brought into the picture. We have now seen how, by treating time periods as pseudo-entities, we can eliminate the second number from this calculation, leaving us with a need for only four C-tables – one for each data element of interest. (Obviously there may be other data elements of interest in a real-world database, besides the four that were mentioned in Chapter 9. However, in most real-world databases, this approach will allow us to place all the aggregate data, for use in after-the-fact analyses, in a fairly small number of C-tables (for example around 20).

Attributes Inherited within Pseudo-Entity Sets

Before leaving this topic, there is one more point that I want to cover. In Chapter 10, when I first talked about aggregation by nested variables, I mentioned that the generalization relationship *is part of* has the following property:

> *The less general entity set inherits all of the attributes of the more general entity set, but the less general entity set may have additional attributes that cannot be possessed by the more general entity set.*

An interesting question that follows from this is: Does this attribute-inheritance rule apply to *day→week→month→quarter→year?* In fact it does; although in practice it is not always necessary to include, in the tables that represent the less-general entity sets, columns that represent the various attributes of the more general entity set. Some judgment is needed in deciding when to apply this rule.

As an illustration of where this rule might be applied, consider the "season" attribute of the pseudo-entity *week*. In the design of the "days" table I did not include a "season" column. As a result, when we needed to perform an aggregation "by year for all Fridays in Spring", we had to include both the "weeks" table and the "days" table in the WHERE clause. However, we might want to recognize that the "season" attribute that applies to "weeks" is inherited by "days", and add a "season" column to the "days" table. This would have simplified the earlier example query, by eliminating the "weeks" table from the query.

By contrast, an example of a theoretically-inherited attribute that does not, in practice, need to "propagate down the nested set" is "leapyear_flag" in the "years" table (which would take a value 'Y' in a leap year or 'N' otherwise). Conceptually we may say that *quarter, month, week,* and *day* also have this attribute, in the sense that each of these time periods, within a leap year, possesses leapyearishness. However, the addition of a "leapyear_flag" to the "days" table serves no useful purpose. As I said, judgment should be used in applying the attribute-inheritance rule. Each attribute of the bigger time-periods should be considered as a possible attribute of the smaller time periods and columns should be included in the tables of those smaller time periods where this seems to be potentially useful; but not otherwise.

Summary

In summary, several useful ideas and techniques come out of thinking of time periods as pseudo-entities. If we treat time periods as pseudo-entities, and represent them as tables in the database design, then:

- We can allow time periods to have attributes, such as "holiday_flag". These attributes are very useful in performing complex time-period aggregations, such as "by weekday (excluding holidays)".

- We can treat the keys of these tables ("day_id", "week_id", and so on) as nested grouping variables during the creation of C-tables, thus making it possible to create a single "multiperiod" C-table that contains all the time-period aggregations for a particular data element of interest (instead of having one C-table for days, one for weeks, one for months, and so on).

- We can add the columns "day_id", "week_id", "month_id", "quarter_id", and "year_id" to transaction-history tables like "orders", thus making it easier to (a) perform time-period aggregation in general and (b) perform complex time-period aggregation with reference to information held in tables like "days" and "weeks", avoiding the need for complex date-manipulation functions in the GROUP BY and SELECT clauses.

This chapter concludes our review of database design practices for storing the type of aggregate data used in after-the-fact analyses of business activity. (In the next chapter we will look at point-in-time aggregate data.)

Before leaving the topic of storing aggregate data for after-the-fact analysis, I have one more point to make. You are likely to hear and read a lot about software products that have been designed specifically for the needs of users who want to perform after-the-fact analyses of transaction-history data. (I will give a brief account of such products in Chapter 14.) While these products may be useful in certain situations, do not make the mistake of thinking that these products are a pre-requisite for dealing with after-the-fact aggregate data. As demonstrated in the last three chapters, there are database design practices that can be followed in order to incorporate, in an organization's "live" database, the tables necessary to efficiently store aggregate data that support after-the-fact analysis of business activity through simple queries. This is often a more powerful and flexible approach than arranging to "export" copies of the live database to an off-the-shelf software package – a package whose underlying database design may be poorly aligned with the data model of the business.

CHAPTER 12

POINT-IN-TIME AGGREGATE DATA

Introduction

In the last three chapters we looked at how aggregate data can be generated from transaction-history tables, and how provision can be made, in the database design, to store aggregate data. I explained that aggregate data may be stored in the database for two reasons: (a) so that it can be quickly and easily retrieved by users for use in after-the-fact analyses of business activity; and (b) for use in day-to-day business operations. I devoted a lot of space in the last three chapters to time-period aggregate data, particularly the most general case of time-period aggregate data, type F (for example, "total sales by product by customer by year for the last five years"), which is used in after-the-fact analysis. I did this because studying type-F time-period aggregate data gives the most comprehensive view of aggregate data. However, this should not be taken to mean that time-period aggregate data is more important than point-in-time aggregate data.

The ability to perform after-the-fact analysis of business activity is important. However, it is not as important as being able to conduct business in the first place. For this reason, point-in-time (or "balance" type) aggregate data, where it is necessary for day-to-day business operations, is the most important application of the concepts covered in the last three chapters. There are many businesses that have always depended on correctly-calculated point-in-time aggregate data, such as companies engaged in banking, credit card operations, and brokerage. These companies need to know how much money there is in customers' accounts; how much money customers owe them; and what securities are in each customer's portfolio. Also, all companies that manufacture or sell tangible goods need accurate point-in-time aggregate data, such as the inventory levels that exist at each stage of manufacturing and the inventory is available for shipment to customers. Companies are growing increasingly dependent on systems that help them manage their complete workflow in an efficient manner; and these systems depend on databases that are designed with point-in-time aggregate-data generation and storage in mind.

In this chapter we now return to the topic of point-in-time aggregate data in order to look at how point-in-time aggregate data is typically represented in database designs.

As explained in Chapter 9, point-in-time aggregate data has the following two characteristics:

- It is a function of a single datetime – the point in time for which the "balance" is calculated.

- For that point in time it represents, *in concept*, the aggregation of all transactions from the initial starting point (for example, the time when an account was opened) to the point in time under consideration.

Although it is theoretically possible to calculate balances by going back to the starting point, *in practice*, a balance is almost always calculated by starting with a balance that has been stored in the database for an earlier point in time (such as the end of the prior month, or the end of the prior business day), and applying all the subsequent debit and credit transactions to this baseline balance – up to the datetime for which the balance is to be calculated. Adopting such an approach is common sense: it would be lunacy to attempt to retain, in a database, every transaction that ever occurred for a particular enterprise (such as a bank) and to calculate balances by aggregating all transactions from the point in time when each account was opened. However, although it would be lunacy to calculate balances in this way, it is important, before you think about practical ways of dealing with balances, to understand that this is the essential nature of many types of "balance".

Certain types of balance information represent a real-world situation, such as the number of items of a particular product in a company's warehouse. In this case we can record, in a database, each physical action that affects this number – such as the withdrawing of stock to fill a customer's order, or the addition of new stock received from a supplier. Each of these physical actions represents a transaction. If we want to know the number of items in stock we can do one of two things. We can either:

(a) use an SQL command to calculate, from the database contents, a point-in-time data aggregate by performing a SUM() operation on all recent transactions (treating a withdrawal of stock as a debit and an addition of stock as a credit), and adding the result to the baseline balance; or

(b) go to the warehouse, look in the storage bin for the items in question, and count them.

Ideally, these two actions would yield the same result. However, sometimes the results will differ, due to items being lost, stolen, or discarded because of damage. In this case, the balance found from the database is wrong because the series of transactions stored in the database is incomplete: it is missing transactions needed to represent the loss or destruction of the stock. Because such "transactions" are not recorded (or cannot be consistently recorded), it becomes necessary to perform periodic stocktaking. What stocktaking does, in effect, is to determine the net effect of all unrecorded "transactions" and record this net effect in the database as a special transaction – a stock-level adjustment – to bring the database back into synchronization with the real world.

Although some types of balance correspond to a physical reality, databases used in some industries, particularly the financial-services industry, have no physical counterparts for balance information: what is in the database is "reality" as far as the bank, credit card company, or brokerage is concerned. Other examples of balances that may have no physical counterpart (apart from paper records of the balances) include the number of vacation days that an employee has left for the remainder of the year and the number of accumulated frequent-flyer miles that an airline customer has in his or her frequent-flier account. For all such cases (where the database contents are treated as "reality"), there is no possibility of stocktaking and therefore no such thing as a stock-level adjustment transaction.

Calculating and Storing Balances

Returning now to the calculation of balances using a practical database design, the construction of the SQL commands used to calculate balances is based on taking an existing balance, whose accuracy we trust, and applying just the most recent transactions to that balance. In other words, the practical process for generating a new piece of point-in-time aggregate data (for example, the current balance of an account) is as follows:

- Take a previously-stored baseline balance.

- Generate a time-period aggregate, using transactions whose datetimes lie between the datetime of the baseline and the datetime for which the new balance is required.

- Add that time-period aggregate to the baseline, and store the result as the new baseline.

Once a series of SQL commands that performs these steps has been executed, the former baseline balance may be deleted from the database. Alternatively, and more commonly, the former baseline is retained in the database. As a result, the table that contains the balance information holds a series of balances, each with a different datetime. This makes it possible for a user to find out what the balance was at any of the previous datetimes for which a balance has been calculated and stored.

The steps shown above apply to a single account. In practice, the generation of a new set of balances is done for all accounts in the database at the same time, rather than one at a time. The time-period aggregation in the second step of the process (as above) would therefore involve a grouping by account. For example, we would generate the aggregate "net change by account for the last month", where "net change" is obtained using the SUM() function applied to all transactions, treating credits as positive values and debits as negative values, and "by account" represents a grouping action (using the SQL "GROUP BY" function).

Where each individual account "balance" is represented by a set of data elements, rather than a single data element, the aggregation command would contain two variables in the GROUP BY clause: (a) the account number, to group the results by account, and (b) the codes that represent the distinct entities held in the account, in order to group the transactions by these entities within each account. For instance, if the accounts hold securities, rather than cash, we would need to generate the time-period aggregate "net changes by security by account for the last twenty-four hours" when working out the change in the position in each account since yesterday. The net changes, for the various securities held in the account, are the result of sales and purchases of securities (stocks, bonds, and other securities). In this case, "net change" for each security is obtained using the SUM() function applied to transactions, treating the purchases of securities as positive values and the sales of securities as negative values.

For example, if the balance of an account at the end of the day yesterday was 500 shares of IBM stock and 1000 shares of Oracle stock, and today the customer bought 500 shares of IBM, then later in the day sold 700 shares of IBM, then bought 500 shares of Oracle, the "net changes" for this account are +500 − 700 = −200 for IBM stock and +500 for Oracle stock. This is a very simple calculation for a single account. However, when the SQL command has to operate for every recognized tradable security, and the results have to be grouped by account for hundreds of thousands (or even millions) of accounts, the execution of the command may take quite a long time and consume a lot of computer processing power. For this reason, the calculation of new balances for all accounts, at a particular point in time each day, is typically done during the night. In this way, the operation does not compete for computer resources with the SQL commands that are recording individual transactions.

The design of the parts of a database used to store point-in-time aggregate data is, at least in principle, simpler that the design of C-tables (used to store aggregated transactional data in a way that allows users to perform after-the-fact analysis of business activity). However, there are various practices used in the design of the "balance" tables that may seem puzzling when you first encounter them. These aspects of the database design are often interwoven with a certain way of designing the parts of the database used to store the raw transaction-history. These design features become necessary because of the need to store both an up-to-the-minute "current balance" and a balance for a specific time each day, combined with the need to take account of exactly how the company's daily or weekly transaction processing cycles are executed. This will be illustrated in the following example.

Storing Bank Balances

For this example we will look at how a bank might store balance information for the checking accounts of its customers. This example shows very small extracts of the contents of four tables − two "balance" tables and two transaction-history tables. These extracts include rows of data for only four accounts. (In practice there would be hundreds of thousands, or even millions, of accounts.) To further simplify the example, I will show data for only three days − January 4 to January 6. In practice there would be data covering several months stored in these tables. (Data older than this would be moved to some form of off-line archive, where data would be stored on magnetic tapes or discs.)

In this example we are going to look at the rows of data that are added to the four tables between 2008-01-04 and 2008-01-06. We start by examining the contents of the two "balance" tables during the early hours of the morning on January 4, after the bank has run its nightly processing cycle for business conducted the day before. (We will look at the two transaction-history tables in a moment.) For simplicity, I have assumed that the nightly processing cycle starts at exactly midnight and ends at exactly 2 a.m. (In practice, the time taken each night to complete nightly processing would vary.) After nightly processing ends at 2 a.m., the contents of the two "balance" tables might look like the following.

Table name: nightly_balance		
account_ number	updated	nightly_ balance
23456700001	2008-01-04 02:00:00	1272.95
23456700002	2008-01-04 02:00:00	528.55
23456700003	2008-01-04 02:00:00	3826.04
23456700004	2008-01-04 02:00:00	-69.22

Table name: memo_balance		
account_ number	updated	memo_ balance
23456700001	2008-01-04 02:00:00	1272.95
23456700002	2008-01-04 02:00:00	528.55
23456700003	2008-01-04 02:00:00	3826.04
23456700004	2008-01-04 02:00:00	-69.22

At this point in time the contents of the two tables are the same. We regard the "nightly_balance" table as holding the "master" version of the balance of each of the four accounts that we are looking at in this example, as at the completion of nightly processing (at 2 a.m.). The "memo_balance" table contains a copy of the information taken from "nightly_balance" at that point in time (2 a.m.).

Suppose that, in the next 22 hours, only one transaction occurs for these four accounts, as follows:

- On January 4, at about 5:32 p.m., the customer whose account number is 23456700001 withdraws $200 in cash at a cash machine.

If we look at the database just before nightly processing for June 4 is started, we will find this transaction has resulted in two changed rows in the database. (We are now looking at all four tables that are involved in recording transactions and balances.)

Table name: nightly_balance		
account_ number	updated	nightly_ balance
23456700001	2008-01-04 02:00:00	1272.95
23456700002	2008-01-04 02:00:00	528.55
23456700003	2008-01-04 02:00:00	3826.04
23456700004	2008-01-04 02:00:00	-69.22

Table name: memo_balance		
account_ number	updated	memo_ balance
23456700001	2008-01-04 17:32:09	1072.95
23456700002	2008-01-04 02:00:00	528.55
23456700003	2008-01-04 02:00:00	3826.04
23456700004	2008-01-04 02:00:00	-69.22

Table name: transaction_journal				
account_ number	transaction_ datetime	amount	transaction_detail_1	transaction_detail_2

Table name: transaction_journal_intraday				
account_ number	transaction_ datetime	amount	transaction_detail_1	transaction_detail_2
23456700001	2008-01-04 17:32:09	-200.00	CASH OUT	MACHINE 01599

The third and fourth tables are transaction-history tables, often referred to in the financial services industry as **transaction journals**, or **TJs** for short. (The term "journal" is commonly used in accounting and financial services to mean "a record of events or transactions, in time order, at the finest level of detail".)

I have shown the "transaction_journal" table as empty because, in this example, I am ignoring all rows with dates prior to January 4 and all rows relating to accounts other than these four accounts.

In spite of the $200 cash withdrawal having taken place during the day, no rows have been added to, or updated in, either the "nightly_balance" table or the "transaction_journal" table. However, the transaction has resulted in changes being made in the two other tables – the "memo_balance" table and the "transaction_history_intraday" table. A row has been added to the "transaction_history_intraday" table, recording the $200 transaction. Also, the row in "memo_balance" for account 23456700001 has been updated, showing the balance reduced by the amount of the withdrawal (from $1272.95 down to $1072.95).

At midnight, nightly processing for the business day January 4 is started. We will suppose that a check for $1,000.00 has been written against account number 23456700003 and presented to the bank for payment. We will assume that checks are cleared as part of nightly processing; they are not processed during the day. At 2 a.m., after processing has been completed, the tables will look like this:

Table name: **nightly_balance**

account_ number	updated	nightly_ balance
23456700001	2008-01-04 02:00:00	1272.95
23456700002	2008-01-04 02:00:00	528.55
23456700003	2008-01-04 02:00:00	3826.04
23456700004	2008-01-04 02:00:00	-69.22
23456700001	2008-01-05 02:00:00	1072.95
23456700002	2008-01-05 02:00:00	528.55
23456700003	2008-01-05 02:00:00	2826.04
23456700004	2008-01-05 02:00:00	-69.22

Table name: **memo_balance**

account_ number	updated	memo_ balance
23456700001	2008-01-05 02:00:00	1072.95
23456700002	2008-01-05 02:00:00	528.55
23456700003	2008-01-05 02:00:00	2826.04
23456700004	2008-01-05 02:00:00	-69.22

Table name: **transaction_journal**

account_ number	transaction_datetime	amount	transaction_detail_1	transaction_detail_2
23456700001	2008-01-04 17:32:09	-200.00	CASH OUT	MACHINE 01599
23456700003	2008-01-05 02:00:00	-1000.00	CHECK	CHECK NUMBER 1588

Table name: **transaction_journal_intraday**

account_ number	transaction_datetime	amount	transaction_detail_1	transaction_detail_2

Examining the contents of the tables above, we find that the following changes have occurred:

- Four rows have been added to "nightly_balance" showing the balances of each account as at the end of nightly processing. (The rows from the day before remain in the table.) Two of these "new" balances are the same as twenty-four hours earlier; but the balance of account 23456700001 has been reduced by $200 because of the cash withdrawal; and the balance of account 23456700003 has been reduced by the amount of the $1,000 check that was cleared during nightly processing.

- The single transaction that had been recorded in "transaction_journal_intraday" has been moved to "transaction_journal" and deleted from "transaction_journal_intraday".

- The check transaction for $1,000 has been added to the "transaction_journal" table. (It is added directly to that table during nightly processing, without appearing in the "transaction_journal_intraday" table.)

- The earlier contents of "memo_balance" have been deleted and replaced by copies of the four rows that were just added to "nightly_balance" (as you can see by the fact that the datetime values in "memo_balance" are now January 5, 2 a.m.).

Suppose that, in the next 22 hours, the following two transactions occur:

- On January 5, at about 12:20 p.m., the customer whose account number is 23456700002 withdraws $100 in cash from a cash machine.

- On January 5, at about 3:12 p.m., an automatic transfer of $500 is made into account 23456700004.

If we look at the database before nightly processing for the business day January 5 starts, we will find the following rows in the four tables:

Table name: nightly_balance

account_number	updated	nightly_balance
23456700001	2008-01-04 02:00:00	1272.95
23456700002	2008-01-04 02:00:00	528.55
23456700003	2008-01-04 02:00:00	3826.04
23456700004	2008-01-04 02:00:00	-69.22
23456700001	2008-01-05 02:00:00	1072.95
23456700002	2008-01-05 02:00:00	528.55
23456700003	2008-01-05 02:00:00	2826.04
23456700004	2008-01-05 02:00:00	-69.22

Table name: memo_balance

account_number	updated	memo_balance
23456700001	2008-01-05 02:00:00	1072.95
23456700002	2008-01-05 12:20:48	428.55
23456700003	2008-01-05 02:00:00	2826.04
23456700004	2008-01-05 15:12:33	430.78

Table name: transaction_journal

account_number	transaction_datetime	amount	transaction_detail_1	transaction_detail_2
23456700001	2008-01-04 17:32:09	-200.00	CASH OUT	MACHINE 01599
23456700003	2008-01-05 02:00:00	-1000.00	CHECK	CHECK NUMBER 1588

Table name: transaction_journal_intraday

account_number	transaction_datetime	amount	transaction_detail_1	transaction_detail_2
23456700002	2008-01-05 12:20:48	-100.00	CASH OUT	MACHINE 01382
23456700004	2008-01-05 15:12:33	500.00	TRANSFER IN	INTERNET BANKING REF 18212

Two rows have been added to "transaction_history_intraday", recording the two transactions that took place during January 5. The rows in "memo_balance" for accounts 23456700002 and 23456700004 have been updated: the balance of account 23456700002 has been reduced by $100 and the balance of account

23456700004 has been increased by $500 – going from $69.22 overdrawn to $430.78 in credit.

At midnight, nightly processing for the business day January 5 is started. At 2 a.m., after processing has been completed, the tables will look like this:

Table name: nightly_balance

account_number	updated	nightly_balance
23456700001	2008-01-04 02:00:00	1272.95
23456700002	2008-01-04 02:00:00	528.55
23456700003	2008-01-04 02:00:00	3826.04
23456700004	2008-01-04 02:00:00	-69.22
23456700001	2008-01-05 02:00:00	1072.95
23456700002	2008-01-05 02:00:00	528.55
23456700003	2008-01-05 02:00:00	2826.04
23456700004	2008-01-05 02:00:00	-69.22
23456700001	2008-01-06 02:00:00	1072.95
23456700002	2008-01-06 02:00:00	428.55
23456700003	2008-01-06 02:00:00	2826.04
23456700004	2008-01-06 02:00:00	430.78

Table name: memo_balance

account_number	updated	memo_balance
23456700001	2008-01-06 02:00:00	1072.95
23456700002	2008-01-06 02:00:00	428.55
23456700003	2008-01-06 02:00:00	2826.04
23456700004	2008-01-06 02:00:00	430.78

Table name: transaction_journal

account_number	transaction_datetime	amount	transaction_detail_1	transaction_detail_2
23456700001	2008-01-04 17:32:09	-200.00	CASH OUT	MACHINE 01599
23456700003	2008-01-05 02:00:00	-1000.00	CHECK	CHECK NUMBER 1588
23456700002	2008-01-05 12:20:48	-100.00	CASH OUT	MACHINE 01382
23456700004	2008-01-05 15:12:33	500.00	TRANSFER IN	INTERNET BANKING REF 18212

Table name: transaction_journal_intraday

account_number	transaction_datetime	amount	transaction_detail_1	transaction_detail_2

The following changes have occurred during nightly processing:

- Four more rows have been added to "nightly_balance", showing the balances of each account as at the end of nightly processing. Two of these balances are the same as twenty-four hours earlier; but the balance of account 23456700002 has been reduced by the $100 cash withdrawal and the balance of account 23456700004 has been increased by $500 – from $69.22 overdrawn to $430.78 in credit.

- The two transactions that had been recorded in "transaction_journal_intraday" have now been moved to "transaction_journal" and deleted from "transaction_journal_intraday". (No checks were cleared against any of the four example accounts in this nightly processing cycle.)

- The contents of "memo_balance" have been deleted and replaced by copies of the rows just added to "nightly_balance" (as you can see by the fact that the datetime now shows 2 a.m. on January 6).

Points Illustrated by the Example

This example illustrates the following points about how point-in-time aggregate data is handled in this database design:

- Two tables are used to hold the balance information. One table (in this example, "nightly_balance") holds information about the balances as at specific, regular points in time – in this case at the end of nightly processing for each business day. This table can be thought of as the "authoritative" balance table. Another table (in this example, "memo_balance") holds information about the current balances – the balances right now. The datetimes that appear in this table are those of the most recent transactions for each account (if there have been any such transactions since the end of the last nightly processing), or the datetime for the end of nightly processing (if there have been no transactions since then).

- Two transaction-history tables are used. One table (in this example, "transaction_journal") holds transactions that have already been taken into account in arriving at the balances in the authoritative balance table. This table can be thought of as the "authoritative" transaction journal. The second transaction-history table (in this example, "transaction_journal_intraday") holds the real-time transactions (such as cash withdrawal) that occurred since the most recent rows were added to the authoritative balance table, up to the present time. This table can be thought of as the "pending" or "temporary" transaction journal.

- The rows that are added to the two "authoritative" tables ("nightly_balance" and "transaction_journal") do not change after they are added: they represent the unchangeable past. (In some databases there may be special situations where a past balance is updated during nightly processing to reflect the effect of a back-dated transaction. This is, in effect, a reworking of the nightly processing for that account. The back-dated transaction is added to the "transaction_journal" table and the balances in the "nightly_balance" table are updated for that account for the one or several nights between the back-value date and the current date.)

- During nightly processing (when processing is done to establish the authoritative baseline balances), the following things happen:
  - Transactions stored in the "temporary" transaction journal are aggregated by account and the results are added to the most recent baseline balances taken from the authoritative balance table. In addition, any transactions that are not processed in real time, but which are recorded as part of the nightly processing (for example, the clearing of checks), are also included in the aggregation of transactions. The result of aggregating all transactions and adding the totals to the baseline balances is a new set of rows. These rows are added to the authoritative balance table. (Existing rows remain unchanged.)

- At the same time, transactions stored in the temporary transaction journal ("transaction_journal_intraday") are copied into the authoritative transaction journal ("transaction_journal") and deleted from the temporary transaction table. Transactions (such as check transactions) that are not processed in real time are entered straight into the authoritative transaction journal.
- All rows in the current-balance table are deleted and replaced by copies of the rows just added to the authoritative balance table. In many cases the rows are replaced with rows that are exactly the same as the ones that were deleted, apart from the updated datetime. However, where non-real-time transactions have been processed during nightly processing, the balances in the current-balance table will differ from their earlier values by the amounts of such transactions.

Thus, the two authoritative tables have rows added to them only during the nightly processing cycle. Existing rows are never deleted from these tables (except when they are archived to off-line storage media). Specifically:

- The authoritative balance table accumulates rows as the new point-in-time baseline balances are added at each processing cycle.

- The transaction journal accumulates rows because every transaction that occurs is represented by another row.

By contrast, the temporary transaction journal is cleared out at each processing cycle, ready for the new business day; and the temporary balance table is cleared out and its earlier contents replaced by the new authoritative end-of-processing balances.

The Example Generalized

If you have not worked with systems used for banking, brokerage, or inventory management, you may wonder why the design has to be this complex. The complexity of the design comes from the fact that, in the real world, (a) "current balances" are never as accurate as we might like them to be, and (b) companies typically need to record reliable "snapshots" of the balances at certain fixed points in time. These point-in-time "snapshots" are needed in order to:

- Provide reliable reference points for the preparation of statements and reports; and

- Make it easy to reconcile the changes in balances that have occurred, between two points in time, with the transactions that have occurred within that period. (This would be difficult if the snapshots were taken at irregular intervals, or not taken at frequent-enough intervals.)

There are many different reasons why a "current balance" may not be completely accurate. In the above example, the clearing of a check represents an event that is not reflected in the current balance because it is not recognized in the database until nightly processing is completed. Suppose that a customer has issued a check for $1,000 and has $1,100 is his account. Before the check has been cleared, that customer goes to withdraw $200 at a cash machine. The balance of the account is notionally only $100; and so the cash withdrawal should, ideally, not be allowed. In practice, the memo balance will not reflect the un-cleared check: the cash withdrawal will be allowed and, as a result of the account then containing only $900, the check may bounce. The current balance of $1,100, at the time the customer withdrew the cash, was therefore "inaccurate", in that it did not reflect the check that had not yet been cleared.

Another example of an inaccurate current balance is in a stock-inventory database. The "current stock level" table may record that there are 12 red stapling machines in stock. Two salespersons may each accept an order for 6 red stapling machines. As the salespersons enter these orders on their workstations, the "current stock level" will be reduced from 12 to 6 and then from 6 to 0. However, when the packer is assembling the first order, he may find that one of the stapling machines is damaged. He will enter an adjusting entry on his workstation and this will reduce the stock level to –1, meaning that there are only 5 items in stock and an outstanding commitment to ship 6 items. He will not now be able to assemble the second order. He will call the second salesperson to tell him the bad news. The second salesperson will then have to call the customer back and apologize for the fact that he was wrong when he said that he could ship six red stapling machines right away. The "current stock level" in the database was inaccurate in this case because nobody knew that one of the red stapling machines was damaged.

Because of situations like this, current balances are therefore generally regarded as good enough to support day-to-day business processes (such as approving cash withdrawals and promising immediate shipment of goods), but not completely reliable. This is why, in a bank's database, the potentially-inaccurate "current balance" (often called a "memo balance") is overwritten with the authoritative nightly-processing balance after nightly processing has been carried out. The authoritative balance takes account of transactions that were not recorded in real time.

In a situation where the database represents a physical situation, such as the level of stock held in a warehouse, the current balance is brought into line with the real world by means of "adjustment" transactions. These represent events that were not recorded in real time (such as an item being damaged) and unobserved events (such as stock theft). The adjustments may be made when someone comes across a damaged stock item or a smaller number of stock items than are needed to fill an order; or adjustments may be made during a periodic stocktaking.

In the example of the bank balances, a single type of authoritative balance ("nightly_balance") was recorded for each account. In many practical database designs there may be two or more separate balance-recording tables, holding similar information but with a different frequency of balance calculation. For example, there may be additional tables that hold only "end_of_month_balance" information and "end_of_year_balance" information. The rows in these tables are copies of particular rows in the "nightly_balance" table. Such additional tables make it easier for users to perform certain after-the-fact-analysis queries, for example, queries to generate reports showing how the total funds in a group of accounts at the end of each month has changed during the year. Having the additional tables in the database also allows the more-detailed information (contained in "nightly_balance" and "transaction_journal") to be archived and taken out of the on-line database. The less-detailed information that is retained in the database can be used in answering customers' questions about their accounts and for queries that analyze long-term trends across groups of customers.

Account-Value Tables

Another type of "balance" table that you may come across in practical database designs is not really a balance table at all; rather, it is a "account value" table. For example, the database design for a brokerage will typically include tables whose "balance" column actually contains a single number representing the total funds that would have been received if all the securities in the customer's account had been sold at the end-of-trading-day prices on the last trading day of the month. The "account value" numbers that are inserted into this column represent the results of multiplying the numbers of each security held in an account at that point in time with the closing prices for each security on that day, and then totaling the results. Such numbers typically appear on the monthly statements sent to customers, in the form of entries showing "Account Value Last Month" and "Account Value This Month". This serves the purpose of showing the customer how much his or her investments have increased or decreased in value during the month just ended. However, the numbers do *not* represent a balance in the normal sense. By themselves, they do not contain enough information to allow us to calculate the balance at a later date (by aggregating subsequent transactions and adding the result to those numbers).

In general, "account value" tables record hypothetical events that did not actually happen, for example, the results of every customer selling all their stocks just before the market closed on the last trading day of the month, or a company selling every item of stock that it holds at list prices on the last business day of the month. They bring together a set of point-in-time aggregate data, representing balances, with a set of market prices at that point in time. In order to calculate such account values, it is important to include, in the database design, a table that records a "snapshot" of the appropriate prices (market prices or list prices) for the same points in time for which the balances are recorded.

Care must be taken in writing the SQL commands used to calculate "account value" information and insert this information into "account value" tables. Care is needed because the datetimes in the "market_prices_history" table will probably not exactly match the datetimes in the "nightly_balance" table that they need to be matched with. For example, the appropriate rows from the "market_prices_history" table may be those with a datetime of 4 p.m. of the last trading day of the month (the time at which the market closed), whereas the appropriate rows from the "nightly_balance" table may have a datetime of 2 a.m. the next day; or, depending on how many days it takes to settle the trades done on the last trading day, several days later. For this reason, it may be necessary to have two datetime columns in a balance table – one to record the datetime at which the balance was actually calculated, and one to record the "as of" datetime. The latter could be the date and time that the market closed for the day for which the "balance" represents the result of having settled all the trades done that day.

For example, if it takes two days to settle trades, and nightly processing is done between midnight and 2 a.m., the balance information entered into the "nightly_balance" table at 2 a.m. on Friday morning would have an actual datetime of 2 a.m. Friday (stored in one column) together with an "as of" datetime of 4 p.m. Tuesday (stored in another column) – indicating that the balance takes account of the effects of trades only up until this "as of" time: any trades done during the Wednesday and Thursday trading days will not have been settled by the time that the Thursday night processing cycle starts.)

Summary

Point-in-time aggregate data is a lot easier to comprehend than time-period aggregate data, because it generally represents something that we are familiar with (like a bank balance). However, the details of practical database designs for storing point-in-time aggregate data take some getting used to. It is common to encounter more than one "balance" table in a database design – because database designs incorporate the idea of "authoritative" tables for balances and transactions as of, and up to, a specific "time of record" each day, plus separate "temporary" or "memo" tables that hold real-time balances and records of transactions that have taken place since the last "time of record".

In many industries, balances consist of not just single quantities, like dollars in an account, but rather of the quantities of several different entities (such as different stocks or different products). In such cases the balance tables have columns for the key attributes of these entities, as well as for the quantities of those entities that represent the balance – in addition to the datetime as of which the balance was calculated and other columns that represent the entities that hold or contain the balances – for example, accounts (represented by the attribute "account_id") or warehouses (represented by the attribute "warehouse_id").

Tables that represent "account *value*" or "stock *value*" should not be confused with true balances. A value is typically the result of multiplying some sort of calculated balance (as of a certain date) by the market price or sales price of the items in question (at that point in time). Such a value is notional – in that the items in question were not actually sold at that point in time and may have a different by the time they are actually sold.

CHAPTER 13

TEMPORAL DATABASES

The Story of Relational Databases, continued

In the last six chapters I have described a number of practices that are widely used in the business world to represent time in relational databases. They address, in a pragmatic way, the various problems that arise in representing time. In this chapter I will continue with the story of the development of database concepts and products from where I left off at the end of Chapter 4. To start with I will look at a body of research work that was started in 1982 and is still going on today – although the ideas it produced became fairly concrete around 1994. In the next chapter, I will look at a somewhat different set of developments that occurred during the 1990s – developments that represent another approach to one aspect of "the time problem". These developments started outside the field of relational databases, but are now starting to converge with relational database practices.

In this chapter I will also attempt to answer a question that may have occurred to you while you were reading the last five chapters, namely: Why are these pragmatic approaches and techniques for representing time in relational database designs widely practiced in the real world of database design but rarely covered by textbooks and courses on relational databases?

University Research from 1982 onwards

In the early 1980s, when practical relational DBMSs were still evolving, people doing research in universities on databases started to think about, and worry about, the representation of time in relational databases from a theoretical point of view. Meanwhile, as relational databases started to be used in commercial applications, database designers encountered the various time-related problems that were being studied in universities. They developed their own solutions to these problems (within the constraints of the relational database model and the syntax of SQL). Although there was some exchange of ideas between the hands-on database designers and the researchers, the two efforts to tackle "the time problem" were largely independent of one another. Most of the energy of academic research on this subject, from about 1982 onwards, came to be focused on re-thinking Codd's relational model. The research concentrated on finding a solution to the problem *within the DBMS itself*, rather than on defining practices and rules for the hands-on database designers to follow when making the best of existing relational DBMS products.

A Quick Re-cap of the Time Problem

Before looking at what emerged from the academic research, it may be useful at this point to summarize "the time problem" (or perhaps, more accurately, the several time problems), as brought out in the various examples in the previous chapters:

(1) Codd's relational database model, in common with earlier models, was based mainly on the idea of storing data about the world as it is in the present. Chen's Entity-Relationship data modeling technique was presented, and used, in a way that reinforced this focus on the present. As a result, a relational database design, based on a "textbook" approach, will make no provision for the retention of data about the past. Such data will be overwritten or deleted as the information in the database is kept up to date.

(2) Nevertheless, there is nothing in the relational database model, nor in the Entity-Relationship model, to rule out a database design that retains data about the past. The following are ways in which provision is made in practical database designs for the recording of data about the past. However, these methods bring out shortcomings in the E-R modeling process, the normalization process, and SQL:

    (a) In some cases we can represent information about the past via relationships. Starting at the Entity-Relationship modeling stage, we can add supplementary relationships that operate "in parallel" with the present-time relationships (that is, they operate between the same pairs of entities as the present-time relationships). For example, for the entities *student* and *course*, we can add a relationship *student has completed course*, which operates in parallel with *student is enrolled in course*. The new "historical" relationship's attributes can be different from those of the present-time relationship. For example, *has completed* has the attribute "grade", which *is enrolled in* does not. (As we saw earlier, when translated into a database design, *is enrolled in* becomes the table "enrollments", and *has completed* becomes the table "grades".)

        • *Shortcoming (as regards normalization):* When this approach is adopted, modification anomalies may arise in connection with the historical table, even when the database design rigorously follows standard normalization rules.

    (b) In other cases we can represent information about the past via transactional entities (such as *order* or *customer_call*) that have one or several datetime attributes.

        • *Shortcoming (as regards normalization):* When these entities are represented in the database design (for example, as tables like "orders" and "customer_calls"), we find that the tables sometimes give rise to modification anomalies, either directly or indirectly, even when the database design rigorously follows standard normalization rules.

    (c) If we want to record the history of the attributes of a particular entity, such as the past values of "price" for the entity *product*, we can include, in the database design, a table like "prices_history" that has columns for "valid from" and "valid to" datetime attributes.

        • *Shortcoming (as regards E-R modeling):* This arrangement is outside the scope of the Entity-Relationship model and so we cannot include it at the data modeling phase of designing the database: we have to tack it on at the end of the design process.

- *Shortcoming (as regards SQL):* Constructing queries that operate on such tables (in combination with other tables) results in very complex queries. These queries are hard to understand and therefore hard to debug.

(d) If we want to hold, in the database, the results of data-aggregating queries that are performed automatically on historical data at set intervals, we can place these results (such as "end-of-day account balance" or "annual sales by branch") in tables in the database. Users can then retrieve information from them as needed. Such tables typically include one or more datetime columns. These datetimes represent the point in time for which the query was performed, or the periods over which aggregation is performed.

- *Shortcoming (as regards E-R modeling):* The creation of such tables is outside the scope of the Entity-Relationship model and has to be tacked on at the end of the design process.

- *Shortcoming (as regards normalization):* In common with the raw historical tables from which they are derived, these tables are not protected from modification anomalies by following standard normalization rules.

- *Shortcoming (as regards SQL):* The queries required to populate aggregate-data tables with data, or to take data from these tables and combine it with data from present-time tables and other historical tables, are complex and hard to debug. SQL was clearly not designed with such queries in mind and is poorly matched to the job. (In fact, Codd made a statement to this effect in 1993.)

Temporal Databases

University research on "the time problem" grew out of concerns about the fact that the normalization rules for avoiding modification anomalies seemed to fail in the parts of a relational database that dealt with the past. In other words, the research tackled "the time problem" (as defined above), excluding the aggregate-date problem (item (d), above). Researchers who had spent a lot of time between 1970 and 1981 thinking about normalization were reluctant to question the principles of normalization that had evolved in that period, particularly Fagin's Domain/Key Normal Form (the holy grail of normalization, defined in 1981). They believed that it was somehow necessary to fix whatever was wrong with the relational model itself, so that the established rules of normalization could then be applied to all tables – rather than re-think normalization within the context of Codd's relational model.

One of the first database experts to examine this problem in depth was James Clifford, who was doing research on this subject at the State University of New York at Stony Brook. His Ph.D. thesis, *A logical framework for the temporal semantics and natural-language querying of historical databases*, was completed in 1982, at which time he joined New York University Business School, later becoming Associate Professor of Information Systems. Clifford continued to develop his ideas over the next thirteen years and helped to establish an international forum on "temporal databases". Sadly, Clifford died suddenly in 1995, just three weeks before he was to chair an international workshop on temporal databases in Zurich.

What Clifford and his colleagues wanted to achieve was a modified version of Codd's relational model that would be such that the user would not have to worry about creating historical tables in order to preserve the earlier values of data elements. Instead, the DBMS itself would preserve all the previous values of every data element. At the same time, the query language (SQL) would be extended to enable the user to specify the required versions of data elements (their present values or their earlier values) when doing a query.

What they came up with was the idea of replacing the two-dimensional tables in the standard relational model with three-dimensional tables or **data cubes** (sometimes also referred to as **time cubes**). The third dimension of these data cubes would be time. You can picture a data cube as follows:

- Imagine that one side of the cube is facing you and that this (the "front face") is a two-dimensional data table, as in the standard relational model, with rows and columns representing the world at the present time.

- Imagine that the depth of the cube is the time dimension.

- Imagine that earlier times are towards the back of the cube.

- Imagine that, behind the side of the cube that is facing you, there are many layers composed of earlier versions of the table that you can see facing you. Thus, if you were to slice off the side of the cube facing you (a thin enough slice to take just one layer of data), the cube that would remain would represent the entire history of the "present-time" version of the table that you have sliced off. The rear side of the cube (the one facing away from you) represents the initial state of the table when it was first created.

This picture is not a perfect analogy, but it will do.

Once Clifford and his colleagues started looking at the best way to record the history of a table, they decided that it would be a waste of storage space in the computer to add to the cube a complete new layer (corresponding to an entire table in the standard relational model) every time the value of a single cell changed. They therefore decided that, rather than build up the cube by adding new layers to the front face, they would add only the updated row to the front face of the cube. This approach makes the resulting "cube" somewhat more difficult to describe pictorially.

One way of picturing this cube is as follows. Imagine that you start with a sheet of paper to act as the back side of the cube. This has the starting values of the whole table printed on it. Each time that a single row is updated, imagine that the new values of the data in that row are written onto a very thin strip of paper. This strip is then glued onto a transparent sheet of plastic the same size as the original piece of paper. This transparent sheet is then added to the front of the cube. The result would be a cube composed mainly of transparent sheets. The data (the thin strips of paper) would be held in the appropriate layer of this cube, based on the date and time at which it was added. Looking at the front face of the cube, you would be able to see the complete present-time table: you would be able to see through the layers of transparent sheet and read the strips of paper that are the most recent (that is, are the nearest to you). To see the state of the table at some earlier point in time you would "cut" the cube at the appropriate layer and look at the front face. You would then see how the table looked when that layer was the front face of the cube.

To store such data cubes, the DBMS would need to contain a mechanism for tagging each newly added version of a row with a start-of-validity timestamp, showing when it was entered into the database. The DBMS would, simultaneously, add an end-of-validity timestamp to the prior version of the row. Thus, every historical row would carry with it a "valid from" and "valid to" timestamp, without the database user having to worry about this.

Various different arrangements for creating the timestamps were discussed. The simplest arrangement was to use the date and time at which the information was actually entered into the database. This came to be called **transaction time**. The second arrangement allowed the user to provide the time of occurrence of the real-world event (the event that led to the need to update the row in the table). This came to be known as **valid time**. A third arrangement allowed each version of a row to have both kinds of timestamp – transaction time and valid time – making a total of four timestamps attached to each historical row.

Turning next to the question of how queries can be performed on a database composed of data cubes, Clifford and his colleagues defined an extended version of SQL, called **TSQL**. TSQL makes a clear distinction between the traditional WHERE part of the query and the part of the query that concerns time. It does this using the new reserved word WHEN, in combination with the following additional new reserved words:

- Eight "temporal comparison operators" that allow conditions to be defined, in the WHEN clause, about the temporal relationship that must apply between the rows in one data cube and the rows in another data cube (in addition to the conditions specified in the WHERE clause). These eight new operators were:

BEFORE	PRECEDES	ADJACENT	DURING
AFTER	FOLLOWS	OVERLAP	EQUIVALENT

- Three "postfix operators". These are reserved words used to refer to an interval (a pair of "valid from" and "valid to" timestamps), or to a single timestamp, in a WHEN clause. In a TSQL command, these operators take the place of a normal column name. For example, for a data cube called "products", the three operators would be appended as follows:

products.INTERVAL	products.TIME-START	products.TIME-END

- A set of "postfix operator qualifiers" that can be added after ".TIME-START" or after ".TIME-END", in order to limit the comparison in the WHEN clause to just part of the timestamp. For example, using a data cube called "products", these qualifiers could be applied to the ".TIME-START" operator as follows:

products.TIME-START.DATE	(to ignore the time and consider only the date)
products.TIME-START.YEAR	(to consider only the year)
products.TIME-START.YEAR.MONTH	(to consider only the year+month)

A TSQL query, operating on a data cube version of the example of an Order and Invoice Management database that we looked at earlier, might look like the following:

```
SELECT
  orders.customer_id,
  order_details.order_number,
  order_details.quantity
FROM
  products,
  orders,
  order_details
WHERE
  (products.product_code = 'D12345' AND products.price = 10.50) AND
  (order_details.product_code = 'N9182R' AND orders.order_number =
order_details.order_number)
WHEN
  order_details.INTERVAL DURING products.INTERVAL
```

What this query says is, "Give me the Customer ID, Order Number, and Quantity for each instance of an order for the item whose product code is N9182R [the Pocket Protector] during the period (or periods) that D12345 [the red stapling machine] was priced at $10.50." This is a rather unlikely query, and not one that brings out the full power of the WHEN clause. However, I have chosen it because it is considerably easier to understand that many of the examples you will find in books and papers on temporal databases.

In executing this query, the DBMS will find the "intervals" (that is, the "valid from" and "valid to" datetimes) of the rows in the "products" data cube that have a "product_code" value of 'D12345' and a "price" value of $10.50. It will then look for rows in the "order_details" data cube whose intervals fall within any of these intervals and for which there is a value in the "product_code" column of 'N9182R'.

Note that it is *not* necessary for any red stapling machines to have been sold at a price of $10.50 for this query to work. The interval is defined with respect to the "products" data cube, which records the price at which the red stapling machine was offered for sale, regardless of whether any sales were made during this interval.

It should be noted that the retention, in a table, of rows that represent situations in the past, and the inclusion of "valid_from" and "valid_to" datetimes in these rows, can be pursued on a table-by-table basis within a standard relational database – as we saw earlier with the example of a "prices_history" table. In this case, the role of the WHEN clause would be played by standard SQL queries operating on the values in the "valid_from" and "valid_to" columns. What distinguishes the temporal database concept from such a practice is that the creation of the "valid from" and "valid to" timestamps is enforced by the DBMS for *all* tables, and is done in a manner that is controlled by the DBMS, without the user having to worry about it.

In order to illustrate the usefulness of a temporal database, Clifford and his colleagues chose examples in which the recording of time and the retention of historical data is important. The example of a University Administration database, widely used in books on standard relational databases, was therefore replaced by other examples in papers and books about temporal databases. One common example is a Human Resources database example, which records information about salaries, salary increases, who works for whom, employees' expense reports, and so on.

Rather than going through the example of the Human Resources database in detail, I will give a short summary of some of the TSQL queries that were illustrated in the various books and papers. This will provide an illustration of the kind of query that TSQL was designed to handle. Examples of these queries are as follows:

- Find the salary of Jones when Smith was his manager.

- Find the manager of Jones who immediately succeeded Smith.

- List the current salaries of all employees whose first manager was Smith.

- Find the period of time for which Jones worked under Smith.

- List the calendar years in which Jones made more foreign business trips than domestic business trips.

Although the ability to perform such queries is clearly useful, there are three points that become obvious if you study these TSQL examples:

- The TSQL queries are extremely hard to understand compared with normal SQL queries. It is hard to form a mental picture of the interplay between the WHERE conditions and the WHEN conditions.

- Even if you have a firm grasp on the interplay between the WHERE and WHEN conditions for a particular query, the "temporal operators" take a lot of getting used to: it takes a lot of thought to decide which operator a particular situation demands, particularly when choosing between OVERLAP, DURING, and EQUIVALENT.

- Although the examples of queries that can be performed using TSQL seem to show how powerful TSQL is in dealing with time, no example stands out as being a query that would be impossible, or even difficult, to do using SQL with a traditional (two-dimensional) database design – provided that the design included the right historical tables (such as "salary_history" and "manager_history"), and provided that these tables included "valid from" and "valid to" datetime columns. In fact, the equivalent SQL examples would, in most cases, be simpler to construct, and easier to understand, than their TSQL counterparts.

Following the definition of TSQL and the operating principles of a data cube-based database, Clifford and his colleagues continued to discuss and develop their ideas. One important point that was recognized early in the development of the data cube concept was that the "valid from" and "valid to" timestamps must be "required" data elements (that is, NOT NULL data elements). The DBMS must have the timestamps in order to be able to know the time order of the rows that form the data cube. However, requiring the timestamps to be NOT NULL gave rise to two problems:

- When the database is new, and data is entered for the first time, there may be no reliable record of when the initial data in a particular row was valid from. For example, we may know an employee's current salary; but the information about the date of his or her last salary increase may have been lost.

- Whenever a new row is added to a data cube, unless the entry represents something with a known end-of-validity date (like the term of a magazine subscription), there is no datetime value to put in the "valid to" column.

In order to satisfy the non-NULL requirement in these cases, four special "values" were defined. (These are not real datetimes, but rather placeholders that the DBMS understands.) The four are as follows:

- If transaction-time timestamps are used, any row for which there is no known "valid from" date will be assigned the special value INITITATION when the database is first populated.

- If valid-time timestamps are used, any row for which there is no known "valid from" date will be assigned the special value BEGINNING when the database is first populated.

- When a new row is added to a data cube and there is no explicit "valid to" datetime to be entered, in both the transaction-time and valid-time cases the standard value assigned to the "valid to" timestamp is NOW. The value NOW means "this is a new row that is valid whenever you look at it, but it can be superseded by a newer row at any time".

- Exceptionally, for valid-time timestamps, when a new row is added, and it is known that the row represents a perpetual situation, the special value FOREVER can be used for the "valid to" timestamp. (This value is not allowed for a transaction-time timestamp.) The value FOREVER might be used, for example, when someone has been granted a lifetime membership or subscription to something. Once a row has such a timestamp, the DBMS will prevent the row ever being superseded. Exactly what happens if the database user changes his or her mind about the FOREVER arrangement is not clear. (What if a subscriber, who has paid for a lifetime subscription, dies?)

The various new features of TSQL (relative to traditional SQL), such as the interplay of WHERE and WHEN, the temporal comparison operators, and the required special timestamp values like BEGINNING, make TSQL much harder to learn than SQL. They clearly increase the amount of training and practice needed before the DBMS can be used without the user making a lot of mistakes. This applies both to programmers who are writing programs that manage interaction with the database for less skilled end users, and to skilled end users who interact directly with the DBMS.

Another drawback of a temporal DBMS is that it takes the retention of data that represents past situations out of the hands of the user. This means that tables for which the past contents of the rows are of no possible interest to any user will needlessly retain their entire history, thus cluttering up the database with unneeded data. By contrast, the pragmatic approach of holding past values selectively, as in the example of the "prices_history" table, gives the database designer control over the extent to which data about the past is retained.

The Development of Temporal DBMS Products

As background to what follows, we will first review what happened between 1961 and the mid-1980s and how this predisposed the database software industry to take new database concepts very seriously.

The idea of computer databases was originated in 1961 by Charles Bachmann at General Electric. General Electric's first DBMS product was called "IDS" (short for "Integrated Data Store"). But, although General Electric pioneered computer databases, by the late-1960s IBM had taken over the leadership of database development and DBMS sales to the business world. When Codd, who was working for IBM, published his paper on relational databases in 1970, the general view was that IBM's leadership position in DBMS products was unassailable and that IBM would continue to be the leader in DBMS products for many years to come.

Even though the idea of relational databases came out of IBM, senior managers at IBM did not at first recognize the importance of the idea and its potential to transform the database software business. Nevertheless, Codd and his colleagues were allowed to start work on the development of a relational DBMS. This work led (after some earlier products) to the important relational DBMS product SQL/DS; and this in turn eventually evolved into DB2. However, this line of development got off to a slower start than relational database development elsewhere. It was a government-funded effort at the University of California at Berkeley that really launched the relational database concept and gave it the intellectual legitimacy required for broad acceptance and commercialization. This work spawned a number of start-up companies, such as Ingres and Oracle, who were faster to react to Codd's paper than IBM. As a result, although IBM's DB2 is a leading DBMS product today, the other vendors (including Oracle and Microsoft) collectively hold about two-thirds of the relational DBMS market share – a situation that would have been unthinkable in 1970.

This transformation of the database software business, as a result of Codd's paper, made everyone in the business acutely aware of the potential for yet another new idea to change the fortunes of DBMS vendors. So, when the work of Clifford and his colleagues started to be published and discussed, most of the vendors paid attention. A number of projects were started in order to explore the temporal database concept and to try to build a working temporal DBMS (or **TDBMS** for short).

So, where are these TDBMSs today? The short version of the progress report on the various efforts to build a TDBMS is, "Gosh, this is harder than we thought". There is no full-function TDBMS on the market today. All that remains of the various efforts to build a TDBMS are:

- A number of experimental pieces of software that act as a "temporal front-end" to a standard relational DBMS. What this software does is to translate queries in one of the temporal query languages (such as TSQL, TSQL2, or ChronoSQL) into standard SQL, operating on two-dimensional tables to which timestamp columns have been added. These pieces of software are really *a demonstration of TSQL*, not a real TDBMS.

- A product called "TimeCube", developed by Beacon IT in Japan, which claims to be an implementation of the TDBMS concept. However, if you read the small print in the product description, you will find that the product "does not support joins" (between data cubes). All you can do with TimeCube is perform queries on one cube at a time. You would find this a fairly major shortcoming if you were hoping to build a temporal database!

Beacon IT should be commended for sticking to their goal of building a TDBMS, even though they have not yet reached it. By contrast, other vendors appear to have given up. Confusingly, some vendors appear to have re-purposed the incomplete results of their work on trying to build a TDBMS as a DBMS product optimized for handling time-series data, retaining the term "data cube" for marketing purposes. In fact, the term appears to have been hijacked by the vendors of this somewhat different class of database (which I will describe in the next chapter).

Summary

University research on solving "the time problem" of relational databases has focused on searching for a solution *within the DBMS itself and within the associated query language*. As a result, little academic research has been done on cataloging, analyzing, and formalizing the various pragmatic solutions for handling time in database designs that have emerged in various industries; and so little attention is paid to such solutions in most textbooks. (I hope that this book goes some way toward remedying this situation.)

There are two significant outcomes from the academic research on temporal databases described in this chapter:

(a) Although the work is, in itself, very interesting, and brings out a lot of important ideas, you cannot go out and buy a full-function TDBMSs – at least not yet. So, whatever problems a TDBMS might have solved for you, your only option today is to use the various pragmatic measures described in the previous chapters.

(b) Some of the terminology of temporal databases, in particular the term "data cube", has been imported into the field of DBMSs designed for handling large volumes of transactional data and supporting complex aggregate data queries. This leads to the potential for confusion when vendors, database designers, and university researchers try to talk to one another about "the time problem" and its solutions.

CHAPTER 14

THE WORLD ACCORDING TO OLAP

Introduction

As mentioned at the end of the last chapter, attempts to implement the concept of a temporal database, as defined by Clifford and colleagues, have not, so far, resulted in a practical TDBMS. However, what did emerge in the 1990s (partly as a result of re-purposed attempts to build a TDBMS, but mainly from attempts to address relational database performance problems) was a series of products designed specifically for the field of high-volume time-series data storage and analysis. Some of these products were created by revamping old, pre-relational DBMSs.

In this chapter I will give a brief overview of how these products differ from standard relational databases. (I am not going to describe particular products. They are adequately covered in other documents, particularly their vendors' marketing materials.) Then I will explore how we can understand some of their characteristics in terms of the pragmatic approaches to dealing with time in relational database designs that we looked at in Chapters 7 to 11.

The Emergence of OLAP

The products and activities that I am going to look at in this chapter belong to a general field of information technology, which, for simplicity, I will refer to generically as **OLAP**. The OLAP field encompasses all activities and products described using the terms **On-Line Analytical Processing** (OLAP), **Data Warehousing**, **Multidimensional Databases**, **Data Mining**, **Business Intelligence**, and **Executive Information Systems** (EISs). The OLAP field emerged in the 1990s as a result of efforts to address the growing demand for after-the-fact analysis of large volumes of transactional data in order to support business decisions. Executives in some companies had found that, when they asked their IT departments to produce reports based on analyses of the transactional information stored in relational databases, the IT departments told them that the queries put such a heavy load on the relational DBMSs that the reports could be run only during the night – not on-demand as some of them wanted. In some cases the IT departments said that the reports could not be run at all. This was because, if the report-generation process were started after the end of business hours, it would not be completed in time for the start of business the next day. Word soon spread that "relational DBMSs are no good for OLAP".

The perception that relational DBMSs are no good for OLAP was seen by a number of vendors as an opportunity to create and sell a different type of DBMS, optimized for OLAP. Such new products would not replace relational DBMSs but would co-exist with them. They were designed to periodically extract, from the relational databases, copies of most of the transactional data, and snapshots of critical non-transactional data. This might happen every night, or perhaps once a week. These OLAP products were launched in the early 1990s and became popular by the mid-1990s.

The perception that relational DBMSs are no good for OLAP was reinforced by the marketing departments of the companies that were trying to sell these new products. It persists in many quarters today. However, this perception was a gross over-simplification of a complex situation:

- First, the queries being used to do OLAP on relational DBMSs operated on many tables. (In the jargon of relational algebra, they involved many table "joins".) This was because the database designers had applied the standard normalization rules to the design of historical tables. They had not realized that, as described in earlier chapters, this would fail to prevent modification anomalies occurring. Also, they had not realized that going against the standard normalization rules, and creating self-contained historical tables, would actually prevent modification anomalies, while also allowing queries directed at historical data to be performed on a smaller number of tables – in some cases on a single table.

- Second, given that OLAP queries were being directed at several tables (in some cases six or more), the queries were exposing weaknesses in the query optimizers in the relational DBMSs of the late 1980s and early 1990s. Query optimizers take users' SQL queries and translate them into specific operational steps (hidden from the user) that are performed on the tables in order to get the required result. The query optimizers of that time were written to cope with queries involving one, two, or three tables. They were not sophisticated enough to optimize the multiple-table queries used in OLAP. As a result, the execution of these queries consumed a lot of processing power.

- Third, even in the absence of the above two considerations, the processing of large amounts of data inevitably places heavy demands on the resources of the computer on which the DBMS is running. The volumes of transactional data that were being analyzed in many "OLAP" queries were so large that even the older, non-relational DBMSs would have slowed to a crawl in processing similar queries.

Nevertheless, the marketing departments of the vendors of most OLAP products chose to describe their products as having, at their center, a DBMS of fundamentally different design to a standard relational DBMS. They claimed that this non-relational design addressed the perceived shortcomings of relational DBMSs when it came to handling queries involving after-the-fact analysis of large volumes of transactional data. The design of these DBMSs was often described as "multidimensional". (This should be regarded as more a marketing term than a well-defined class of DBMS, as I will explain later.)

The Impact of Improved Technology

By the late 1990s, all of the issues that had led to the initial perception of relational DBMS as being "no good for OLAP" had been addressed:

- More powerful hardware platforms were available at much lower prices. Companies started to buy hardware that was a lot more powerful on which to run databases of all kinds, including those used for OLAP-type queries.

- Some (but not all) database designers had started to include self-contained historical tables in their database designs, thus reducing the number of tables that need to be operated on in a data-aggregation query.

- The leading relational DBMS vendors of the 1990s, such as Oracle and IBM, had greatly improved their query optimizers, so that their DBMSs could optimize queries involving a greater number of tables.

As a result of these technology improvements, some OLAP software vendors started to turn to relational DBMSs as the foundation of their OLAP applications. However, they continued to promote the practice, established in the early days of OLAP, of keeping these databases separate from the main operational databases from which their contents were extracted. This was done for the following reasons:

- First, the products in the OLAP field had evolved considerably since they first appeared on the market. An important part of most OLAP products is a software module that performs data extraction and transformation. This software (nowadays referred to Extract-Transform-Load software, or "ETL" for short) allows a central OLAP database to import data from several operational databases in different parts of a company or consortium. The software does this by periodically extracting copies of the data and rendering the extracted data in a common format, and according to a common set of rules (for example, reconciling the fact that one source uses 'Male' and 'Female' but another uses 'M' and 'F'), before inserting it into the central OLAP database. This makes it possible for the data from the different sources to be brought together without inconsistencies and clashes arising.

- Second, the products also included querying tools that are useful in performing the types of queries that most users want to perform against these databases. In particular, many products had sophisticated Graphical User Interfaces (GUIs) that are much better for OLAP-type queries than standard SQL or SQL-based query tools.

- Third, the vendors of these products, having established a market for their products, were not going to surrender that market to anyone else without a fight.

There is now a well-established trend towards basing OLAP products on relational DBMSs. Such OLAP systems, consisting of querying tools, data extraction and mapping tools, and a standard relational DBMS, are referred to as **ROLAPs** (short for "relational-DBMS-based OLAPs"). The older systems, based on non-relational DBMSs, are now referred to as **MOLAPs** (short for "multidimensional-DBMS-based OLAPs").

With the move to basing OLAP systems on relational DBMSs, we would hope to see the well-established ideas and terminology of relational databases starting to be applied to the design of OLAP databases. This may well happen eventually; but exchange of ideas between the two fields has been limited.

Barriers to OLAP/Relational Re-Unification

In spite of the migration of OLAP systems from so-called multidimensional databases to standard relational databases, the OLAP field keeps its distance from the standard relational world. This separation is reinforced not only by OLAP product sales staff, but also by (a) differences in terminology, and (b) separatist sentiment among leading practitioners and experts in the OLAP field.

Examples of hostile feelings toward standard relational database ideas and solutions can be found in many OLAP textbooks. For instance, Chapter 1 of the well-known book on data warehousing, *The Data Warehouse Toolkit*, by Ralph Kimball, is thought-provokingly entitled "Two Different Worlds" and includes the following statement:

> *"Entity relation [sic] data models are a disaster for querying because they cannot be understood by users and they cannot be navigated usefully by DBMS software."*

Not only does this statement express gratuitous hostility towards the standard relational model, it also seems to reflect confusion, in the mind of the writer, between Chen's Entity-*Relationship* modeling process, standard relational database designs, and the SQL query language. Referring to Chen's model as an "entity relation" model also shows a lack of familiarity with the subject matter being attacked. (We might have given the writer the benefit of the doubt, and assumed that "entity relation" was a typographical error, had the error not appeared seven times in the chapter.)

This hostility towards the standard relational model is a great pity. The representation of time is a critical aspect of OLAP databases. Database designers from the two fields – OLAP databases and standard relational databases – could benefit from an exchange of ideas about the representation of time in database designs. Unfortunately, the use of special OLAP terminology by experts and salespeople in the OLAP field, reinforced by the promotion of hostility towards standard relational database ideas, gets in the way of such an exchange of ideas.

Understanding OLAP Terminology

I will now attempt to translate some of the concepts and terminology of the OLAP field into standard relational database concepts and terminology. I will start by simply summarizing, or paraphrasing, the textbook definitions of the most important OLAP terms. After that, I will attempt to provide translations and explanations. If you find the following definitions confusing, please bear with me. (They *are* confusing.)

- **Multidimensional**. The databases that were used, at least initially, as the core of OLAP systems, were described by their builders as "multidimensional" databases. This term was sometimes used to describe OLAP systems as a whole, that is, the DBMS plus the specific OLAP-oriented database designs. In other cases it was used as a description of only the underlying DBMS. The marketing materials of many OLAP software vendors portray "multidimensional" as the antithesis of "relational". However, as explained in Chapter 1, the term "relational" means "based on relations", that is, "based on tables". OLAP databases are based on tables too; so it is incorrect to say that they are "not relational". Since the internal workings of the DBMS were hidden from the user, all that distinguished MOLAPs (OLAP databases running on OLAP-oriented DBMSs) from standard relational databases was the different practices that were followed in designing the tables. However, now that the practices that were followed in designing the tables in MOLAPs have been carried over into ROLAPs, they can no longer be regarded as distinguishing characteristics of a "multidimensional" DBMS. The term "multidimensional" thus seems to lack any useful definition, other than "described as 'multidimensional' in the vendor's marketing materials".

- **Dimensional**. The practices followed in designing the tables in OLAP databases (including databases that run on "multidimensional" DBMSs and those based on standard relational DBMSs) are generally described as "dimensional", or sometimes "based on the dimensional model". In the dimensional model there are said to be two classes of data: "dimensions" and "facts". Aside from this statement, the dimensional model has little in the way of a formal definition.

- **Dimension**. A dimension is "an index by which you can access facts". Examples of dimensions are "customer", "product", and "distribution channel". In a dimensional database design, dimensions are represented as dimension tables.

- **Fact**. A fact is "an instance of an occurrence or event and the properties of that instance". Examples of facts are "sales fact" and "shipments fact". In a dimensional database design, facts are represented as fact tables.

- **Dimension tables**. Dimension tables hold "information about the dimensions of the business", in the form of values of a number of "dimensional attributes", such as "product_name", "SKU_number", "brand", "product_type", and "weight". (If you examine where the data inserted into dimension tables is imported from in the operational databases that feed the OLAP database, you will find that it is derived from entity-representing tables.)

- **Fact table**. Fact tables hold information about facts. This information takes the form of "numerical measurements", such as "units sold", "sales (in dollars)", and "profits". Fact tables are very large tables. Dimension tables are small by comparison, but there tend to be many more dimension tables than fact tables. (If you examine where the data inserted into fact tables is imported from in the operational databases that feed the OLAP database, you will find that it is derived mainly from transaction-history tables, and sometimes from aggregate-data tables.)

- **Dimensional hierarchies**. Some dimensions belong to dimensional hierarchies, such as the dimension "product→product_type→product_family". Dimensional hierarchies allow users to perform "drill-down" (to finer levels of detail) when looking at the results of analyses.

- **Slowly changing dimensions**. The contents of dimension tables are typically snapshots of the contents of tables in the operational databases. Sometimes the information in the operational databases changes. For example, customers may change their names, or the specifications of products may change. When new snapshots are taken, and the old contents of dimension tables are overwritten, mismatches may be created between historical data in the fact tables and the new information in the dimension tables. This problem can be avoided by either (a) retaining the old contents of the dimension tables and adding the new contents with a new value of the dimensional key, or (b) adding the new contents with the same dimensional key, while retaining the old contents, but tagging the old and new contents with "effective dates". One of the most commonly reported problems of this type is the distortion of past sales and sales-related results by the reorganization of sales teams, areas, and regions.

- **Star schema**. A star schema is the basic database design structure for an OLAP database. In a star schema, a fact table "sits in the middle of the schema" and is "radially connected" to the surrounding dimension tables, like a star.

Before we try to understand these definitions in terms of standard relational database terminology and concepts, I want to briefly mention one general point about the data in an OLAP database: from the user's point of view, all data is *read-only* data. In practical terms, this is because it is a copy of data, extracted from one or more operational databases. It is extracted for querying purposes only, never for updating. In addition, most of it was definitionally read-only *before* it was extracted, because it was already information about the past (that is, transaction-history data and aggregated transactional data). The small amount of data that was not already read-only before it was extracted is the data taken from tables that represent entities.

Now I will try to translate the above OLAP definitions into standard relational database ideas and terminology:

- When OLAP experts talk about "dimensions", they are talking about *entities that are commonly used as grouping entities in transactional data aggregation.* These are entities such as *customer, product, salesperson,* and *branch.* Dimension tables are extracts (from the operational databases) of the tables that represent these grouping entities. The attributes of a dimension are some, or all, of the columns of the entity-representing table in the operational database.

- When OLAP experts talk about "facts" and "fact tables", they are talking about one or more of the following:
  - Extracts of transaction-history tables from the operational databases.
  - Extracts of aggregate-data tables from the operational databases.
  - Tables of aggregate data, created within the OLAP database by performing aggregation on historical data extracted from the operational databases.

- When OLAP experts talk about the "numerical measurements" in "fact tables", they are talking about what I called the *data elements of interest* in data aggregation, such as unit sales, sales (in dollars), costs, profits, or number of calls to the Customer Service desk.

- When OLAP experts talk about "dimensional hierarchies", they are talking about *sets of nested grouping entities,* like the geographical set *branch→area→region→country.* The way that these hierarchies are represented in dimension tables is somewhat similar to the example I gave in Chapter 10, when describing nested grouping variables. In Chapter 10, I showed how these geographical entities could be represented by the tables "branches", "areas", "regions", and "countries". In an OLAP database, nested grouping entities like *branch→area→region→country* are similarly represented in sets of dimension tables.

- When OLAP experts talk about "slowly changing dimensions", they are talking about entities whose attributes change from time to time in a manner that gives rise to modification anomalies with respect to the contents of historical tables. (We saw this kind of anomaly in Chapter 7 with respect to the entity-representing "products" table. We saw what happened to a re-created invoice after the price of a product had changed and the price information in the "products" table no longer reflected the price at the time of the customer's order.) Any entity that is represented in an OLAP database as a "dimension" has the potential to give rise to this kind of anomaly.

- When OLAP experts talk about solutions to the slowing-changing-dimensions problem, based on retention of the old versions of the information in the dimension tables, together with "effective date" attributes, they are talking about the same techniques that we looked at in Chapter 8, in the example of the "prices_history" table – where "valid from" and "valid to" columns are included in the table. This is also the same concept that lies at the heart of TDBMSs. (Some OLAP textbooks refer to this approach for handling slowly changing dimensions as the "Type 3" approach.)

- When OLAP experts talk about a "star schema", they are simply observing that dimension tables can be associated with fact tables (by way of key attributes like "customer_id"), but dimension tables cannot be associated with one another. (They never have keys in common.) There is nothing remarkable or special about this aspect of the database design. It is the same design that can be found in a standard relational database design if you look only at the tables from which data is extracted by the OLAP system, that is, grouping-entity tables, transaction-history tables, and aggregate-data tables.

Thus, OLAP database design largely mimics design approaches that, by the early 1990s, had already started to appear within the field of standard relational databases (to handle the storage of transactional data and the storage of aggregate data). What made these approaches seem new, when OLAP databases started to appear on the market, was the new terminology of OLAP and the OLAP marketing materials.

It should be noted that the existence of the "slowly changing dimensions" problem in OLAP databases, and the fact that it becomes necessary to retain old values of dimensional information (for instance, using the "Type 3" approach), highlights the fact that the pragmatic solution to this basic time-related anomaly, as described in Chapter 7, is not utilized in the standard OLAP database design. In other words, OLAP database designers have not applied the technique of including as-it-was-then values for the attributes of entities in rows of transactional data.

The Representation of Time in OLAP Databases

There is one aspect of OLAP databases that I omitted from the earlier definitions of OLAP terms because I wanted to address it separately. This is the way that time is represented. In the OLAP field, *time is treated as a dimension*, just like "product". Although this idea might, at first sight, seem to have some kind of Einsteinian validity, stated like this (in the way it is commonly stated in OLAP textbooks), it is not only confusing but also wrong.

When OLAP experts talk about "time", what they really mean is "time periods", not time as a continuous variable, nor a point in time represented as a single datetime value. Also, they are not talking about time periods in general, but rather *time periods in the context of aggregate data*. Once we understand that this is what OLAP experts really mean by "time", the idea of representing time periods as "dimensions" (equivalent to entities) seems less alien. We saw in Chapter 11 that, in the context of aggregate data, it is possible to treat time periods as though there are "pseudo-entities", even though this is outside the scope of the Entity-Relationship model. This is exactly what is going on in an

OLAP database. Thus, a better way of stating how time is treated in an OLAP database is as follows:

In an OLAP database, strictly in the context of data aggregation, a collection of similar time periods, such as weeks, is treated as a pseudo-dimension.

We also saw that time periods can be said to form a set of nested pseudo-entities. So, describing the set of different time periods "days→weeks→months→quarters→years" as a "dimensional hierarchy" is something that is easily understood in standard relational database terms. A better way of talking about the dimensional hierarchy of time is therefore as follows:

In an OLAP database, strictly in the context of data aggregation, a set of nested time periods such as days→weeks→months→quarters→years is treated as a set of nested pseudo-dimensions.

Another characteristic of the way that time periods (and also other dimensions, such as "product" or "customer") are represented in an OLAP database is that there are no relationship-representing tables in the database design. Instead, a direct link is established between the dimension (entity) tables and the fact (aggregate-data) tables, by way of columns in the fact tables that correspond to the key attributes of the dimension tables. This is similar to the way that aggregate-data tables, like "unit_sales_multiperiod_multifactor_v3", were associated with the nested pseudo-entity tables "days", "weeks", "months", and so on, in Chapter 11. In the example of Chapter 11 we saw how the associations could be established by placing "day_id", "week_id", "month_id", "quarter_id", and "year_id" in the aggregate-data table. This is exactly the same arrangement used in an OLAP database. Each time period is assigned a key value (equivalent to the keys like "day_id" in our earlier example); and this key value associates the time period with appropriate "fact" (equivalent to a row in an aggregate-data table).

The Choice of Keys

There is one point on which OLAP database design practices genuinely differ from those used in most standard relational database designs, and it is worthwhile to examine it in some detail. This is the choice of the key attributes that are used to associate the contents of dimension tables with the contents of fact tables.

We saw in earlier chapters how the key attribute of an entity, such as "branch_code", can be included as a non-key column in a transaction-history table like "orders" in order to support data aggregation. The value of this key attribute thus ties "orders" (the contents of which would become part of an OLAP fact table) with the entity *branch* (which would be represented as an OLAP dimension table). However, this arrangement is not carried over into an OLAP database. This is because there is a significant risk that a key like "branch_code" will not be unique when data is extracted from several different operational databases and inserted into the OLAP database. For example, two different parts of the company may administer their own numbering schemes for various entity sets, such as branches, employees, products, and customers; and the values assigned in the different parts of the company may clash. There are various ways that this could be handled. One way would be to check for uniqueness of values when the data is being extracted from the operational databases, before insertion into the OLAP database. When clashes are detected they could be referred to an administrator, who would find a way of resolving them. Another way would be to add a prefix to the extracted values of the key attribute, identifying the source of the data. A third way – which is the one generally used in the OLAP field – is to programmatically generate a completely new artificial key. This artificial key becomes the key of the dimension table. The original key attribute of the entity (as used in the source database) is retained as a *non-key* attribute of the dimension.

After values for the artificial key have thus been assigned to the entries represented in the dimension tables, these key values are used to replace the values of the key attributes of entities (such as "customer_id" or "product_code") that appear in the transactional data that is imported into the fact tables.

Note that the values of these artificial keys are *for internal use within the OLAP database*, associating facts (that is, transactional data and aggregate data) with dimensions (that is, entities and time periods). These artificial keys need not, and ideally should not, appear in the results of users' queries. Where the real key attributes (such as "customer_id" or "product_code") are needed in OLAP reports, their *original* values are taken from the appropriate non-key columns of the dimension tables that hold these original values.

Summary

The practices followed in the design of OLAP databases were not really new when OLAP systems started to appear in the early 1990s. Very similar designs could be seen in standard relational databases. The existence of such OLAP-like designs becomes apparent in standard relational databases if you ignore the present-time parts of the database design and look only at the following tables:

- Transaction-history tables.

- Aggregate-data tables.

- Tables representing grouping entities (individual or nested).

- Tables representing time periods as pseudo-entities, for use as nested grouping entities.

The lack of novelty in the concepts underlying OLAP databases is camouflaged by the use of OLAP-specific terminology, much of which is poorly defined and inconsistently used. Nevertheless, a study of OLAP database design practices is informative. It underscores the usefulness of the practical database design techniques that we examined in Chapters 9 to 11, when looking at ways to facilitate queries directed at large volumes of aggregated transactional data in standard relational database designs.

The translations of OLAP terminology into standard relational-database terminology, presented in this chapter, are summarized in the table below.

OLAP Term	Translation
Dimensions	Grouping entities in transactional data aggregation.
Dimension tables	Entity-representing tables for entities that are used as grouping entities in transactional data aggregation.
Dimensional hierarchies	Sets of nested grouping entities (for example, *branch→area→region→country*).
Time (as a dimension)	Time periods, treated as pseudo-entities for the purpose of data aggregation.
Fact tables (and their contents, "facts")	Tables in an OLAP database containing extracts, from operational databases, of transaction-history tables and/or aggregate-data tables.
Numerical measurements in fact tables	Data elements of interest in data aggregation, for example, unit sales, sales (in dollars), and profits.
Slowly changing dimensions	The attributes of entities which may change and give rise to modification anomalies with respect to transaction-history tables (for example, the prices of products which change after orders have been fulfilled) – assuming that the historical tables do not include as-it-was-then values of these attributes.
Type 3 solution to the slowing-changing-dimensions problem	Keeping a record of the history of the values of an attribute of an entity, with "valid from "and "valid to" datetimes for each of its earlier values.
Star schema	A pictorial representation of the relationships between fact tables and dimension tables in an OLAP database. The "star" description recognizes that fact tables (at the hub of the "star") share keys with several dimension tables (which are viewed as "surrounding" that hub).
Multidimensional	Described as "multidimensional" in the vendor's marketing materials. (As explained in this chapter, no other useful translation is possible.)

CHAPTER 15

CUBESPEAK

Data Cubes

The various OLAP terms that I discussed in the last chapter may be confusing for someone who has been involved only in standard relational database design. They certainly take a bit of getting used to. However, on the whole they do not directly clash with the terminology of other disciplines. But when it comes to use of the term "data cube", or "cube", by the vendors of OLAP systems, there is much greater potential for confusion. The term "data cube", as we saw in Chapter 13, has a specific meaning for those who have worked on, or at least studied, the ideas underpinning temporal databases. However, the term has passed into the realm of OLAPs, and has taken on a different meaning. Typical definitions of data cubes in books and papers on OLAP systems can be paraphrased as follows: "A cube is a three-dimensional view of data with a dimension forming each side of the cube. A dimension is a structural attribute of a cube, that is, a list of members, all of which are of a similar type in the user's perception of the data. Typical dimensions for a human resources cube are time, jobs, and components."

This definition clearly refers to something very different from the term "data cube" as used in the context of temporal databases. In a temporal database, one dimension is always time and the other two are simply the rows and columns of a single table that represents one entity or one relationship.

In some vendors' marketing materials the term "hypercube" also appears, but this seems to be used as a synonym for "data cube".

Cubes According to Microsoft

Another, rather different, use of the term "cube" has been has been promulgated by Microsoft. Hearing that "cube" was a big thing in the OLAP field, Microsoft decided that their relational DBMS (Microsoft SQL Server) needed to have a CUBE function. What they did was to add a feature to their product that implements a new argument for the SQL function GROUP BY. When used in conjunction with aggregation functions like SUM(), AVG(), and MAX() in the SELECT clause, the new CUBE argument causes the query to create a C-table. This saves the user a great deal of trouble. *It reduces, to a single step, the several steps required to create a C-table using standard SQL.*

The CUBE function was added to Microsoft SQL Server at version 6.5, in April 1996. Microsoft subsequently submitted the feature to the ANSI SQL Committee (which controls the official definition of the SQL query language) for incorporation in standard SQL. Other vendors have since incorporated the CUBE function into their DBMS products.

The syntax for CUBE is best illustrated by revisiting the example, from Chapter 9, of the query required to generate the C-table "unit_sales_annual_multifactor". In that example, I showed the query that would be required to perform the first step of the process, in which aggregation by year is performed using all three grouping variables: "product_code", "customer_id", and "salesperson". Then, without showing the fairly-complex multi-part SQL query needed to do it, I described how this initial result could be further aggregated to produce a much larger table, featuring the value 'ALL' wherever a grouping variable has been eliminated by further aggregation. By making use of Microsoft's CUBE function, we can take the first-step SQL command from that example and modify it to generate the final C-table in a single command. Specifically, we add WITH CUBE to the GROUP BY clause, as follows:

```
INSERT INTO unit_sales_annual_multifactor
SELECT
  SUM(order_details.quantity) AS number_sold,
  YEAR(orders.date_of_order) AS sales_year,
  order_details.product_code,
  orders.customer_id_aiwt AS customer_id,
  orders.salesperson_aiwt AS salesperson
FROM
  order_details,
  orders
WHERE
  orders.order_number = order_details.order_number
GROUP BY
  YEAR(orders.date_of_order),
  order_details.product_code,
  orders.customer_id_aiwt,
  orders.salesperson_id_aiwt
WITH CUBE
```

The complexity of the superaggregation process is now handled by the DBMS itself, when interpreting this SQL query. The bad news about the way CUBE has been implemented is that, rather than inserting the word 'ALL' in the appropriate places in the result (as in our earlier example), Microsoft SQL Server places a NULL in those positions. This is rather an clumsy arrangement, with the obvious drawback that it is not immediately clear whether a particular NULL has been generated by the CUBE operation or is a NULL that existed in the raw data.

Reportedly, Microsoft originally hoped to create an ALL placeholder, like NULL, but different from NULL. ALL would have been stored in the database in a distinct way, rather than as the three-letter text string 'ALL', so that the ambiguity problem with a variable that actually had the value 'ALL' would not arise. But in the end, Microsoft released the feature using the NULL approach. However, they did this in such a way that the DBMS "knows", internally, the difference between an ALL-style NULL and a true NULL. To make this knowledge accessible to the user, Microsoft added another function that can be used to test what kind of NULL a NULL is. This is the GROUPING() function, which takes a column name as its argument. (I wish that they had used a less-confusing name than "GROUPING".)

The GROUPING() function is basically an "ALL-detector" which:

- Returns a value of TRUE for an ALL-style NULL.
- Returns a value FALSE for a true NULL.
- Returns a value FALSE for any real value, like 'D12345'.

Cubes and Nested Grouping Variables

The Microsoft CUBE function is clearly useful in generating C-tables. It can be used to prepare data for export to an OLAP system, where the data would be used to build a fact table. However, CUBE should be used with some caution. It works correctly *only when all the grouping variables are independent of one another*, like "customer", "product", and "branch", and where aggregation is done by only one time-period, such as "years". If you are trying to produce a C-table that includes two or more variables that belong to a set of nested grouping variables, then the results will include unwanted rows that are useless and potentially confusing to users who query the C-table. This applies to nested time-period variables, as well as normal (entity-related) grouping variables. I mentioned the need to take special steps to prevent unwanted rows appearing in C-tables when I first introduced the idea of data aggregation with nested grouping variables. To emphasize this point I will repeat the example from Chapter 10, but this time using CUBE.

Suppose that the results of the CUBE operation are going to be placed in a table with the following columns:

Table name: **unit_sales_annual_multifactor_v3**								
number_ sold	sales_ year	product_ code	customer_ id	salesperson	branch_ code	area_ code	region_ code	country_ code

The CUBE function does not "know" that a branch is part of an area, an area is part of a region, and a region is part of a country. As far as the CUBE function is concerned, these are just grouping variables, no more alike than "products" and "customers". The resulting table will therefore include many rows that are, in reality, duplicates – even though they contain apparently-different data values in certain columns. For example, we can look at the results of using CUBE in a query to find the number of items with product code 'D12345' that were purchased by the customer with customer ID '49123', through the New York branch, and handled by Alice. We would expect to find a single row for this number in a normal C-table. However, in the results of the CUBE operation we find eight rows instead of one:

number_ sold	sales_ year	product_ code	customer_ id	salesperson	branch_ code	area_ code	region_ code	country_ code
49	2008	D12345	49123	Alice	NYC	NYTRI	USNE	US
49	2008	D12345	49123	Alice	NYC	NYTRI	USNE	NULL
49	2008	D12345	49123	Alice	NYC	NYTRI	NULL	US
49	2008	D12345	49123	Alice	NYC	NULL	USNE	US
49	2008	D12345	49123	Alice	NYC	NYTRI	NULL	NULL
49	2008	D12345	49123	Alice	NYC	NULL	USNE	NULL
49	2008	D12345	49123	Alice	NYC	NULL	NULL	US
49	2008	D12345	49123	Alice	NYC	NULL	NULL	NULL

Note that all the NULLs here really ALLs. These eight rows are really all the same row. There are seven "duplicates", because the New York branch can only be in one area, region, and country, namely, those it is actually in. Thus, the appearance of 'NULL' in any column to the right of the "branch_code" column, when "branch_code" does not contain 'NULL', does not really change the level of geographical aggregation.

A similar problem exists in rows that have 'NULL' in "branch_code", but do not have 'NULL' in "region_code". In this case there will be three "duplicates" as follows:

number_ sold	sales_ year	product_ code	customer_ id	salesperson	branch_ code	area_ code	region_ code	country_ code
49	2008	D12345	49123	Alice	NULL	NYTRI	USNE	US
49	2008	D12345	49123	Alice	NULL	NYTRI	USNE	NULL
49	2008	D12345	49123	Alice	NULL	NYTRI	NULL	US
49	2008	D12345	49123	Alice	NULL	NYTRI	NULL	NULL

With all these duplicates, the resulting C-table is thus quite a lot larger than it needs to be. Also, users will need to be aware of these duplicates when they perform queries directed at this table – particularly if they are using queries that calculate subtotals and totals. These subtotals and totals will be wrong, because they will include the values of "number_sold" in all the duplicate rows.

Summary

The CUBE function is a very powerful addition to SQL. It allows a C-table to be generated by a single SQL statement. However, it should be used with care. It produces unwanted duplicate rows when any of the grouping variables are the key attributes of a set of nested grouping entities (including time-period pseudo-entities). Therefore:

> If you want to create a C-table that includes nested variables, it is probably a better idea to write the multi-part query yourself, and avoid using the CUBE function.

Useful though the Microsoft CUBE function is in many situations, the use of the term "cube" for this function has further added to the general confusion about the meaning of the term.

CHAPTER 16

REPRESENTING TIME – EXAMPLES FROM VARIOUS INDUSTRIES

Introduction

In this book I have concentrated on a small number of examples, going into detail on only two (the Order and Invoice Management database and the University Administration database). I did this in order to allow you to follow the various lines of thought that run through the book, without having to start from scratch with a completely new example in each chapter.

In this chapter I will give you a brief overview of a few other situations in which the various approaches for the representation of time in database designs is important. This is by no means an exhaustive list. Almost all databases contain some representation of events, transactions, the historical values of attributes, time-series information, or aggregate data. I picked the following examples because the need for handling time is immediately obvious when you start to think about the nature of each enterprise or activity and the information on which it depends.

Manufacturing and Distribution

We have already looked at the Order and Invoice Management database example. This is typical of a range of business applications where the manufacture, selling, and distribution of goods need to be tracked. In these applications you will find extensive use made of historical tables to record events such as the following:

- The purchase of raw materials
- The delivery of raw materials
- The completion of various stages in manufacture
- The entering of finished goods into inventory
- The ordering of goods
- The shipment of goods
- The generation of invoices
- The receipt of payments

The databases that support those activities are often tied to, or fully integrated with, the company's bookkeeping system (discussed later). The need to correctly record the values of unit costs and prices, *as at the time of purchase, manufacture, or sale*, is critical in accurately tracking where the company is making or losing money. It is therefore vital to avoid time-related modification anomalies when present-time data is updated. Another important characteristic of databases in manufacturing and distribution is the storing, in the database, of balance-type aggregate data. This aggregate data relates to stock levels at various points in the supply chain, including raw materials, work in progress, and finished goods. Good management of inventory levels is critical in ensuring profitability and the ability to promptly fulfill customers' orders.

Banking and Credit Cards

The operations of banks and credit card companies rely heavily on historical tables. Wherever money is involved, the accurate and reliable recording of transactions is essential. Transaction data describes debits and credits to customers' accounts, along with the date of the recording of the transaction and the "value date" of the transaction (which is generally the same as the recording date, but may be an earlier date for back-valued transactions or a later date for forward-valued transactions). As mentioned in Chapter 12, a basic record of transactions is generally referred to as the transaction journal, or TJ for short. ("Journal" is a commonly used term in accounting and financial services. A journal is "a record of events or transactions, in time order, at the finest level of detail".)

In the database designs for banking and credit card applications, besides the tables that hold TJs, there are many balance-type aggregate-data tables to record account balances. These are derived from the data in the TJs, as described in Chapter 12. To briefly re-cap: the balance information is typically stored, not as a single value for each account, but as a set of values as at various points in time, such as the end of nightly processing or the end of the month. The end-of-the-month balance provides a baseline from which the next month's statement can be prepared. The end-of-day balance provides a baseline from which the current balance can be calculated when needed (for example, when a customer wants to withdraw cash from a cash machine). In each case, starting with the appropriate baseline balance, the subsequent debits and credits from the TJ are then applied, in order to get the end-of-month balance or the current balance.

Further levels of aggregation occur in banking and credit card databases to allow the organization's overall situation to be assessed, and to provide top-level aggregations to feed into the organization's own bookkeeping process.

As explained in earlier chapters, aggregate data lies outside the E-R model; therefore much of the business of banks and credit card businesses cannot be modeled in this way. However, there is a great deal of other data that *does* fall within the E-R model. This includes information about customers, their accounts (excluding balance information), services, fees, and rates. Having a good database design for all this data helps to improve the performance of the organization. Unfortunately, because of the consolidation that has taken place in the financial services industry in the last thirty years, many organizations have ended up with separate databases for each line of business. A major challenge facing many large banks is the integration of those databases. Although banks love to talk about having an integrated view of each customer's business with them, they are notoriously bad at delivering on this promise (as you will know if you have ever had to notify, individually, several different parts of a single bank about a change in your address). Because they have separate databases for each line of business, separate loosely-coupled copies of your address and other information appear in each database.

General Bookkeeping (All Enterprises)

Bookkeeping is a vital function in every business and professional enterprise. Bookkeeping has many of the same characteristics as banking, although with a much smaller number of "accounts". The financial condition of an enterprise as a whole, and the aggregate changes to that condition, are represented in the general ledger accounts (such as asset, liability, stockholders' equity, revenue, expense, and dividend accounts).

The concept of a transaction journal is fundamental to any bookkeeping database. Each journal entry contains information about the amount of the entry, the direction of the effect (debit or credit), the general ledger accounts affected, the profit-center/cost-center code with which the transaction is to be associated, a description of the entry, and a code that defines the general category into which the entry falls (for example, "stationery expense" or "rental income"). As in banking, the account balances are data aggregates which are, conceptually, the aggregation of all relevant transactions from the time the enterprise came into existence to the present. In practice, each balance is calculated by applying recent transactions to a baseline balance, stored in the database.

The reports that are required by the users of a bookkeeping system consist almost entirely of combinations of different sets of aggregate data. There are two basic types of report: (a) balance-type aggregate data (for the balance sheet), and (b) aggregates of transactions over a month or a year (for income statements and other statements describing recent operations). The top-level reports (with the least detail) are used by senior management and in the preparation of information for shareholders, such as annual reports. Lower-level reports, covering parts of the enterprise in more detail, are required by the managers of profit centers and departments.

In the creation of aggregate data for the income-statement style of report, the codes used to define the general category of each journal entry are used as grouping variables in the various forms of income statement, so that the required level of detail can be given for a particular user. For example, reports sent to profit-center managers typically include a detailed breakdown of each individual category of income and expense (salaries, stationery, maintenance, sales, fee income, and so on). In the top-level reports these are aggregated into more-general categories.

Bookkeeping databases consist, in large part, of historical tables (representing transactions), plus a small number of tables representing (a) basic entities (such as accounts, profit centers, and transaction categories) and (b) relationships between these entities.

Brokerage and Securities-Custody

Brokerage and Securities-Custody operations use databases that have many of the features of banking databases, but with two added complications:

- First, the portfolio "balance" (in the sense of what is in the account) is not a single value. As mentioned in Chapter 9, these balances include (a) the security identifier codes for each security held and (b) the numbers of each security held (separately recorded for each different occasion on which a purchase was made). Information, either explicit or implicit, about the date that each lot of securities was bought is also considered to form part of the balance information. Without this, the lots cannot be separately identified. This information may take the form of a lot identification code or a date of purchase.

- Second, customers are very interested in knowing the market value of their securities holdings (that is, what the securities could be sold for). As explained in Chapter 12, this is related to the portfolio "balance"; but it is not the same thing as the balance. It is derived from the portfolio balance by multiplying the quantities of the various securities held by the market prices of those securities at a particular datetime. The datetime of the market prices may be different from the datetime of the balance. For example, the balance may have been calculated at the close of business yesterday; but the market prices may be today's prices at some point in the trading day. So, whereas the balance for a particular datetime does not change once it has been determined, the market value of that balance continues to change whenever the securities markets are open.

In producing statements and reports for customers about the past state of their portfolios, the securities prices as at the close of trading are used in combination with the portfolio balance as at the end of that day, when calculating portfolio values. Care must be therefore be taken in the database design to ensure that different pieces of historical data (such as securities held at a point in time and their market value at a point in time) are correctly matched according to date when this type of valuation calculation is performed – even if the datetime of the calculation of the numbers of each security held and the datetime at which their market values were recorded differ slightly.

Healthcare and Healthcare-Related Enterprises

The healthcare profession, including hospitals, clinics, healthcare practices, support services, and insurers, have applications that make extensive use of historical tables. These record patient examinations, test results, treatments, operations, and so on. The high incidence of lawsuits against doctors and hospitals in the USA has provided the motivation for "defensive" record-keeping. The information demanded by insurers has provided the motivation for codifying every treatment and procedure according to standardized schemes. As a result, the "historical" elements of healthcare databases (recording who did what to whom, when, where, and why) are well-developed.

Pharmaceutical Industry

The pharmaceutical industry, particularly in the USA, is the frequent target of lawsuits regarding bad outcomes of treatments using their products. Also, the industry is subject to close supervision by regulators. As a result, the applications used by the industry make even more extensive use of historical tables than hospitals and clinics. If something goes wrong with a particular patient, the company that manufactured the medication given to the patient needs to be able to retrieve information about every event related to the particular packet or bottle of medication administered to (or taken by) the patient. This includes information such as the following: which production plant the batch was made at; when it was made; when and from where every chemical component was acquired; when and where the components of the components came from; and so on. This information has to be accurately recorded all the way back to the start of every thread of the supply chain, for everything that ultimately went into each batch of each product. To store all this information requires a large number of interrelated historical tables.

On top of this, the company needs to know whether the doctor who prescribed the medication called the company's "doctors' helpline" to ask for information relating to that medication. Such a call may have taken place at any time prior to the administration of the medication to the patient. The company needs to know on what day the doctor called. If a notice was sent to the doctor about possible side-effects and contraindications, the company needs to know exactly which version of the notice (out of possibly dozens of versions over the life of the product) was sent to the doctor, and by what means it was sent.

Needless to say, the need to avoid modification anomalies across all these historical tables is paramount. We saw in Chapter 7 how time-related modification anomalies can be avoided by including as-it-was-then data in every row of historical data. However, in the pharmaceutical industry this data consists of many numerical values and long text strings. As a result, it is not generally practical to repeat it in every transactional record. Instead, it is necessary to use the "tracking changes in present-time data" approach described in Chapter 8. In this approach (illustrated in the "prices_history" table), each row of information about something whose characteristics change from time to time must include a "valid_from" and "valid_to" datetime. If ever there were an industry that could make good use of a temporal DBMS, this would be it!

CHAPTER 17

OVERVIEW OF EXAMPLES

Adding Columns to Tables

We now return to the pragmatic approaches, described earlier, for the representation of time in relational database designs and for solving various time-related problems. As described in Chapter 13, efforts aimed at creating a full-function TDBMS have not, so far, been successful. In any case, a TDBMS does not tackle all of the "problems with time". Therefore, the pragmatic approaches described in Chapters 7 to 12 represent the only solutions available to relational database designers today.

In the various examples in Chapters 7 to 12, presented earlier, it may have seemed to you that hardly a page went by without a new column being added to one of the tables. This is certainly a common feature of many of these approaches. This stands in stark contrast to what happens during standard normalization. During standard normalization carried out with database designs that aim to represent the present state of a part of the real world, the number of columns in each table tends to shrink, as "troublesome" tables are split into two or more tables; but when time-related modification anomalies are being addressed, the number of columns in certain tables tends to grow.

You should not, however, think of the addition of columns as a cure-all when it comes to addressing time-related problems in a database design. The additional columns are certainly a necessary part of many of the solutions; but they must be the right additional columns added to the right tables.

A Summary of the Examples

In order to leave you with a clearer mental picture of what happened in the examples of the various pragmatic approaches, the following two tables summarize the changes that we made to the original database design in the two main examples, and the reasons for these changes. The two summaries are structured as follows:

- The first section of each summary shows "Tables in the original design". Only those tables that were discussed in the examples are shown: the complete database design would consist of many more tables than the few considered in these examples. Note that, in the Order and Invoice Management database example, some of the tables included in this section were not mentioned when the example was first introduced in Chapter 7. I introduced these tables one by one, as the example progressed. However, they are represented here as part of the "original" design, before it was changed to better represent time in the database. (Some of the tables were mentioned only briefly, but I have included them anyway.)

- The second section of each summary shows "Tables added". In this section I show those tables that were added specifically to solve a time-related problem.

- The third section of each summary shows the *columns* that were added to various tables. In this section I show columns that were added to both the tables of the "original" design and to tables that were added in the first stages of refining the original design.

When you look at the examples of tables that hold aggregate data you will notice that I have not underlined any of the column names (to identify columns as key columns). The reason for this is that, although *all* the columns *except* the one that holds the data element of interest (like "number_sold") are technically key columns, it is not essential to define them as key columns: the SQL commands used to fill the table with aggregate data (assuming that they are not flawed in some way) will never insert duplicate rows. However, the Database Administrator will probably mark generate of sorting indices for all these columns in order to speed the retrieval of rows by users.

University Administration Database Example

Tables in the original design	Columns (key columns underlined)	
students	student_id, first_name, last_name, sex, date_of_birth	
courses	course_number, course_title, credits	
enrollments	student_id, course_number, term, year	

Tables added	Columns	Explanation
grades	student_id, course_number, grade, year, term	The "grades" table represents the historical relationship *has completed* between *student* and *course*. This relationship operates "in parallel" with *is enrolled in* (represented by the "enrollments" table). The "grades" table was added to the database design in order to preserve historical information (namely, the courses that students have completed), after rows are deleted from the "enrollments" table at the end of the term.

Columns added to:	Columns added	Explanation
grades	course_title_aiwt, credits_aiwt	These columns were subsequently added to the "grades" table in order to preserve information about courses that students have completed in the past, in case courses are removed from the curriculum and deleted from the "courses" table.

Order and Invoice Management Database Example

Tables in the original design	Columns (key columns underlined)
customers	customer_id, customer_name, line_of_business, credit_status, address_line1, address_line2, address_line3
products	product_code, product_description, price
orders_placed	customer_id, order_number, sales_channel_code
orders	order_number, status, purchase_order_number, date_of_order, shipping_date, invoice_date, payment_due_date, branch_code
order_details	order_number, line_number, quantity, product_code
customer_calls	csvc_call_id, customer_id, call_starttime, agent_id, problem_description
branches	branch_code, branch_name
branches_by_area	branch_code, area_code
areas	area_code, area_name
areas_by_region	area_code, region_code
regions	region_code, region_name
regions_by_country	region_code, country_code
countries	country_code, country_name
customers_by_group	customer_id, customer_group_code
customer_groups	customer_group_code, customer_group_description
products_by_product_type	product_code, product_type_code
product_types	product_type_code, product_type_description
product_type_by_product_family	product_type_code, product_family_code
product_families	product_family_code, product_family_description
products_by_product_manufacturer	product_code, product_mfr_id
product_manufacturers	product_mfr_id, product_mfr_name
sales_credits	salesperson_id, order_number
salespeople	salesperson_id, first_name, last_name

Tables added	Columns	Explanation
prices_history	product_code, price, valid_from, valid_to	This table was added in order to preserve the past values of the prices at which products were offered for sale. These would otherwise be lost when the "products" table is updated. This information is preserved so that it will continue to be available for analyses of prices over time and/or to comply with industry regulations about retention of such information.
days	day_id, year, month_number, day_number_in_month, day_number_in_year, week_id, day_of_week, weekday_flag, last_day_of_month_flag, holiday_flag	This table was added in order to represent the time-period pseudo-entity day, and to hold information that might be useful in using this as a grouping entity during time-period data aggregation.
weeks	week_id, year, week_number_in_year, year_id, first_day_of_week_day_id, season	This table was added in order to represent the time-period pseudo-entity week, and to hold information that might be useful in using this as a grouping entity during time-period data aggregation.
months	month_id, year, month_number, year_id	This table was added in order to represent the time-period pseudo-entity month, and to hold information that might be useful in using this as a grouping entity during time-period data aggregation.
quarters	quarter_id, year, quarter_number, year_id	This table was added in order to represent the time-period pseudo-entity quarter, and to hold information that might be useful in using this as a grouping entity during time-period data aggregation.
years	year_id, year, leapyear_flag	This table was added in order to represent the time-period pseudo-entity year, and to hold information that might be useful in using this as a grouping entity during time-period data aggregation.

sales_by_product_annual	product_code, total_sales, sales_year	Aggregate-data tables are created in the database to allow users to perform simple queries, directed at these tables, to obtain aggregate data without putting a heavy load on the DBMS during business hours. This table was the first example of an aggregate-data table for the data element of interest "total sales (in dollars)".
unit_sales_multiperiod_multifactor	number_sold, year_id, quarter_id, month_id, week_id, day_id, product_code, product_family_code, † product_type_code, † product_mfr_id, † customer_id, customer_group_code, † salesperson_id, † department_code, † branch_code, area_code, region_code, country_code	Aggregate-data tables are created in the database to allow users to perform simple queries, directed at these tables, to obtain aggregate data without putting a heavy load on the DBMS during business hours. This table was the last, and most-comprehensive, example of an aggregate-data table for the data element of interest "unit sales". This table is a C-table, covering all possible grouping variables, including the time-period grouping variables year, quarter, month, week, and day. (Various example tables, not summarized here, were presented as we built up to this final example.) † These six columns, mentioned in earlier chapters, were omitted from the simplified version of the this table presented in Chapter 11.
Columns added to:	**Columns added**	**Explanation**
order_details	price_aiwt, product_description_aiwt	These columns were added to the "order_details" table in order to capture information about the price and description of the product as these stood at the time of an order, thus preserving this information in the face of subsequent changes to these values in the "products" table.

order_details	product_family_code_aiwt, product_type_code_aiwt, product_mfr_id_aiwt	These columns were added to this table in order to (a) make sure that the assignment of products to these categories, as at the time of the order, are captured in the table, and not lost when changes are later made to present-time tables; and (b) speed up aggregating queries, by eliminating the need for these queries to refer to various relationship-representing tables, like "products_by_product_type", when performing aggregations by product family, by product type, and by product manufacturer.
orders	customer_id_aiwt, sales_channel_code_aiwt	These columns were added to this table in order to speed up aggregating queries, by eliminating the need for them to refer to the "orders_placed" table when performing aggregations using "customer_id" or "sales_channel_code" as a grouping variable. The presence of "customer_id_aiwt" also prevents modification anomalies arising in aggregate data if customers are deleted from the database. Note that "orders_placed" continues to be used for day-to-day operational queries and updates. These new columns are strictly for after-the-fact analyses.
orders	salesperson_id_aiwt	This column was added to this table in order to speed up aggregating queries, by eliminating the need for them to refer to the "sales_credits" table when performing aggregations using salesperson_id as a grouping variable. It also prevents modification anomalies arising in aggregate data if salespeople are deleted from the database. Note that "sales_credits" continues to be used for day-to-day operational queries and updates. This new column is strictly for after-the-fact analyses.

orders	area_code_aiwt, region_code_aiwt, country_code_aiwt	These columns were added to this table in order to (a) make sure that the assignment of branches to areas, regions, and countries, as at the time of the order, are captured in the table, and are not lost when changes are later made to present-time tables like "branches_by_area"; and (b) speed up aggregating queries, by eliminating the need for them to refer to tables like "branches_by_area" when performing aggregations by area, by region, and by country.
orders	customer_group_code_aiwt	This column was added to this table in order to (a) make sure that the assignment of customers to customer groups, as at the time of the order, is captured in the table, and is not lost when changes are later made to the "customers_by_group" table; and (b) speed up aggregating queries, by eliminating the need for them to refer to the "customers_by_group" table when performing aggregations by customer group.
orders	day_id, week_id, month_id, quarter_id, year_id	These columns were added to this table in order to (a) allow completed orders to be easily associated with the "days", "weeks", "months", "quarters", and "years" tables when performing complex time-period data aggregation that uses information contained in those tables; and (b) allow time-period data aggregation and superaggregation to operate more efficiently, by avoiding the need to use date-manipulation functions within GROUP BY clauses.

CHAPTER 18

CONCLUSION

In the early 1980s, as relational DBMSs moved from university research departments into the business world, relational databases were used first in applications that involved storing data about the present time. But database designers who developed real-world database designs soon recognized that the needs of the business demanded that they represent time in their database designs.

The basic tool for representing time in a relational database is the datetime format, which was defined in SQL early in its development. This was at first used mainly for the attributes of entities, such as "date of birth" or "date of purchase". However, as the range of applications of relational databases expanded, database designers had to figure out how to do more complicated things involving dates, such as recording transactions, calculating interest charges, tracking price movements, and so on. The *mathematical operations* involved in queries that do these things are fairly easy to do in SQL (even though SQL is not an ideal language for calculation-intensive programs). By contrast, it was much harder to figure out how best to represent (in database designs) the relevant parts of the real world in which such mathematical operations had meaning. Database designers had to tackle this much-harder problem with very little help. Textbooks on databases, university database courses, and vendors' database courses, did little to prepare database designers for solving these problems.

The time-related problems that database designers had to tackle included:

(1) How do you prevent time-related modification anomalies occurring with respect to historical data when the attributes of entities change? The standard normalization rules do not seem to prevent this.

(2) What is the best way to store time-stamped "transaction" data and avoid modification anomalies relative to this information?

(3) What is the best way to generate and store aggregated transactional data?

(4) For queries that aim to produce aggregate-data reports, what is the best way to minimize the load placed on the DBMS at the time of users' queries?

(5) How can you represent time periods as nested grouping variables for aggregate data?

Over the last two decades a number of practices and techniques have become established in the business world for the representation of time in relational databases. However, little of the knowledge and experience thus accumulated has found its way into the textbooks and courses that are being used to train new generations of database designers. As a result, approaches in different companies vary greatly. The less lucky companies may suffer from:

- Poor database performance, or needlessly large investments in powerful computer hardware to overcome performance problems.

- Business-impacting data inconsistencies, or the need for large numbers of staff to manually fix data inconsistencies so that they do not affect business operations.

- Costly and time-consuming database re-design efforts whenever new user requirements demand the addition of new tables to the design.

Meanwhile, luckier companies may be very happy with their databases. In the absence of a way to share best practices, the outcome is largely determined by the effectiveness of the solutions that the database designers develop, often working in isolation from their peers in other companies.

Work on Problems (3), (4), and (5), in the context of the generation reports to support business decisions, initially led to frustration with the performance of relational DBMSs. This, in turn, led to a number of "OLAP" vendors building special-purpose, "multidimensional" DBMSs, together with data extraction and transformation software modules, and querying tools for aggregate-data queries. These products subsequently evolved to use relational databases for the underlying DBMS. Although work in the OLAP field has generated some interesting and useful solutions to some of the "time problems", the terminology that has evolved in the OLAP field is a barrier to incorporation of those solutions into the general body of relational database knowledge.

In the early 1980s, while databases designers in the business world were starting to grapple with all the above-mentioned problems, theoretical research (on representing time in database designs) set off in a specific direction, namely, the pursuit of a solution to Problem (1) within the DBMS itself. This led to the idea of a "temporal DBMS", the basic requirements for which were worked out in the mid-1980s, along with a specification for a first-generation temporal query language (TSQL). However, subsequent attempts to build a working temporal DBMS met with limited success, and most were eventually abandoned.

Pursuit of the time problem in universities, with no practical full-function TDBMS to show for over 20 years of research and development, has distracted researchers from looking at what has been going on in the business world, where relational DBMSs are still the systems of choice for all day-to-day operational functions. Such an examination might have led to a codifying of the various pragmatic approaches to representing time in relational databases and, very probably, to improvements in these pragmatic approaches. More importantly, it might have led to their appearance in textbooks and database courses, thus better preparing database students for the database design work that they will be asked to do when they start to apply what they have learned. I hope that this book will be of help to such students and that it will also help to promote interest in developing a better theoretical foundation for the subject.

GLOSSARY

Aggregate Data Data that is derived by applying mathematical functions to the values of a particular "data element of interest" in a series of transactions. The transactions are those that occurred within a particular time span for which the aggregate is being derived. The "data element of interest" is a numerical attribute of those transactions, for example, the value of each order in a series of orders. The mathematical function that is most commonly applied to these numerical attributes is SUM(), although it could be another function that operates on a series of values, such as AVG(). An example of aggregate data is "total sales by product for the last twelve months".

Artificial Key A key that is not a naturally-occurring attribute of an entity but which is assigned to the entity by the database designer because (a) the entity lacks a suitable key attribute, or (b) use of an otherwise suitable candidate key is not permissible. For example, students may be assigned the artificial key "Student ID" because students' names are not unique, and also because use of students' Social Security Numbers is not allowed for reasons of privacy. Artificial keys are typically sequential integers assigned automatically as data about the entities is entered into the database. Most artificial keys are used only for the purposes of storing data in the database. However, in a few cases, such as the Student ID example, the artificial key may be forced on the real world (for instance, printed on student ID cards and used by students in course enrollment and other transactions with the university).

Attribute A property, in which we are interested, of the entities in an entity set; or a property, in which we are interested, of the instances of a relationship between two sets of entities. For example, attributes of the entity *student*, in which we might be interested, are "name", "sex", and "date of birth". Attributes, in which we might be interested, of the relationship *is enrolled in* (which operates between the entities *student* and *course*) are "term" (or "semester") and "year". The term "attribute" is also sometimes used as an alternative to "column" when talking about the tables in a relational database. (The columns of tables derive from the real-world attributes of the entities or relationships represented by those tables.) The term "attribute" is also used when referring to the fact that two columns, in different tables, represent the same thing. Thus, we talk about the "student_id" columns in the "students" and "enrollments" tables as representing the same attribute.

Boyce-Codd Normal Form (BCNF) The next level of normalization after Third Normal Form in the seven steps to full normalization of a relational database design. (See Normalization.) The definition of BCNF came out of work done by Ray Boyce, who defined the BCNF level as being achieved if a database design meets all the requirements for the prior three levels and, in addition, meets the condition that "every determinant must be a candidate key". A candidate key is an attribute that could be used as a key. A determinant is an attribute whose value determines what value another attribute will have. The next level of normalization after BCNF is called Fourth Normal Form (even though it is really the fifth level).

Business Intelligence   A branch of what I have called "the OLAP field" that focuses on analysis of transactional data in order to discover previously unrecognized correlations between consumers' actions, choices, and activities, or in order to predict future trends and events. (See OLAP.)

Candidate Key   An attribute of an entity that could be used as a key because it takes a unique value for each entity. In many cases there is only one candidate key, which is selected to become the actual key in the database design. In a few cases there may be two or more candidate keys: a choice has to be made between them. For example, "student ID" and "social security number" (if they are different) are candidate keys for the entity *student*: they both uniquely define a student. We might choose to use "student ID" as the actual key (to preserve the confidentiality of the Social Security Number).

Cardinality (of a Relationship)   A description, in a data model, of a real-world rule that governs whether one entity, or more than one entity, can be on each end of each instance of a relationship. There are three possible cardinality rules, one of which will apply to a specific relationship: one-to-one, one-to-many, many-to-many. In some cases the real-world situation may change over the life of a database, so that the rule that is applied in the database will need to be revised.

Cascading Delete   A situation, intentionally brought about by the database designer, in which the deletion of a row from one table causes rows to be automatically deleted from one or several other tables, wherever the rows in those other tables contain the same value of the key attribute of the first table. The aim of a cascading delete is to preserve referential integrity within the database, that is, to prevent rows being "marooned" in the database. A marooned row is a row that can no longer be associated, via a key attribute, with a row in the "master" table for that attribute. For example, suppose that the "courses" table is regarded as the master representation of courses in the database. In this case the deletion of a course from the database, by way of the deletion of a row from the "courses" table, could be made to also delete a row from the "course_teachers" table. (The "course_teachers" table represents the relationship *is teaching* between *teacher* and *course*.) The cascading delete removes, from "course_teachers", the row that associates a teacher with the now-deleted course. It prevents the row being marooned in the "course_teachers" table, with a no-longer-recognized value of "course_number" in its "course_number" column. The mechanism by which cascading deletes are made to occur is one version of the "foreign key" feature. (See Foreign Key.)

Cell   The contents of a particular column in a particular row of a table, that is, a single data element. The term "cell" is widely understood because of its use in the context of spreadsheet programs like Microsoft Excel. However, there seems to be an aversion to using the term "cell" in the context of relational databases – even though it is a sensible and very useful term. I have used it in this book.

C-Table
(Combinatorially-
Superaggregated
Transaction-
History Table)

The result of performing data aggregation on a series of historical transactions in an iterative manner, including, in the result set, the results of each of these iterative steps. The final result set, which is typically stored in a table in the database, contains many possible aggregations that users might be interested in. For example, the first iteration might produce the aggregate "total sales for the last twelve months by product by customer by branch". The next level will aggregate the results by each of the grouping variables in turn, to give total sales for the last twelve months "by product by customer (for all branches)"; "by product by branch (for all customers)"; and "by customer by branch (for all products)". The next iteration will aggregate the results further, giving total sales for the last twelve months "by product", "by customer", and "by branch". The last iteration will give simply "total sales for the last twelve months". The C-table would contain all eight of these combinations of grouping variables: the case with all three variables, the three cases of pairs of variables, the three cases of single variables, and the case with no variables. The columns in the C-table corresponding to a variable that has been eliminated by an aggregation step contain the value 'ALL'. A user can extract the required rows from the C-table by applying the condition that certain columns must contain 'ALL'; and that other columns must not contain 'ALL'.

CUBE (the SQL
function)

An SQL function which is used in combination with a mathematical function such as SUM() to generate a C-table in a single step, thus avoiding the need to write SQL statements to perform the various iterative steps with different combinations of grouping variables. (See C-table.) The CUBE function does not, however, generate a value of 'ALL' where a variable has been eliminated through aggregate: instead it generates a NULL.

Data Cube

A term, introduced in research on temporal databases, to describe the construct that, in a temporal database, takes the place of a table in a standard relational database. A data cube is like a table, with rows and columns, but with a third dimension that represents time. The "front face" of a data cube represents the current contents of a table. The layers behind that front face represent the complete history of the values held in that table, back to the time when the database was created. (The initial values are found on the rear face of each data cube.) The term "time cube" is also sometimes used to mean the same thing. (See Temporal Databases.) In spite of its established use in the field of temporal databases, the term "data cube" has also been used (since the mid-1990s), in the OLAP field, to refer to the ability to readily retrieve aggregate data based on different grouping variables – which are described as "dimensions". (See OLAP.) Even when there are exactly three variables, the use of the term "data cube" to describe the stored aggregate data is potentially confusing. More recently, the term "data cube" has also been used to refer to a C-table – a table used to store aggregate data, grouped by all possible combinations of grouping variables, in a standard relational database. (See C-table.) Use of the term "data cube" for a C-table is also confusing, because a C-table is a standard two-dimensional table, not a three-dimensional or multi-dimensional construct; and, even when it has exactly three grouping-variable columns, it cannot easily or usefully be represented as a three-dimensional array of values.

Data Element	A particular value of an attribute, that is, the contents of a particular cell in a table, at the intersection of a row and a column. The term "attribute" is sometimes also used to mean "data element", although the term "attribute" is better used to refer to the whole column. Note also that the term "cell", universally understood because of the use of spreadsheet programs like Microsoft Excel, is not very often used in the context of databases. However, "cell" is a useful term, and I see no reason why it should not be used.
Data Element of Interest (in Data Aggregation)	The numerical attribute which is the subject of a data aggregation, for example, the value of an order, to which the SUM() function is applied to get "total sales". (See Aggregate Data.)
Data Entity (or Entity)	Something, in which we are interested, that exists and which is distinguishable from other similar things, for example, a student, who is distinguishable from other students. (As a counter-example, a grain of sand is not an entity because there is no practical way of distinguishing one grain of sand from another.)
Data Mining	A branch of what I have called "the OLAP field" that focuses on analysis of transactional data in order to discover previously unrecognized correlations between consumers' actions, choices, and activities, and to predict future trends and events. (See OLAP.)
Data Warehousing	The underlying processes, for all parts of what I have called "the OLAP field", in which copies of data are extracted from one or several operational databases and placed in a read-only database for the purpose of running various types of after-the-fact analysis on that data. Where data is taken from several different sources, one of these processes is the transformation of the data in such a way that differences in the way it is represented in the various databases are resolved, and duplication of key attribute values are prevented. (See OLAP.)
Database Design (Relational)	The specification of the empty database, before any data is inserted into it. The design consists of the table names, column names, the column formats (or datatypes), and designation of key columns.
Database View	A view of a database, presented to a group of users, in which they can see, and update, only a subset of the data contained in the database. Sometimes also referred to as a subschema.
Datatype (or Type)	The class of the data elements that will be stored in a particular column of a table. In a mathematical context, and in some programming languages, "type" means things like "integer", "real number", or "text string". In SQL, "type" is more specific than this. It defines the number of characters or digits used to represent the data in the database, for example, "text string of nine characters", or "real number represented as up to six digits to the left of the decimal point and up to four digits after the decimal point". Because of the greater specificity of the data descriptions in SQL, I prefer to use the term "format". This emphasizes the fact that there may not be an exact mapping between "type" in some programming languages and "format" in a database. However, most books and DBMS manuals use the term "type" or "datatype".

Datetime Format (or Datetime Datatype)   The SQL format (or datatype) of a column that is used to hold dates or dates-plus-times, for example, '2002/4/1 10:28am'. A date may be represented by omitting the time, in which case the DBMS will set the time part of the datetime to midnight (00:00:00). The internal representation of a datetime used by a DBMS is independent of how a database user elects to display datetimes (day/month/year, year/month/day, or month/day/year) so that comparisons between datetimes entered by users with different datetime-display settings will always operate correctly.

DBMS   Database Management System – a suite of software that manages the storage of data in a computer in an organized way (that is, as a database), so that data can be easily inserted, retrieved, and updated by many users sharing the database.

Deletion Anomaly   A situation in which, because of the database design, the deletion of one piece of data causes another still-needed piece of data to be deleted, or to be rendered inaccessible via any reasonable query.

Dimension Table   A table, in an OLAP system, that represents a grouping entity in transactional data aggregation, for example, *customer*, *product*, or *branch*. A dimension table is based on an extract, from an operational database, of an entity-representing table in a standard relational database design. (See OLAP.)

Domain/Key Normal Form (DK/NF)   The seventh and last step to full normalization of a relational database design. DK/NF represents a state of complete normalization. (See Normalization.) The definition of DK/NF came out of work done by Ronald Fagin, who defined DK/NF as being achieved if, for every table in the database design, "every constraint on the table is a logical consequence of the definition of the keys and the domains [of all the attributes]". (See Chapter 4 for an attempt at explaining this condition.) Note that Domain/Key Normal Form is abbreviated as DK/NF, not D/KNF or DKNF. I do not know the reason for this; we seem to be stuck with it.

Domain (of an Attribute)   The full set or range of possible values that an attribute may take. For example, a binary attribute has a domain consisting of the two values 0 or 1. A day-of-the-week attribute has a domain consisting of seven possible values (Monday, Tuesday, Wednesday, and so on). Attributes of these types have a domain consisting of a finite number of values; and so do integers within a fixed range, such as "integers between 0 and 10,000". Integers in general, and all real numbers, have domains containing an infinite number of possible values: there are an infinite number of integers, and there are an infinite number of real numbers, even within a fixed range (such as between 1 and 2). However, specific representations of real numbers, within a defined range, may have domains consisting of a finite number of possible values. For example, a number that can take any positive value between 0 and 1000, represented to two decimal places, has a domain consisting of 100,001 possible values, starting with 0.00, 0.01, 0.02, and 0.03, and ending with 999.98, 999.99, and 1000.00. The concept of a domain is closely related to the concept of the format (or datatype) of an attribute. (See Format.) However, the two are not the same thing. A representation of the day of the week using the digits 1 to 7 has a format "integer"; but its domain is "1, 2, 3, 4, 5, 6, or 7".

Dual-use Historical Table	A table, in a database design, that represents transactions and is (a) utilized as a present-time table while those transactions are in progress (for example, while an order is being assembled and shipped), and (b) utilized as an historical table for completed transactions (for example, in analyses of business activity over the last year). An alternative to a design with dual-use tables is one with separate present-time and historical tables. Such a design requires an automated process, triggered once a transaction is completed (for example, after the invoice is paid), to delete the row that represents the transaction from the present-time table and insert it into the historical table.
EIS	See Executive Information System.
Entity (or Data Entity)	Something, in which we are interested, that exists and which is distinguishable from other similar things, for example, a student, who is distinguishable from other students. (As a counter-example, a grain of sand is not an entity because there is no practical way of distinguishing one grain of sand from another.)
Entity Set	A collection of all similar entities, for example, all students at a particular university.
Entity-Relationship Model (E-R Model)	A data-oriented description of the piece of the real world for which a database is to be designed. The concept of an Entity-Relationship model was introduced by Peter Chen in 1976. An Entity-Relationship model is written down in the form of an Entity-Relationship Diagram (or E-R Diagram).
Executive Information System (EIS)	A system belonging to a branch of what I have called "the OLAP field" that focuses on analysis of transactional data in order to produce a limited number of key indicators for managers who want to be able to get a quick report on the condition of a particular aspect of a business. These key indicators are typically displayed on a single screen or a single printed page, and reviewed on a weekly basis. (See OLAP.)
Fact Table	A table, in an OLAP system, that holds historical data about transactions, either as individual transactional data or as aggregated transactional data. A fact table is based on an extract, from an operational database, of transactional entity tables and transactional relationship tables in a standard relational database design. (See OLAP.)
FFD	See Fully Functionally Dependent.
Forced-key System	A scheme for assignment of values to an attribute in such a way that the attribute can be used as a key, even though the attribute is not truly a key attribute (that is, duplicate values of the attribute may occur in the real world). This is done by preventing the use of a value that has already been used. A common example of a forced-key system is an email address scheme. There may be two John Smiths in a company. The first one will be allowed to take the email address john.smith@bigcompany.com; but the second John Smith will be forced to take a different address, such as john.smith.2@bigcompany.com.

Foreign Key   A permanent designation of a column in one table as representing the same key attribute (of an entity) as a key column in another table (typically the entity-representing table for that entity). For example, the "course_number" column in the "course_teachers" table could be designated as a "foreign key", whose master version appears in the entity-representing table, "courses". Although it is consistent with Codd's original description of the relational model, the foreign key arrangement violates the final relational model that emerged in the 1970s. In the final model, the equivalence of two columns in different tables is established only at the time of a query. A foreign key reference violates this concept by permanently defining the equivalence of two columns. Foreign key references are used to prevent a breakdown of referential integrity within a database, by preventing rows in relationship-representing tables being marooned in the database when the row to which they relate in an entity-representing table has been deleted. Foreign key references can be used in one of two ways: (a) in the triggering of a cascading delete (see Cascading Delete), or (b) in preventing the deletion of a row in an entity-representing table, at the "master" end of the foreign key reference, until all rows in the relationship-representing tables that are associated with that row have first been deleted.

Format (of an Attribute)   The "type" or "datatype" of the data elements that will be stored in a particular column of a table. In a mathematical context, and in some programming languages, "type" means things like "integer", "real number", or "text string". However, in SQL, "type" is more specific than this. It defines the number of characters or digits used to represent the data in the database, for example, "text string of nine characters", or "real number represented as up to six digits to the left of the decimal point and up to four digits after the decimal point". Because of the greater specificity of the term in SQL, I prefer to use the term "format". This emphasizes the fact that there may not be an exact mapping between "type" in some programming languages and "format" in a database. However, most books and DBMS manuals use the term "type" or "datatype".

Fully Functionally Dependent (FFD)   A real-world association between different attributes of an entity such that the value of one determines the value of the other. An attribute of an entity is said to be "fully functionally dependent" (FFD) on another attribute when the value of the first attribute is directly and completely determined by the value of the second attribute. For example, if we know the chassis number of a car we can find out what color the car is painted. The attribute "color" is thus fully functionally dependent on the attribute "chassis_number". In some cases the value of an attribute may be fully functionally dependent on the values of two or more other attributes, taken together. For example, for a DVD player, the attribute "color" might be fully functional dependent on "manufacturer_id" and "serial_number", taken together. Full functional dependency is important in the process of normalization of a database design. (See Normalization.) One of the several requirements to be met for a database design to be normalized is that the non-key attributes of every table must be fully functionally dependent on the table's key attribute or attributes. A simpler way of stating this is to say that non-key attributes must depend on "the key, the whole key, and nothing but the key".

Generalization Relationship

A relationship, in an Entity-Relationship model (or shown on an Entity-Relationship diagram), that indicates that members of one entity set are members of a broader entity set, for example, the relationship *student is a universitymember*. This type of relationship is often referred to as an "is a" relationship, sometimes written as an "isa" relationship. Another form of generalization relationship an *is part of* relationship, where members of the more-general entity contain members of the less-general entity set, for example, *area is part of region*.

Grouping Entity

An entity whose key attribute is used as the grouping variable in the aggregation of transactional data. For example, in the aggregate "total sales by product for the last twelve months", the entity *product* is the grouping entity. In this example, the grouping variable, that is, the attribute by whose values the transactions are grouped, is "product_code", which is the key attribute of *product*. (See Grouping Variable.)

Grouping Variable

An attribute by whose values transactions are grouped during the aggregation of transactional data, for example, the attribute "product_code", used in the creation of the aggregate "total sales by product for the last twelve months". Grouping variables are normally the key attributes of grouping entities, such as *product*.

Hierarchical Model

The earliest database model according to which the first DBMSs were designed (in the 1960s). In a hierarchical database, the user has to navigate a tree-like logical structure, within which the data is placed, in order to retrieve or update data. For example, in order to find an employee's telephone number, the user may be required to navigate the path company→division→department→employee→phonenumber to get to the telephone number. The hierarchical model was superseded by the network model, which in turn was superseded by the relational model. (See Network Model and Relational Model.)

Insertion Anomaly

A situation in which it is impossible, because of the design of the database, to insert a piece of data into a database without first inserting another piece of data.

Join

A condition in a WHERE clause that associates two tables (named in the FROM clause) with one another. Originally (in the 1970s and early 1980s), in relational-algebra query languages, the reserved word JOIN was used to instruct the DBMS to create a temporary table, while executing a query, by combining two tables via matching attribute values. When relational-calculus query languages emerged, such as the present-day SQL, the term "join" continued to be used and acquired its present meaning.

Join Condition

An alternative name for the present-day meaning of "join", that is, a condition in a WHERE clause that associates two tables (named in the FROM clause) with one another.

Key

A shorthand for one of the following: (a) the key attribute of an entity; (b) the two or more key attributes, taken together, of an entity that has a multi-attribute key; (c) a specific value of a key attribute; (d) a specific combination of values of the two or more key attributes of an entity that has a multi-attribute key; (e) the two or more key attributes of a relationship, taken together ("the relationship key"); (f) specific values of the two or more key attributes of the relationship, taken together; (g) the key column of an entity-representing table that has a single key column; (h) the two or more key columns of an entity-representing table or a relationship-representing table that has two or more key columns, taken together; (i) a specific value in a key column that identifies a specific row in a table; or (j) a specific combination of values in the two or more key columns that identifies a specific row in a table with two or more key columns. Thus, we can say "the key is manufacturer_id plus serial_number" when talking about an entity or about the table that represents that entity in the database design; or we can say "the key is LG and 1072410553" when talking about a specific value of this two-attribute key.

Key Attribute

An attribute whose value uniquely identifies an individual entity within an entity set and which occurs only once among the members of the set. For example, the chassis number of a car uniquely identifies a particular car and distinguishes it from all other cars. It is therefore a key attribute of the entity *car*. For some entities there are two attributes which, taken together, form "the key". For example, the key attributes for a DVD player might be "manufacturer_id" and "serial_number", taken together – because the serial number alone may not be unique across all DVD players. (In very rare cases, there may be more than two attributes required to establish a key.) Relationships have two or more key attributes. At a minimum, a relationship's key attributes are all the key attributes of the two entities between which the relationship operates. In some cases a relationship may have an additional key attribute, besides those of the entities, for example, a datetime attribute or transaction number. This is typically the case where the relationship is a transactional relationship that might be repeated with the same two entities, like *customer rented car*.

Key Column(s)

Within the context of a relational database, a designated column of a table (or a designated set of columns), each value (or set of values) of which may occur only once in the table, so that each row of the table is sure to be unique; and so that the key uniquely identifies a particular row. An example of a single key column is "student_id" which, by itself, uniquely identifies students. An example of a two-column key is "manufacturer_id" plus "serial_number" for a DVD player: the serial number alone may not be unique across all DVD players. In some tables the set of columns that forms the key may be *all* the columns. (This is particularly the case in two-column tables that represent relationships.)

Key-based Query   A query, made of a database, in which data is retrieved from a table based on the value of the key. For example, if the key of the "students" table is "student_id", a query that retrieves a row from that table, containing a particular value in the "student_id" column, is a key-based query. Key-based queries retrieve a single row of data because each value of the key can appear only once: the key uniquely identifies a particular row in the table. (See Non-key-based Query.)

Lookup Table   A table that is used (mainly by application programs) to control the accuracy of data inserted into the database, and to enhance information retrieved from the database when presenting it to users. It is treated as an adjunct to the main database: information in the main database can be successfully retrieved or updated without any reference to a lookup table; and the integrity of the main database would not be affected by the deletion of a lookup table. The key column of a lookup table represents an attribute that, in the main database, is a non-key column of one or several tables.   The contents of a lookup table change infrequently and can be changed only by privileged users. An example of a lookup table that performs both functions – controlling data input and enhancing information as stored in the main database tables – is a table like "faculties" that has two columns, "faculty_code" and "faculty_full_name", and which holds the official list of recognized faculties and the translations of the abbreviated faculty code as used in the database (such as 'MAT') to the full faculty name ('Mathematics').

Modification Anomaly   A generic term that encompasses "insertion anomaly", "deletion anomaly", and "update anomaly".   (See Insertion Anomaly, Deletion Anomaly, and Update Anomaly.)

MOLAP   Multidimensional OLAP system – an OLAP system (On-Line Analytical Processing system) based on a "multidimensional" DBMS, that is, a DBMS that is non-relational and designed specifically for use in OLAP systems.   MOLAPs were largely superseded by ROLAPs, which are OLAP systems based on standard relational DBMSs. The term "MOLAP" was introduced when the first ROLAPs started to appear, in order to distinguish between the two types of OLAP system. (See OLAP.)

Multidimensional   A term that was used to describe the non-relational DBMSs that formed the foundation of early OLAP systems, prior to the later trend towards using standard relational DBMSs in this role.   Because OLAP systems as a whole are still sometimes referred to as "multidimensional", and given the evolution of OLAP systems to systems based on relational DBMSs, the term "multidimensional" now seems to lack a useful definition, other than "described as multidimensional in the vendor's marketing materials". (See OLAP.)

Nested Entities (Nested Entity Sets)

A collection of two or more entity sets that are interrelated by a chain of generalization relationships, such as *is a* relationships or *is part of* relationships. The more-general entity sets contain the less-general entity sets, in terms of identity, space, or time. An example of a collection of nested entity sets is *products→product_types→product_families*, where products (such as pencils) are also products of a more-general product type (such as writing implements), which in turn are products of the most-general product family (stationery). In this case nesting is based on identity. An example of a collection of nested entity sets based on space is the geographical collection *branches→areas→regions→countries*, in which entities in one set are geographically contained within in the entities of the more-general entity set.

Nested Grouping Entities

Two or more entities which belong to a nested entity set and which are used as grouping entities in the aggregation of transactional data. (See Grouping Entities.) For example, in the nonsensical aggregate "total sales by region by area for the last twelve months", the grouping entities *region* and *area* are not independent, like the entities *product* and *area*. Instead, they belong to the chain of nested entity sets *branches→areas→regions→countries*. This non-independence of nested grouping entities has important consequences when generating C-tables. (See Chapter 10.)

Nested Grouping Variables

The key attributes of nested grouping entities by whose values transactions are grouped during the aggregation of transactional data. For example, geographic variables such as "branch_code", "area_code", "region_code", and "country_code" are nested grouping variables: the entities of which they are the key attributes are related via the nested entity sets *branches→areas→regions→countries*.

Network Model

A database model according to which the second-generation DBMSs were designed. The network model improved on the earlier hierarchical model by allowing horizontal and diagonal links to be defined in the logical database structure, thus making it possible for users to navigate the structure more easily when retrieving and updating data. The network model was superseded by the relational model. (See Hierarchical Model and Relational Model.)

Non-key-based Query

A query, made of a database, in which data is retrieved from a table based on the value of data in columns other than the key column (or columns). For example, if the key of the "students" table is "student_id", a query that retrieves the rows that contain a particular date in the "date_of_birth" column (in order to find all students with a particular birthday) is a non-key-based query. Because values in non-key columns are not necessarily unique, non-key-based queries often return several rows of data from a table.

Normal Form One of the seven steps to full normalization of a relational database design. (See Normalization.) The seven steps are First Normal Form (1NF), Second Normal Form (2NF), Third Normal Form (3NF), Boyce-Codd Normal Form (BCNF), Fourth Normal Form (4NF), Fifth Normal Form (5NF), and Domain/Key Normal Form (DK/NF) – which represents full normalization. Each normal form is defined in terms of requirements that must be met by individual tables in the database design or, for the higher levels, all the tables in the database design taken together. The requirements for each normal form are cumulative. In other words, for a normal form to be achieved, all the requirements for the lower normal forms must be met, in addition to the requirements for the level in question.

Normalization Tinkering with an initial relational database design to eliminate the possibility of modification anomalies. (See Modification Anomalies and Normal Form.)

NULL A reserved word in SQL that designates the "value" of an empty cell in a table. Although the results of retrieving data from an empty cell may be displayed in the result set as the text-string 'NULL', the DBMS recognizes the value NULL as distinct from the four letters 'NULL'. Thus, a WHERE clause that includes the condition "WHERE student.middle_name IS NULL" will result in the selection of rows where the "middle_name" column is empty. In the unlikely event that a student is called John Null Smith, his row would not be selected. Also, if a space character had been entered in the "middle_name" column then that row would not be selected: a space is not a NULL. (Note that the reserved words "IS" and "IS NOT" are used in a WHERE clause when performing a comparison with NULL. An equals sign cannot be used in combination with NULL, to avoid confusion between the value NULL and the text string 'NULL'.) In most DBMSs there are now two types of NULL that can occur in a result set: a standard NULL, and a NULL that stands in for the value ALL in the results of a CUBE operation. (See CUBE.) An ALL-style NULL can be distinguished from a true NULL (within an SQL command or stored procedure) by use of the GROUPING() function, which is essentially an "ALL detector". However, once printed out, or displayed on a screen, an ALL-style NULL cannot be distinguished from a true NULL.

NULL/NOT NULL Constraint A condition, applied to a column of a table, that allows the column to contain a NULL (the so-called "NULL constraint", meaning "NULL allowed") or prevents the column from having a NULL in it (the "NOT NULL constraint"). (See NULL.)

Object Name The name of a table, a column, or a temporary variable (in an SQL command or stored procedure). Note that the term "object" has a number of different meanings in the world of software and data. Only within the specific context of a relational database can you be sure that "object name" means "table name, column name, or temporary variable name". The term is not particularly important. Its main use is to allow the writers of DBMS manuals to avoid having to repeatedly write "table name, column name, or temporary variable name" when writing about topics like naming standards and case-sensitivity settings.

On-Line Analytical Processing (OLAP)
The after-the-fact analysis of transactional data and aggregated transactional data, typically using a read-only copy of data extracted periodically from operational databases and placed in a central data repository or "data warehouse". The results of OLAP queries could, in many cases, be obtained from the relational databases from which the data is extracted, using standard SQL commands. However, such commands tend to place a heavy load on the computer on which the database resides and take a long time to execute. Also, in some cases, the desired results may require data that is stored in two or more separate databases. For these reasons, OLAP is done on an extracted copy of the operational database or databases. OLAP queries are typically performed using a specialized query interface, such as a graphical user interface (GUI). In this book I have used the term "OLAP field" to refer collectively to the various disciplines that follow or support OLAP practices, including Executive Information Systems (EIS), Data Mining, Data Warehousing, and Multidimensional Databases.

Outer Join (or Outer Join Condition)
A join condition, in a WHERE clause, that associates one table with another in such a way that unmatched rows are selected. (A normal join condition, sometimes called an inner join, selects only the rows in the two tables for which there is a match between the value of the attributes on the two sides of the equals sign in the join condition.) An outer join condition is written in various ways in different versions of SQL. One way is to place a wildcard symbol (an asterisk) to the left of the equals sign, for example:

    WHERE grades.course_number *= courses.course_number

The effect of the wildcard in this position is to add to the rows selected from the "grades" table all those rows for which there is no match for the value of "course_number" in the "courses" table. If the SELECT clause contains columns from the "courses" table (for example, "courses.course_name") then the value of these will appear as NULL for courses that appear in the "grades" table but have no match in the "courses" table. Outer joins are useful when writing test queries to check a database design for possible deletion anomalies. However, they should be used with caution in operational SQL queries and stored procedures. It is generally a bad idea to use them to mask an inadequately normalized database design.

Point-In-Time Aggregate Data

Aggregate data (that is, data that is derived by applying a mathematical function to the values of a particular "data element of interest" in a series of transactions), where the series of transactions is defined by a single datetime. A point-in-time data aggregate typically represents a "balance" of some sort, such as the balance of a bank account; and the single datetime is the datetime for which that balance has been calculated. The "data element of interest" is a numerical attribute of those transactions, for example, the value of a debit or a credit. The mathematical function that is most commonly applied to these numerical attributes is SUM(), with debits or withdrawals treated as negative values, and credits or deposits treated as positive values. In concept, a point-in-time data aggregate represents the aggregation of all transactions from the initial starting point (for example, the time when an account was opened). In practice, a balance is calculated by starting with a baseline balance that has been stored in the database for an earlier datetime; then aggregating the data element of interest for all subsequent transactions up to the datetime for which the new balance is required; and then adding the result to the previous baseline. Another category of aggregate data is *time-period* aggregate data. (See Time-Period Aggregate Data.)

Primary Key

The attribute or attributes chosen to be the actual key column or columns for a table in a relational database design. The word "primary" is redundant in most contexts: the term "key" is generally adequate. The term "primary key" may be used to indicate which of several candidate keys has been selected to be the key. (See Candidate Key.) A key may be a single column of a table, such as "student_id"; or two or more columns taken together, such as "serial_number" and "manufacturer_id". In the SQL commands used to create new tables, the reserved words used to specify a key column are PRIMARY KEY. In this case the word PRIMARY must be included.

Pseudo-Entity

Something in the real world that does not fall within the definition of an entity, and therefore falls outside the scope of the Entity-Relationship Model, but which can usefully be incorporated into a database design as though it were an entity. The example that appears in this book (Chapter 11) is a time period. We can treat all time periods of a specific length, such as all days or all weeks, as though they were entity sets; and we can number them to give them a convenient key attribute. Note that this number must be unique for the lifetime of the database; so we cannot start each year with Week 1: the second year must start with Week 53. Time periods are not true entities because they do not participate in relationships with other entities. (Note: this is *not* because they are intangible. Many entities are intangible, such as a doctor's appointment or an airplane flight.) Time periods, viewed as pseudo-entities, belong to a chain of nested sets of pseudo-entities:
days→weeks→months→quarters→years. (See Nested Entities.)

Query Language   A language, similar to a programming language, by means of which users or programs interact with a database. When users interact directly with a database they type instructions written in the query language: the DBMS executes those instructions. When a computer program interacts with a database, the program incorporates the necessary instructions, written in the query language, within the program. A query language is used not only to retrieve data from a database but also to insert, update, or delete data; so, although it is called a "query" language, it is really a "command" language. It is therefore common, when talking about a specific query language like SQL, to talk about "SQL commands" (rather than "SQL queries").

Referential Integrity, Breakdown of   The "marooning" of rows in relationship-representing tables after a row in an entity-representing table has been deleted. For example, if a course is deleted from the "courses" table, but a row is left in the "course_teachers" table that contains the value of "course_number" for the deleted course, that row is now "semi-marooned". It can still be associated with a teacher in the "teachers" table; but it can no longer be associated with a row in the "courses" table. The referential integrity that existed between the row in the "course_teachers" table and the now-deleted row in the "courses" table has broken down. If the teacher who was teaching the now-deleted course leaves the university, and the corresponding row is deleted from the "teachers" table, the row in "course_teachers" becomes completely marooned. Breakdowns of referential integrity in a database can be handled in various ways. (See Chapter 5.) One way is to use the Foreign Key feature of the DBMS (see Foreign Key). Although, in a normalized database design, breakdowns of referential integrity generally affect only relationship-representing tables, in a non-normalized database design (where the key column of one entity-representing table has been turned into a non-key column of another entity-representing table), a breakdown of referential integrity can occur between two entity-representing tables.

Relation   A table (used to hold data in a relational database). "Relation" was the term used by E.F.Codd when he defined the relational model; but nowadays the more down-to-earth term "table" is used instead. However, databases based on Codd's model are still called *relational* databases, meaning "databases based on tables".

Relational Algebra   An early type of query language for relational databases, superseded in the 1980s by query languages of the relational calculus type (like SQL). A relational algebra language is procedural; that is, the query tells the DBMS how to go about retrieving the data. (By contrast, relational calculus query languages are declarative; that is, a query simply tells the DBMS what data is required, and the DBMS figures out how best to retrieve that data.) The early query languages, based on relational algebra, used reserved words like SELECT, PROJECT, and JOIN. (By contrast, relational *calculus* query languages used reserved words like RETRIEVE, FROM, and WHERE. RETRIEVE was later changed to SELECT, as in present-day SQL.)

Relational Calculus	A type of query language for relational databases which is declarative; that is, a query tells the DBMS what data is required, and the DBMS figures out how best to retrieve that data. SQL is a relational calculus type of query language. Relational calculus query languages superseded those based on relational algebra (which are procedural, that is, the query tells the DBMS how to go about retrieving the data). Relational calculus query languages originally used reserved words like RETRIEVE, FROM, and WHERE, although RETRIEVE was later changed to SELECT. (See Relational Algebra.)
Relational Database	A database organized according to the relational model, under which data is stored in a set of tables. The term derives from "relation", meaning "table". The concept of a relational database was introduced by E.F.Codd in 1970.
Relational DBMS	Relational Database Management System – a DBMS that operates according to the relational model, under which data is stored in a set of tables. (See DBMS and Relational Model.)
Relational Model	The model according to which a database is formed as a set of tables. The relational model was introduced by E.F.Codd in 1970. The term "relational" derives from "relation", meaning "table".
Relationship	The formal definition of a relationship is "an association between two entity sets". A clearer way of explaining this is to say that a relationship is the generalization of the possible associations that may occur, in the real world, between individual entities in one entity set and individual entities in another entity set. For example, the relationship *is enrolled in*, between the entity sets *students* and *courses*, is an expression of the fact that any individual student may be enrolled in any individual course. It is normally less confusing if a relationship is expressed using single entities, as in "*student is enrolled in course*", even though the formal definition of a relationship is based on sets.
Result Set	The results of an SQL query, which typically take the form of several rows of data. The term is used even when the query produces a single row, or even a single data element. A result set may be displayed on a screen, printed on a printer, or inserted into a table in the database.
ROLAP	Relational OLAP system – an OLAP system (On-Line Analytical Processing system) based on a standard relational database. ROLAPs superseded the older MOLAPs, that is, OLAP systems based on non-relational, "multidimensional" DBMSs. (See OLAP.)
Schema	A database design, that is, the table names, column names, the column formats (or datatypes), and designation of key columns. This is an old term which has evolved into a technology buzzword: it is therefore advisable to avoid it and to use the term "database design". The term "schema" is still used in some technical papers, and by database designers who are trying to impress their managers.

SQL   Structured Query Language – the name given to the query language
                        which is now a universal standard for interacting with relational
                        databases. SQL has been progressively refined and extended since
                        it became the *de facto* standard in the late 1980s, displacing other
                        relational-calculus query languages such as QUEL. (See Relational
                        Calculus.)

Stored Procedure   A program, written in an extended form of SQL (such as Oracle's
                        PL/SQL or Microsoft's Transact-SQL), which is stored in the
                        database and given a unique name, such as "sp_GetSalesResults".
                        Once a stored procedure has been stored in the database, a user (or
                        a user's application software) can execute the stored procedure by
                        using the SQL command EXECUTE, followed by the name of the
                        stored procedure and, if required, one or several input parameters.
                        For example, the user could type EXECUTE sp_GetSalesResults
                        @year='2001'. What this means to the DBMS is "execute the set of
                        SQL commands contained in the stored procedure known as
                        'sp_GetSalesResult', assigning the value '2001' to that stored
                        procedure's input parameter, known within the stored procedure as
                        @year". Stored procedures were introduced so that frequently-used
                        sequences of SQL commands could be thoroughly tested and
                        debugged and kept in one place, rather than being incorporated in
                        many different application programs. Stored procedures also
                        allowed changes to the database design to be masked from users
                        and from application software: stored procedures could be modified
                        to cope with a changed database design, while keeping the input
                        parameters and result set of the stored procedure unchanged.
                        Some DBMSs optimize the way that stored procedures are executed
                        to a greater extent than they optimize the execution of ordinary SQL
                        commands. The use of stored procedures has broadened from the
                        time of their first introduction: in some organizations significant
                        pieces of business logic have been moved from application software
                        to stored procedures. Some stored procedures are now twenty or
                        more pages long when printed out.

Subschema   A database view, that is, a view of a database, presented to a group
                        of users, in which they can see and update only a subset of the data
                        contained in the database. This is an old term (but it is still used in
                        some technical papers). The term "database view" can be used
                        instead, but not "view", which is now generally understood to mean
                        "table view". (See Table View and View.)

Superaggregation   The aggregation of data, stored in the database or in a temporary
                        table, which is already aggregate data, rather than raw transaction-
                        history data. For example, users may perform aggregating queries
                        on the aggregate "total sales by month" in order to get "total sales by
                        quarter" if this there is no such aggregate already stored in the
                        database. An important example of superaggregation is the
                        aggregation of data in a series of iterative steps to produce a C-
                        table. (See C-table.)

Table Alias   An abbreviation (such as "s" for "students") assigned to the name of a table in the FROM clause of an SQL command or stored procedure, so that the abbreviation can be used in the SELECT and WHERE clauses, in place of the full table name. Use of table aliases saves the person who is writing the SQL command or stored procedure a few keystrokes; but it makes the command or stored procedure less easily understood by others. My recommendation is that table aliases should never be used.

Table View   A virtual table that is defined by an SQL command that operates on one or several real tables. Once a table view has been defined, SQL commands can be written to operate on the virtual table, defined by that view, as though it were a real table. The DBMS will translate these commands into operations performed on the real tables referenced in the table-view definition.

Temporal DBMS (TDBMS)   A database management system (DBMS) that is designed to store not only the current versions of each row in a table but also all the previous values, back to the time when the database was first created. Using a temporal query language, such as TSQL, users can retrieve the values of data elements as they were at any point in the past. (See TSQL.) In a TDBMS, the tables of a standard relational database are replaced by data cubes. (See Data Cube.) TDBMSs were intended to solve some of the problems with the representation of time that were found in standard relational database designs, particularly the failure of normalization to prevent time-related modification anomalies. Although the concepts underlying TDBMSs have been described in detail, and TSQL (as well as a number of alternative query languages) has been fully defined, attempts to build a practical TDBMS have met with limited success. (For example, a TDBMS called TimeCube was developed by Beacon IT of Japan; but it was a limited implementation of the model and more of a demonstration of the TDBMS concept than a practical TDBMS.)

Time Cube   An alternative name for a data cube in a temporal database. (See Temporal Database.) Note that TimeCube (without a space) is a trademark of Beacon IT.

Time-Period Aggregate Data   Aggregate data, that is, data that is derived by applying a mathematical function to the values of a particular "data element of interest" in a series of transactions, where the transactions are those that occurred within a particular time span for which the aggregate is being derived. The "data element of interest" is a numerical attribute of those transactions, for example, the value of each order in a series of orders. The mathematical function that is most commonly applied to these numerical attributes is SUM(), although it could be another function that operates on a series of values, such as AVG(). An example of time-period aggregate data is "total sales by product for the last twelve months". Another category of aggregate data is point-in-time aggregate data. (See Point-In-Time Aggregate Data.)

Time Span (in Data Aggregation)

The overall period of time used to select transactions for use in a data aggregation, for example, "from January 2000 to December 2006". As part of the aggregation process, transactions may be grouped according to shorter periods of time within the overall time span, such as "each full month within the time span". This leads to aggregates such as "total sales by month for 2000 to 2006".

Transaction Journal (TJ)

A record of transactions stored in a database, such as the database of an accounting or financial services organization. "Journal" is a commonly used term in accounting and financial services, meaning "a record of events or transactions, in time order, at the finest level of detail".

Transaction Time (in Temporal Databases)

A type of datetime tag, attached to rows in a temporal database, in order to record the date and time when an updated row was added to a data cube. (See Temporal Database.) Datetime tags in a temporal database may, alternatively, be based on "valid time". (See Valid Time.)

Transactional Data

The values of the attributes of entities that represent transactions, or of relationships that represent transactions. Transactional entities and transactional relationships are records of events that take place, or are concluded, at a specific point in time. They possess at least one datetime attribute, the value of which represents the conclusion or completion of the action. Transactional entities and relationships are of continuing operational importance in the activity for which the database is to be used. For example, when you take money from a cash machine, your bank is going to be using the record of that transaction perhaps dozens of times after it is completed, at least up until the preparation of your next monthly bank statement. By contrast, *non-transactional* entities and relationships generally have no datetime attribute or, if they have one, have an end datetime which is unpredictable or revisable; and, once they are "concluded" (for instance, by account closure or employee retirement), the rows that represent them are either deleted from the table or retained only for occasional reference purposes. (See Transactional Entity and Transactional Relationship.)

Transactional Entity

A transaction that is represented, in an Entity-Relationship model, as an entity (as opposed to a relationship), for example, the entity *order*. Transactions are records of events that take place, or are concluded, at a specific point in time. Transactions may, in some situations, be represented as relationships; but transactional entities are the most common representation of transactions.

Transactional Relationship

A transaction that is represented, in an Entity-Relationship model, as a relationship (as opposed to an entity), for example, the relationship *has purchased*, which operates between *customer* and *airplane* in *customer has purchased airplane*. This is a less common representation of a transaction.

TSQL

Temporal SQL – a query language defined for use with a Temporal DBMS. TSQL allows the user to refer to either the current value of any row in any table in the database, or to any of its former values, all of which are retained in the database. This is done by way of a WHEN clause, which operates in conjunction with the WHERE clause. (See Temporal DBMS.)

Tuple
A row of data in a table in a relational database. "Tuple" (pronounced "too-pull") is the term used by E.F.Codd when he defined the relational model; but nowadays the more down-to-earth term "row" is used instead.

UNIQUE Constraint
A constraint, applied in a table, to a column (or several columns taken together) in order to cause the DBMS to prevent the same value (or set of values) appearing in more than one row. It is not necessary to designate single key columns as UNIQUE: key columns are, by definition, unique. Non-key columns may be designated as UNIQUE for various reasons. For example, they may be candidate keys, such as Social Security Number, that have not been chosen as actual keys but for which duplicate values (entered in error) should be rejected. Another use of the UNIQUE constraint is to enforce relationship cardinality rules in the database. (See Chapter 3.)

Update Anomaly
A situation in which the updating of a piece of data in a database has unintended, undesirable effects on the results of certain subsequent queries, as a consequence of the database design that has been used. (The term is also sometimes used to describe a situation where, because the database design has the same piece of information appearing in more than one place, the updating of one copy of that piece of information leaves the other copy or copies unchanged, resulting in incorrect results when queries are performed that refer to the non-updated copy or copies.)

Valid Time (in Temporal Databases)
A type of datetime tag, attached to rows in a temporal database in order to record the date and time of the real-world event that gave rise to the updated row being added to the data cube. (See Temporal Database.) Datetime tags in a temporal database may, alternatively, be based on "transaction time". (See Transaction Time.)

View (Table View)
A virtual table that is defined by an SQL command that operates on one or several real tables. Once a table view has been defined, SQL commands can be written to operate on the virtual table defined by that view, as though it were a real table. Although the shorter term, "view", is nowadays understood to mean "table view", "view" was originally understood to mean a "database view" (also called a subschema), that is, a view of a database, presented to a group of users, in which they can see and update only a subset of the data contained in the database. To avoid misunderstandings, it is better to always use the full terms "table view" and "database view".

Made in the USA
Middletown, DE
21 January 2022

59331091R00136